CAMBRIDGE LIBRARY COLLECTION

Books of enduring scholarly value

Literary Studies

This series provides a high-quality selection of early printings of literary works, textual editions, anthologies and literary criticism which are of lasting scholarly interest. Ranging from Old English to Shakespeare to early twentieth-century work from around the world, these books offer a valuable resource for scholars in reception history, textual editing, and literary studies.

Robin Hood

A controversial literary critic and commentator, Joseph Ritson (1752–1803) made his reputation identifying and exposing literary forgeries. His enduring legacy, however, stems from his interest in the legend of Robin Hood. The combination of his passion for collecting literary antiquities, particularly medieval ballad poetry, and his political convictions in support of republican government, drew him to the tale of the English outlaw. This two-volume work, first published in 1795, is an important collection of texts relating to the legend. Ritson's aim was to present all the known poems and songs, and his research was so thorough that very little further material has been found since. This work helped transform the perception of the Robin Hood tradition, encouraging its serious study. As well as a selection of texts, Volume 1 contains a lengthy scholarly discussion of the tradition.

Cambridge University Press has long been a pioneer in the reissuing of out-of-print titles from its own backlist, producing digital reprints of books that are still sought after by scholars and students but could not be reprinted economically using traditional technology. The Cambridge Library Collection extends this activity to a wider range of books which are still of importance to researchers and professionals, either for the source material they contain, or as landmarks in the history of their academic discipline.

Drawing from the world-renowned collections in the Cambridge University Library and other partner libraries, and guided by the advice of experts in each subject area, Cambridge University Press is using state-of-the-art scanning machines in its own Printing House to capture the content of each book selected for inclusion. The files are processed to give a consistently clear, crisp image, and the books finished to the high quality standard for which the Press is recognised around the world. The latest print-on-demand technology ensures that the books will remain available indefinitely, and that orders for single or multiple copies can quickly be supplied.

The Cambridge Library Collection brings back to life books of enduring scholarly value (including out-of-copyright works originally issued by other publishers) across a wide range of disciplines in the humanities and social sciences and in science and technology.

Robin Hood

A Collection of All the Ancient Poems, Songs, and Ballads, Now Extant, Relative to That Celebrated English Outlaw

VOLUME 1

EDITED BY JOSEPH RITSON

CAMBRIDGE
UNIVERSITY PRESS

CAMBRIDGE
UNIVERSITY PRESS

University Printing House, Cambridge, CB2 8BS, United Kingdom

Cambridge University Press is part of the University of Cambridge.
It furthers the University's mission by disseminating knowledge in the pursuit of education, learning and research at the highest international levels of excellence.

www.cambridge.org
Information on this title: www.cambridge.org/9781108078160

This edition first published 1795
This digitally printed version 2015

ISBN 978-1-108-07816-0 Paperback

ROBIN HOOD:

A

COLLECTION

OF ALL THE ANCIENT

POEMS, SONGS, AND BALLADS,

NOW EXTANT,

RELATIVE TO THAT CELEBRATED

ENGLISH OUTLAW:

TO WHICH ARE PREFIXED

HISTORICAL ANECDOTES OF HIS LIFE.

IN TWO VOLUMES.

VOLUME THE FIRST.

In this our ſpacious iſle I think there is not one,
But he 'of ROBIN HOOD hath heard' and Little John;
And to the end of time the tales ſhall ne'er be done
Of Scarlock, George a Green, and Much the miller's ſon,
Of Tuck, the merry friar, which many a ſermon made
In praiſe of ROBIN HOOD, his out-laws, and their trade.

DRAYTON.

LONDON:

PRINTED FOR T. EGERTON, WHITEHALL, AND J. JOHNSON, ST. PAULS-CHURCH-YARD.

MDCCXCV.

PREFACE.

THE ſingular circumſtance, that the name of an outlawed individual of the twelfth or thirteenth century ſhould continue traditionally popular, be chanted in ballads, and, as one may ſay,

Familiar in our mouth as houſehold words,

at the end of the eighteenth, excited the editors curioſity to retrieve all the hiſtorical or poetical remains concerning him that could be met with: an object which he has occaſionally purſued for many years; and of which purſuit he now publiſhes the reſult. He cannot, indeed, pretend that his reſearches, extenſive as they muſt appear, have been attended with all the ſucceſs he could have wiſhed; but, at the ſame time, it ought to be acknowleged that many poetical pieces, of great antiquity and ſome merit, are deſervedly reſcued from oblivion.

The materials collected for "the life" of this celebrated character, which are either preſerved at large, or carefully refered to, in the "notes and illuſtrations," are not, it muſt be confeſſed, in every inſtance, ſo important, ſo ancient, or, perhaps, ſo authentic, as the ſubject ſeems to demand; although the compiler may be permitted to ſay, in humble ſecond-hand imitation of the poet Martial:

Some there are good, ſome middling, and ſome bad;
But yet they were the beſt that could be had.

Desirous to omit nothing that he could find upon the subject, he has everywhere faithfully vouched and exhibited his authorities, such as they are: it would, therefor, seem altogether uncandid or unjust to make him responsible for the want of authenticity of such of them as may appear liable to that imputation.

The justice or candour, however, which he has reason to expect from the professed critic, who is allowed to dictate or influence the public opinion, may be easyly conceived; since the author of an article in the *Critical review,* for the month of January, 1792, who was necessaryly an entire stranger to the particular contents of these volumes, was pleased, by way of anticipation, it would seem, of his own criticism, (too frequently exercised on subjects he is equally ignorant of,) to pronounce them "the refuse of a stall." To the impartial critic, whether hireling or volunteer, who points out errors that might be corrected, and faults that might be remedyed, in a word, who, instead of abusing books for being what they are, shews what they should have been, an author or editor is not less, and, perhaps, even much more, indebted and obliged than the public at large; but, to adopt the words of the great Milton, one must always "ABOMINAT THE CENSURE OF RASCALS."

THE

LIFE

OF

ROBIN HOOD.

IT will ſcarcely be expected that one ſhould be able to offer an authentic narrative of the life and tranſactions of this extraordinary perſonage. The times in which he lived, the mode of life he adopted, and the ſilence or loſs of contemporary writers, are circumſtances ſufficiently favorable, indeed, to romance, but altogether inimical to hiſtorical truth. The reader muſt, therefor, be contented with ſuch a detail, however ſcanty or imperfect, as a zealous purſuit of the ſubject enables one to give; and which, though it may fail to ſatisfy, may poſſibly ſerve to amuſe.

No aſſiſtance has been derived from the labours of his profeſſed biographers (a); and even the induſtrious ſir John Hawkins, from whom the public might have expected ample gratification upon the ſubject, acknowleges that "the hiſtory of this popular hero is but little known, and all the ſcattered fragments concerning him, could they be brought together, would fall far ſhort of ſatisfying ſuch an enquirer as none but real and authenticated facts will content. We muſt," he ſays, "take his ſtory as we find it." He accordingly gives us nothing but two or three trite and trivial extracts, with which every one, at all curious about the ſubject, was as well acquainted as himſelf. It is not, at the ſame time, pretended, that the preſent attempt promiſes more than to bring together the ſcattered fragments to which the learned hiſtorian alludes. This, however, has been done, according to the beſt of the compilers information and abilities; and the reſult is, with a due ſenſe of the deficiency of both, ſubmitted to the readers candour.

ROBIN HOOD was born at Locksley, in the county of Nottingham, (A) in the reign of king Henry the ſecond, and about the year of Chriſt 1160 (B). His extraction was noble, and his true name ROBERT FITZOOTH, which vulgar pronunciation eaſyly corrupted into ROBIN HOOD (C). He is frequently ſtiled, and commonly reputed to have been EARL OF HUNTINGDON; a title to which, in the latter part of his life, at leaſt, he actually appears to have had ſome ſort of pretenſion (D). In his youth he is reported to have been of a wild and extravagant diſpoſition; inſomuch that, his inheritance being conſumed or forfeited by his exceſſes, and his perſon outlawed for debt, either from neceſſity or choice, he ſought an aſylum in the woods and foreſts, with which immenſe tracts, eſpecially in the northern parts of the kingdom, were at that time covered (E). Of theſe he chiefly affected Barnſdale, in Yorkſhire, Sherwood, in Nottinghamſhire, and, according to ſome, Plompton-park, in Cumberland (F). Here he either found, or was afterward joined by, a number of perſons in ſimilar circumſtances;

> "Such as the fury of ungovern'd youth
> Thruſt from the company of awful men;" (*F)

who appear to have conſidered and obeyed him as their chief or leader, and of whom his principal favourites, or thoſe in whoſe courage and fidelity he moſt confided, were LITTLE JOHN, (whoſe ſurname is ſaid to have been *Nailor*,) WILLIAM SCADLOCK (Scathelock or Scarlet), GEORGE A GREEN, pinder (or pound-keeper)of Wakefield, MUCH, a millers ſon, and a certain monk or frier named TUCK (G). He is likewiſe ſaid to have been accompanyed in his retreat by a female, of whom he was enamoured, and whoſe real or adopted name was MARIAN (H).

His company, in proceſs of time, conſiſted of a hundred archers; men, ſays Major, moſt ſkilful in battle, whom four times that number of the boldeſt fellows durſt not attack (I). His manner of recruiting was ſomewhat ſingular; for, in the words of an old writer, "wherſoever he hard of any that were of unuſual ſtrength and 'hardines,' he would deſgyſe himſelfe, and, rather then fayle, go lyke a begger to become acquaynted with them; and, after he had tryed them with fyghting; never give them over tyl he had uſed means to drawe [them] to lyve after his faſhion" (J): a practice of which numerous inſtances are recorded in the more common and popular ſongs, where, indeed, he ſeldom fails to receive a ſound beating. In ſhooting with the long bow, which they chiefly practiſed, "they excelled all the men of the land; though, as occation required, they had alſo other weapons" (K).

In theſe foreſts, and with this company, he for many years reigned like an independant ſovereign; at perpetual war, indeed, with the king of England, and all his ſubjects, with an exception, however, of the poor and needy, and ſuch as were "deſolate and oppreſſed," or ſtood in need of his protection. When moleſted, by a ſuperior force, in one place, he retired to another, ſtill defying the power of what was called law and government, and making his enemies pay dearly, as well for their open attacks, as for their clandeſtine treachery. It is not, at the ſame time, to be concluded that he muſt, in this oppoſition, have been guilty of manifeſt treaſon or rebellion; as he moſt certainly can be juſtly charged with neither. An outlaw, in thoſe times, being deprived of protection, owed no allegiance: "his hand 'was' againſt every man, and every mans hand againſt him" (L). Theſe foreſts, in ſhort, were his territories; thoſe who accompanyed and adhered to him his ſubjects:

The world was not his friend, nor the worlds law;

and what better title king Richard could pretend to the territory and people of England than Robin Hood had to the dominion of Barnſdale or Sherwood is a queſtion humbly ſubmitted to the conſideration of the political philoſopher.

The deer with which the royal foreſts then abounded (every Norman tyrant being, like Nimrod, "a mighty hunter before the lord") would afford our hero and his companions an ample ſupply of food throughout the year; and of fuel, for dreſſing their veniſon, or for the other purpoſes of life, they could evidently be in no want. The reſt of their neceſſaries would be eaſyly procured, partly by taking what they had occaſion for from the wealthy paſſenger, who traverſed or approached their territories, and partly by commerce with the neighbouring villages or great towns.

It may be readyly imagined that ſuch a life, during great part of the year, at leaſt and while it continued free from the alarms or apprehenſions to which our foreſters, one would ſuppoſe, muſt have been too frequently ſubject, might be ſufficiently pleaſant and deſireable, and even deſerve the compliment which is payed to it by Shakſpeare, in his comedy of *As you like it*, (Act 1. ſcene 1.) where, on Olivers aſking, "where will the old duke live?" Charles anſwers, "They ſay he is already in the foreſt of Arden, and a many merry men with him;

and there they live like the OLD ROBIN HOOD OF ENGLAND; . . . and fleet the time carelesly as they did in the golden world." Their gallant chief, indeed, may be presumed to have frequently exclaimed with the banished Valentine, in another play of the same author:*

" How use doth breed a habit in a man!
This shadowy desert, unfrequented woods,
I better brook than flourishing peopled towns:
Here can I sit alone, unseen of any,
And, to the nightingale's complaining notes,
Tune my distresses, and record my woes."

He would, doubtless, too often find occasion to add:

" What hallooing and what stir is this to-day?
These are my mates, that make their wills their law,
Have some unhappy passenger in chace:
They love me well; yet I have much to do,
To keep them from uncivil outrages."

But, on the other hand, it will be at once difficult and painful to conceive,

——— When they did hear
The rain and wind beat dark December, how,
In that their pinching cave, they could discourse
The freezing hours away! (M)

Their mode of life, in short, and domestic œconomy, of which no authentic particulars have been even traditionally preserved, are more easyly to be guessed at than described. They have, nevertheless, been elegantly sketched by the animating pencil of an excellent, though neglected poet.

" The merry pranks he play'd, would ask an age to tell,
And the adventures strange that Robin Hood befell,

* *Two gentlemen of Verona*, act 5. scene 4.

When Mansfield many a time for Robin hath been laid,
How he hath coufen'd them, that him would have betray'd;
How often he hath come to Nottingham difguis'd,
And cunningly efcap'd, being fet to be furpriz'd.
In this our fpacious ifle, I think there is not one,
But he hath heard fome talk of him and little John;
And to the end of time, the tales fhall ne'er be done,
Of Scarlock, George a Green, and Much the miller's fon,
Of Tuck the merry friar, which many a fermon made
In praife of Robin Hood, his out laws, and their trade.
An hundred valiant men had this brave Robin Hood,
Still ready at his call, that bow-men were right good,
All clad in Lincoln green, (N) with caps of red and blue,
His fellow's winded horn not one of them but knew,
When fetting to their lips their little beugles fhrill,
The warbling ecchos wak'd from every dale and hill.
Their bauldricks fet with ftuds, athwart their fhoulders caft,
To which under their arms their fheafs were buckled faft,
A fhort fword at their belt, a buckler fcarce a fpan,
Who ftruck below the knee, not counted then a man:
All made of Spanifh yew, their bows were wondrous ftrong;
They not an arrow drew, but was a cloth yard long.
Of archery they had the very perfect craft,
With broad-arrow, or but, or prick, or roving fhaft,
At marks full forty fcore, they us'd to prick, and rove,
Yet higher than the breaft, for compafs never ftrove;
Yet at the fartheft mark a foot could hardly win:
At long-outs, fhort, and hoyles, each one could cleave the pin:
Their arrows finely pair'd, for timber, and for feather,
With birch and brazil piec'd to fly in any weather;
And fhot they with the round, the fquare, or forked pile,
The loofe gave fuch a twang, as might be heard a mile.
And of thefe archers brave, there was not any one,
But he could kill a deer his fwifteft fpeed upon,
Which they did boil and roaft, in many a mighty wood,
Sharp hunger the fine fauce to their more kingly food.
Then taking them to reft, his merry men and he
Slept many a fummer's night under the greenwood tree.
From wealthy abbots chefts, and churls abundant ftore,
What oftentimes he took, he fhar'd amongft the poor:
No lordly bifhop came in lufty Robin's way,
To him before he went, but for his pafs muft pay:
The widow in diftrefs he graciously reliev'd,
And remedied the wrongs of many a virgin griev'd: (O)

He from the husband's bed no married woman wan,
But to his mistress dear, his loved Marian,
Was ever constant known, which wheresoe'er she came,
Was sovereign of the woods; chief lady of the game:
Her clothes tuck'd to the knee, and dainty braided hair,
With bow and quiver arm'd, she wander'd here and there,
Amongst the forests wild; Diana never knew
Such pleasures, nor such harts as Mariana slew."*

That our hero and his companions, while they lived in the woods, had recourse to robbery for their better support is neither to be concealed nor to be denyed. Testimonies to this purpose, indeed, would be equally endless and unnecessary. Fordun, in the fourteenth century, calls him, "*ille famosissimus siccarius*," that most celebrated robber, and Major terms him and Little John, "*famatissimi latrones*." But it is to be remembered, according to the confession of the latter historian, that, in these exertions of power, he took away the goods of rich men only; never killing any person, unless he was attacked or resisted: that he would not suffer a woman to be maltreated; nor ever took any thing from the poor, but charitably fed them with the wealth he drew from the abbots. I disapprove, says he, of the rapine of the man; but he was the most humane and the prince of all robbers(*O). In allusion, no doubt, to this irregular and predatory course of life, he has had the honour to be compared to the illustrious Wallace, the champion and deliverer of his country; and that, it is not a little remarkable, in the latters own time (P).

Our hero, indeed, seems to have held bishops, abbots, priests, and monks, in a word, all the clergy, regular or secular, in decided aversion.

"These byshoppes and thyse archebyshoppes,
Ye shall them bete and bynde,"

was an injunction carefully impressed upon his followers:

* Draytons *Polyolbion*, song xxvi.

and, in this part of his conduct, perhaps, the pride, avarice, uncharitableness, and hypocrisy of these clerical drones, or pious locusts, (too many of whom are still permitted to prey upon the labours of the industrious, and are supported, in pampered luxury, (Q) at the expence of those whom their useless and pernicious craft tends to retain in superstitious ignorance and irrational servility,) will afford him ample justification. The abbot of Saint Marys, in York, (R) from some unknown cause, appears to have been distinguished by particular animosity; and the sherif of Nottinghamshire, (S) who may have been too active and officious in his endeavours to apprehend him, was the unremitted object of his vengeance.

Notwithstanding, however, the aversion in which he appears to have held the clergy of every denomination, he was a man of exemplary piety, according to the notions of that age, and retained a domestic chaplain (frier Tuck no doubt) for the diurnal celebration of the divine mysteries. This we learn from an anecdote preserved by Fordun, as an instance of those actions which the historian allows to deserve commendation. One day, as he heard mass, which he was most devoutly accustomed to do, (nor would he, in whatever necessity, suffer the office to be interrupted,) he was espyed by a certain sherif and officers belonging to the king, who had frequently before molested him, in that most secret recess of the wood where he was at mass. Some of his people, who perceived what was going forward, advised him to fly with all speed, which, out of reverence to the sacrament, which he was then most devoutly worshiping, he absolutely refused to do. But the rest of his men having fled for fear of death, Robin, confiding solely in him whom he reverently worshiped, with a very few, who by chance were present, set upon his enemies, whom he easyly vanquished; and, being enriched with their spoils and ransom, he always held the ministers of the church and masses in greater veneration ever after, mindful of what is vulgarly said:

> Him god does surely hear
> Who oft to th' mass gives ear. (T)

They who deride the miracles of Moses or Mahomet are at full liberty, no doubt, to reject those wrought in favour of Robin Hood. But, as a certain admirable author expresses himself, "an honest man and of good judgment believeth still what is told him, and that which he finds written."

Having, for a long series of years, maintained a sort of independant sovereignty, and set kings, judges, and magistrates at defiance, a proclamation was published, offering a considerable reward for bringing him in either dead or alive; which, however, seems to have been productive of no greater success than former attempts for that purpose (U). At lengh, the infirmities of old age increasing upon him, and desirous to be relieved, in a fit of sickness, by being let blood, he applyed for that purpose to the prioress of Kirkleys-nunnery in Yorkshire, his relation, (women, and particularly religious women, being, in those times, somewhat better skilled in surgery than the sex is at present,) by whom he was treacherously suffered to bleed to death. This event happened on the 18th of November, 1247, being the 31st year of king Henry III. and (if the date assigned to his birth be correct) about the 87th of his age. (V) He was intered under some trees, at a short distance from the house; a stone being placed over his grave, with an inscription to his memory (W).

Such was the end of Robin Hood: a man who, in a barbarous age, and under a complicated tyranny, displayed a spirit of freedom and independence, which has endeared him to the common people, whose cause he maintained, (for all opposition to tyranny is the cause of the people,) and, in ſpite of the malicious endeavous of pitiful monks, by whom hiſtory was conſecrated to the crimes and follies of titled ruffians and ſainted idiots, to ſuppreſs all record of his patriotic exertions and virtuous acts, will render his name immortal.

> "*Dum juga montis aper, fluvios dum piſcis amabit,*
> *Dumque thymo paſcentur apes, dum rore cicadæ,*
> *Semper honos, nomenque tuum, laudeſque manebunt.*"

With reſpect to his perſonal character: it is ſufficiently evident that he was active, brave, prudent, patient; poſſeſſed of uncommon bodyly ſtrength, and conſiderable military ſkill; juſt, generous, benevolent, faithful, and beloved or revered by his followers or adherents for his excellent and amiable qualities. Fordun, a prieſt, extols his piety, and piety, by a prieſt, is regarded as the perfection of virtue; Major (as we have ſeen) pronounces him the moſt humane and the prince of all robbers; and Camden, whoſe teſtimony is of ſome weight, calls him "*prædonem mitiſſimum*," the gentleſt of thieves. As proofs of his univerſal and ſingular popularity: his ſtory and exploits have been made the ſubject as well of various dramatic exhibitions (X), as of innumerable poems, rimes, ſongs and ballads (Y): he has given riſe to divers proverbs (Z); and to ſwear by him, or ſome of his companions, appears to have been a uſual practice (AA): his ſongs have been prefered, on the moſt ſolemn occaſions, not only to the pſalms of David, but to the new teſtament (BB); his ſervice to the word of god (CC): he may be regarded as the patron of archery (DD): and, though not actually canonized, (a ſituation to which the miracles wrought in his favour, as well in his lifetime as after his death, and the ſupernatural powers he is, in ſome parts, ſuppoſed to have poſſeſſed (EE), give him an indiſputable claim,) he obtained the principal diſtinction of ſainthood, in having a feſtival allotted to him, and ſolemn games inſtituted in honour of his memory, which were celebrated till the latter end of the ſixteenth century; not by the populace only, but by kings or princes and grave magiſtrates; and that as well in Scotland as in England; being conſidered, in the former country, of the higheſt political importance, and eſſential to the civil and religious liberties of the people, the efforts of government to ſuppreſs them frequently producing tumult and inſurrection (FF): his bow, and one of his arrows, his chair, his cap, and one of his ſlippers, were preſerved, with peculiar veneration, till within the preſent century (GG); and not only places which afforded him ſecurity or amuſement, but even the well at which he quenched his thirſt, ſtill retain his name (HH): a name which, in the middle of the preſent century, was confered as an honorable diſtinction upon the prime miniſter to the king of Madagaſcar (II).

After his death his company was diſperſed (JJ). Hiſtory is ſilent in particulars: all that we can, therefor, learn is, that the honour of Little Johns death and burial is contended for by rival nations (KK); that his grave continued long "celebrous for the yielding of excellent whetſtones;" and that ſome of his deſcendants, of the name of *Nailor*, which he himſelf bore, and they from him, were in being ſo late as the laſt century (LL).

NOTES AND ILLUSTRATIONS

REFERED TO IN THE

FOREGOING LIFE.

(a) "FORMER biographers, &c."] Such, that is, as have already appeared in print, ſince a ſort of manuſcript life in the Sloane library will appear to have been of ſome ſervice. The firſt of theſe reſpectable perſonages is the author, or rather compiler, of "The noble birth and gallant atchievements of that remarkable outlaw Robin Hood; together with a true account, of the many merry extravagant exploits he played; in twelve ſeveral ſtories: newly collected by an ingenious antiquary. London, printed by W. O." [William Onley.] 4to. black letter, no date. Theſe "ſeveral ſtories," in fact, are only ſo many of the ſongs in the common *Garland* tranſproſed; and the "ingenious antiquary," who ſtrung them together, has known ſo little of his trade, that he ſets out with informing us of his heros baniſhment by king Henry the *eighth*. The above is ſuppoſed to be the "ſmall merry book" called *Robin Hood*, mentioned in a liſt of "books, ballads, and hiſtories, printed for and ſold by William Thackeray at the Angel in Duck-lane", (about 1680,) preſerved in one of the volumes of old ballads (part of Bagfords collection) in the Britiſh muſeum.

Another piece of biography, from which much will not be expected, is, "The lives and heroick atchievements of the renowned Robin Hood, and *James Hind*, two noted robbers and highwaymen. London, 1752." 8vo. This, however, is probably nothing more than an extract from Johnſons *Lives of the highwaymen*, in which, as a ſpecimen of the authors hiſtorical authenticity, we have the life and actions of that noted robber, SIR JOHN FALSTAFF.

The principal if not ſole reaſon why our hero is never once mentioned by Matthew Paris, *Benedictus abbas*, or any other ancient Engliſh hiſtorian, was moſt probably his avowed enmity to churchmen; and hiſtory, in former times, was written by none but monks. From the ſame motives that Joſephus is pretended to have ſuppreſſed all mention of Jeſus Chriſt, they were unwilling to praiſe the actions which they durſt neither misrepreſent nor deny. Fordun and Major, however, being foreigners, have not been detered by this profeſſional ſpirit from rendering homage to his virtues.

(A) "—was born at Locksley in the county of Nottingham."] "Robin Hood," ſays a MS. in the Britiſh Muſeum, (*Bib. Sloan.* 715.) written, as it ſeems, toward the end of the ſixteenth century, "was borne at Lockesley in Yorkſhyre, or after others in Notinghamſhire." The writer here labours under manifeſt ignorance and confuſion, but *the firſt row of the rubric* will ſet him right:

> "In *Lockſly town*, in merry *Nottinghamſhire*,
> In merry ſweet Lockſly town,
> There bold Robin Hood was *born* and was bred,
> Bold Robin of famous renown."*

Dr. Fuller (*Worthies of England*, 1662, p. 320.) is doubtful as to the place of his nativity. Speaking of the "Memorable Perſons" of Nottinghamſhire, "Robert Hood," ſays he, "(if not by *birth*) by his chief *abode* this country man."

The name of ſuch a town as *Locksley*, or *Loxley* (for ſo, we ſometimes find it ſpelled), in the county of Nottingham or of York, does not, it muſt be confeſſed, occur either in ſir Henry Spelmans *Villare Anglicum*, in Adams's *Index villaris*, in Whatleys *Englands gazetteer*,†

* See part II. ballad 1.

† All three mention a *Loxley* in Warwickſhire, and another in Staffordſhire ("near Needwood-foreſt; the manor and ſeat of the Kinardsleys").

in Thorotons *Hiſtory of Nottinghamſhire*, or in the *Nomina villarum Eboracenſium* (York, 1768, 8vo). The ſilence of theſe authorities is not, however, to be regarded as a concluſive proof that ſuch a place never exiſted. The names of towns and villages, of which no trace is now to be found but in ancient writings, would fill a volume.

(B)—" in the reign of king Henry the ſecond, and about the year of Chriſt 1160.] " Robin Hood," according to the Sloane MS. " was borne . . . in the dayes of Henry the 2nd, about the yeare 1160." This was the 6th year of that monarch; at whoſe death (*anno* 1189) he would, of courſe, be about 29 years of age. Thoſe writers are therefor pretty correct who repreſent him as *playing his franks* (Dr. Fullers phraſe) in the reign of king Richard the firſt, and, according to the laſt named author, " about the year of our lord 1200."* Thus Major (who is followed by Stowe, *Annales* 1592, *p.* 227.) " *Circa hæc tempora* [ſci. *Ricardi I.*] *ut auguror*, &c." A MS. note in the Muſeum (*Bib. Har.* 1233.) not, in Mr. Wanleys opinion, to be relyed on, places him in the ſame period, " *Temp.* Rich. I. " Nor is Fordun altogether out of his reckoning in bringing him down to the time of Henry III. as we ſhall hereafter ſee; and with him agrees that " noble clerke maiſter Hector Boece," who in the nineteeth chapter of his " threttene buke, "ſays, " About this tyme was that waithman Robert Hode with his fallow litil Johne, *&c.*" (*Hyſtory of Scotland*, Edin. 1541. fo.) A modern writer, (*Hiſtory of Whitby*, by Lionel Charlton, York, 1779, 4to.) though of no authority in this point, has done well enough to ſpeak of him as living " in the days of abbot Richard and Peter his ſucceſſor; " that is, between the years 1176 and 1211. The author of the two plays up-

* It is 1100 in the original, but that is clearly an error of the preſs.

on the ſtory of our hero, of which a particular account will be hereafter given, makes him contemporary with king Richard, who, as well as his brother prince John, is introduced upon the ſcene; which is confirmed by another play, quoted in note (D). Warner, alſo, in his *Albions England*, 1602. p. 132. refers his exiſtence to " better daies, firſt Richards daies." This, to be ſure, may not be ſuch evidence as would be ſufficient to decide the point in a court of juſtice; but neither judge nor counſel will diſpute the authority of that oracle of the law ſir Edward Coke, who pronounces that " This Robert Hood lived in the reign of king R.I." (3 *Inſtitute*, 197.)

We muſt not therefore regard what is ſaid by ſuch writers as the author of " George a Greene, the pinner of Wakefield," 1599, (ſee note (G) who repreſents our hero as contemporary with king Edward IV. and the compiler of a fooliſh book called " The noble birth, &c. of Robin Hood," (ſee note (a) who commences it by informing us of his baniſhment by king Henry VIII. As well indeed might we ſuppoſe him to have lived before the time of Charlemagne, becauſe ſir John Harington, in his translation of the *Orlando furioſo*, 1590. p. 391. has made

> " Duke ' Ammon in great wrath thus wiſe ' to' ſpeake,
> *This is a tale indeed of* ROBIN HOOD,
> Which to beleeve, might ſhow my wits but weake:"

or to imagine his ſtory muſt have been familiar to Plutarch, becauſe in his *Morals*, translated by Dr. Philemon Holland, 1603. p. 644. we read the following paſſage: " Evenſo [*i. e.* as the crane and fox ſerve each other in Æſop], when learned men at a table plunge and drowne themſelves (as it were) in ſubtile problemes and queſtions interlaced with logicke, which the vulgar ſort are not able for their lives to comprehend and conceive; whiles they alſo againe for their part come in with their *fooliſh ſongs*, and *vain ballads* of ROBIN-HOOD and LITTLE JOHN, telling *tales of a tubbe*, or of a *roaſted horſe*, and ſuch like."

Who, indeed, would be apt to think that his ſkill in archery was known to Virgil? And yet, as interpreted by our facetious friend Mr. Charles Cotton, he tells us, that

" Cupid was a little tyny,
Cogging, lying, peeviſh nynny;
But with a bow the ſhit-breecht elf
Would ſhoot like ROBIN HOOD himſelf."

In a word, if we are to credit translators, he muſt have exiſted before the ſiege of Troy: for thus, according to one of Homers:

" Then came a choice companion
Of ROBIN HOOD and LITTLE JOHN,
Who many a buck and many a doe,
In *Sherwood foreſt*, with his bow,
Had nabb'd; believe me it is true, ſir,
The fellows Chriſtian name was TEUCER."

Iliad, by Bridges, 4to. p. 231.

This laſt ſuppoſition indeed, has even the reſpectable countenance of dan Geoffrey Chaucer:

" Pandarus anſwerde, it may be well inough,
And held with him of all that ever he ſaied,
But in his hart he thought, and ſoft lough,
And to himſelfe full ſoberly he ſaied,
From *haſellwood* there JOLLY ROBIN plaied,
Shall come all that thou abideſt here,
Ye, farewell all the ſnow of ferne yere."

TROILUS (B. 5.) Speghts edition, 1602.

(C) " His extraction was noble, and his true name ROBERT FITZOOTH".] In " an olde and auncient pamphlet," which Grafton the chronicler had ſeen, it was written that " This man diſcended of a noble parentage." The Sloane MS. ſays " He was of .... parentage;" and though the material word is illegible, the ſenſe evidently requires *noble*. So, likewiſe, the Harleian note: "It is ſaid that he was of noble blood." Leland alſo has expreſsly termed him " *nobilis*." (*Collectanea*, I. 54.) The following account of his family will be found ſufficiently particular. Ralph Fitzothes or Fitzooth, a Norman, who had come over to England with William Rufus, marryed Maud or Matilda, daughter of Gilbert de Gaunt earl of Kyme and Lindſey, by whom he had two ſons: Philip, afterward earl of Kyme, that earldom being part of his mothers dowry, and William. Philip the elder, dyed without iſſue; William was a ward to Robert de Vere earl of Oxford, in whoſe houſehold he received his education, and who, by the kings expreſs command, gave him in marriage to his own niece, the youngeſt of the three daughters of the celebrated lady Roiſia de Vere, daughter of Aubrey de Vere, earl of Guiſnes in Normandy, and lord high chamberlain of England under Henry I. and of Adeliza, daughter to Richard de Clare, earl of Clarence and Hertford, by Payn de Beauchamp baron of Bedford her ſecond huſband. The offspring of this marriage was, our hero, ROBERT FITZOOTH, commonly called ROBIN HOOD. (See Stukeleys *Palæographia Britannica*, No. I. *paſſim.*)

A writer in the *Gentlemans magazine*, for March 1793, under the ſignature D. H. pretends that *Hood* is only a corruption of "*o' th' wood,* q. d. *of Sherwood.*" This, to be ſure, is an abſurd conceit; but, if the name were a matter of conjecture, it might be probably enough refered to ſome particular ſort of *hood* our hero wore by way of diſtinction or diſguiſe. See Scots *Diſcoverie of witchcraft,* 1584. p. 522. It is unneceſſary to add that *Hood* is a common ſurname at this day.

(D) "He is frequently ſtiled . . EARL OF HUNTINGDON, a title to which, for the latter part of his life at leaſt, he actually appears to have had ſome ſort of pretenſion."] In Graftons "olde and auncient pamphlet," though the author had, as already noticed, ſaid "this man diſcended of a noble parentage," he adds, "or rather beyng of a baſe ſtocke and linage, was for his manhood and chivalry advaunced to the noble dignitie of an erle."

In the MS. note (*Bib. Har.* 1233) is the following paſſage: "It is ſaid that he was of noble blood no leſſe then an earle." Warner, in his *Albions England*, already cited, calls him "a county." The titles of Mundys two plays are: "The downfall," and "The death of ROBERT EARLE OF HUNTINGTON." He is likewiſe introduced in that character in the ſame authors *Metropolis coronata*, hereafter cited. In his epitaph we ſhall find him expreſsly ſtiled "ROBERT EARL OF HUNTINGTUN."

In "A pleaſant commodie called *Looke about you*," printed in 1600, our hero is introduced, and performs a principal character. He is repreſented as the young earl of Huntington, and in ward to prince Richard, though his brother Henry, the young king, complains of his having "had wrong about his wardſhip." He is deſcribed as

"A gallant youth, a proper gentleman;"

and is ſometimes called "pretty earle," and "little wag."

"*Fau.* But welcome, welcome, and young HUNTINGTON,
Sweet ROBYN HÙDE, honors beſt flowing bloome."

"——an honourable youth,
Vertuous and modeſt, Huntingtons right heyre."

And it is ſaid that

"*His father* GILBERT was the ſmoothſt fac't lord
"That ere bare armes in England or in Fraunce."

In one ſcene, "Enter Richard and Robert with coronets."

"*Rich.* Richard the Prince of England, with his ward,
The noble ROBERT HOOD, EARLE HUNTINGTON,
Preſent their ſervice to your majeſtie."

Dr. Percys objection, that the moſt ancient poems make no mention of this earldom, but only call him a yeoman, will be conſidered in another place. How he founded his pretenſions to this title will be ſeen in his pedigree. Here it is.

" The pedigree of Robin Hood earl of Huntington.

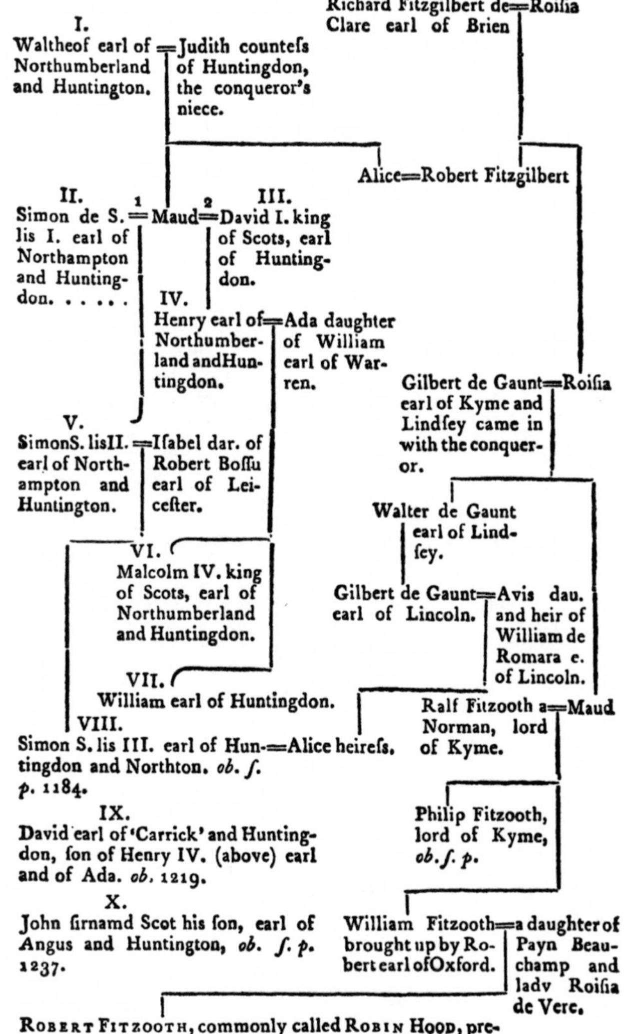

* Stukeleys *Palæographia Britannica*, No. II. p. 115. In an interleaved copy of *Robin Hoods garland* formerly belonging to Dr. Stukeley, and now in the possession of Francis Douce esquire, opposite the 2d page of the 1st song, is the following note in his own hand:

" Guy earl of Warwick.

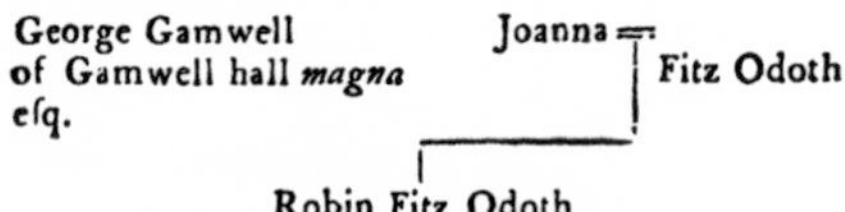

Gamwell the kings forester in Yorkshire, mentioned in Camden.

See my answer No. II. of lady Roisia, where is Robin Hoods TRUE PEDIGREE."

The doctor seems, by this pedigree, to have founded our heros pretensions on his descent from Roisia, sister of Robert Fitzgilbert, husband of Alice, youngest daughter of Judith countess of Huntingdon; which, whatever it might do in those times, would scarcely be thought sufficient to support such a claim, at present. Beside, though John the Seot dyed without issue, he left three sisters, all marryed to powerful barons, either in Scotland or in England, none of whom, however, assumed the title. It is, therefor, probable, after all, that Robin Hood derived his earldom in some other way.

Dr. Stukeley, whose learned labours are sufficiently known and esteemed, was a professed antiquary, and a beneficed clergyman of the church of England. He has not, it is true, thought it necessary to cite any ancient or other authority in support of the above representations; nor is it in the editors power to supply the deficiency. Perhaps, indeed, the doctor might think himself intitled to expect that his own authority would be deemed sufficient: upon that, however, they must be content to rest. Mr. Parkin, who published " A reply to the peevish, weak, and malevolent objections brought by Dr. Stukeley, in his *Origines Roystonianæ*, No. 2. (Norwich, 1748. 4to.) terms " his pedigree of Robin Hood quite jocose, an original indeed!" (see pp. 27, 32.)

Otho and *Fitz-Otho*, it must be confess d, were common names among the Anglo-Normans, but no such name as *Othes*, *Ooth*, *Fitz-Othes*, or *Fitz-Ooth*, has been elsewhere met with. *Philip de Kime*, also, was certainly a considerable landholder in the county of Lincoln, in the time of king Henry II. but it no where appears, except from Dr. Stukeley, that his surname was *Fitz-Ooth*.

The doctor likewise informs us that the arms of Ralph Fitzooth, and consequently of our hero, were " *g.* two bends engrailed, *o.*"

(E) "In his youth he is reported to have been of a wild and extravagant diſpoſition, *&c.*"] Graftons pamphlet, after ſuppoſing him to have been "advaunced to the noble dignitie of an erle," continued thus: "But afterwardes he ſo prodigally exceeded in charges and expences, that he fell into great debt, by reaſon whereof, ſo many actions and ſutes were commenced againſt him whereunto he anſwered not, that by order of lawe he was outlawed."* Leland muſt undoubtedly have had good authority for calling him "*nobilis ille exlex.*"† Fordun ſuppoſes him in the number of thoſe deprived of their eſtates by K. Hen. III. "*Hoc intempore,*" ſays he, "*de* exheredatis *ſurrexit & caput erexit ille famoſiſſimus ſiccarius* Robertus Hode & littill Johanne *cum eorum complicibus.*" (p. 774.) The Sloane MS. ſays he was "ſo ryotous that he loſt or ſould his patrimony & for debt became an outlawe:" and the Harleian note mentions his "having waſted his eſtate in riotous courſes." The former authority, however, gives a different, though, it may be, leſs credible, account of his being obliged to abſcond. It is as follows: "One of his firſt exployts was the going abrode into a forreſt & bearing with him a bowe of exceeding great ſtrength he fell into company with certayne rangers or woodmen, who fell to quarrel with him, as making ſhowe to uſe ſuch a bowe as no man was able to ſhoote withall. Wherto Robin replyed that he had two better then that at Lockeſley, only he bare that with him nowe as a byrding bowe. At length the 'contention' grewe ſo hote that there was a wager layd about the kyllyng of a deere a greate diſtance of, for performance whereof Robin offered to lay his head to a certayne ſome of money, the advantage of which raſh ſpeach the others preſently tooke. So the marke being found out, one of them, both to make his hart faynt and hand unſteady, as he was about to ſhoote

* Graftons chronicle, p. 85. † *Collec.* I. 54.

urged him with the losse of head if he myst the marke. Notwithstanding Robyn kyld the deare, and gave every man his money agayne, save to him which at the poynt of shooting so upbraided him with danger to loose his hed for that wager; & he sayd they would drinke togeyther: whereupon the others stomached the matter and from quarelling they grewe to fighting with him. But Robin, getting him somewhat of, with shooting dispatch them, and so fled away; and then betaking himselfe to lyve in the woods, *&c.*"*

That he lurked or infested the woods is agreed by all. "*Circa hæc tempora,*" says Major, "*Robertus Hudus Anglus & parvus Joannes, latrones famatissimi, in nemoribus latuerunt.*"

Dr. Stukeley says that "Robin Hood took to this wild way of life, in imitation of his grandfather Geoffrey de Mandeville, who being a favorer of Maud empress, K. Stephen took him prisoner at S. Albans, and made him give up the tower of London, Walden, Plessis, &c. upon which he lived on plunder." (*MS. note in his copy of* Robin Hoods garland.)

(F) "Of these he chiefly affected Barnsdale, *&c.*"] "Along on the lift hond," says Leland, "a iii. miles of betwixt Milburne and Feribridge I saw the wooddi and famose forrest of *Barnesdale*, wher thay say that Robyn Hudde lyvid like an owtlaw." *Itinerary*, V. 101.

"They haunted about *Barnsdale forrest*, *Compton* [r. *Plompton*] *parke*,† and such other places." *MS. Sloane.*

* See *Robin Hoods progress to Nottingham*, part II. ballad 2.

† Plompton park, upon the banks of the Peterill, in Cumberland, was formerly very large, and set apart by the kings of England for the keeping of deer. It was disafforested or disparked, by Henry the 8th. See Camdens *Britannia*, by bishop Gibson, who seems to confound this park with Inglewood forest, a district of sixteen miles in length, reaching from Carlile to Penrith, where the kings of England used to hunt, and Edward I. is reported to have killed 200 bucks in one day. *Ibi.*

"His principal reſidence," ſays Fuller, "was in *Shirewood forreſt* in this county [Notts], though he had another haunt (he is no fox that hath but one hole) near the ſea in the North-riding in Yorkſhire, where *Robin Hoods bay* ſtill retaineth his name: not that he was any pirat, but a land-thief, who retreated to thoſe unſuſpected parts for his ſecurity." *Worthies of England*, p. 320.

In Thorotons *Nottinghamſhire*, p. 505. is ſome account of the ancient and preſent ſtate of Sherwood foreſt; but one looks in vain, through that dry detail of land-owners, for any particulars relating to our hero. "In *anno domini* 1194. king Richard the firſt, being a hunting in the forreſt of Sherwood, did chaſe a hart out of the forreſt of Sherwood into Barneſdale in Yorkſhire, and becauſe he could not there recover him, he made proclamation at Tickill in Yorkſhire, and at divers other places there that no perſon ſhould kill, hurt, or chaſe the ſaid hart, but tha the might ſafely retorne into forreſt againe, which hart was afterwards called a *hart-royall proclaimed.* (Manwoods *Foreſt laws*, 1598, p. 25. from "an auncient recorde" found by him in the tower of Nottingham caſtle.)*

(*F) "Here he either found, &c."] After being outlawed, Grafton tells us, "for a lewde ſhift, as his laſt refuge, [he] gathered together a companye of royſters and cutters,† and practiſed robberyes and ſpoyling of the

* Drayton, (*Polyolbion*, ſong 26.) introduces Sherwood in the character of a nymph, who, out of diſdain at the preference ſhewn by the poet to a ſiſter-foreſt,

"All ſelf praiſe ſet apart, determineth to ſing
That luſty Robin Hood, who long time like a king
Within her compaſs liv'd, and when he liſt to range,
For ſome rich booty ſet, or elſe his air to change,
To Sherwood ſtill retir'd, his only ſtanding court."

† Cutters.] See the gloſſary to volume I. The word is ſometimes uſed as ſynonimous with bravos or aſſaſſins. So in the old play of *Arden of Feverſham*, b. l. n. d.

"And they are *cutters* and may *cut* your throat."

kinges ſubjects, and occupied and frequented the foreſtes or wild countries." See alſo the following note.

(G) "LITTLE JOHN, WILLIAM SCADLOCK, GEORGE A GREEN, pinder of Wakefield, MUCH a millers ſon, and a certain monk or friar named TUCK."] Of theſe the preeminence is inconteſtably due to *Little John*, whoſe name is almoſt conſtantly coupled with that of his gallant leader, "*Robertus Hode* & littill Johanne," are mentioned together by Fordun, as early as 1341; and later inſtances of the connection would be almoſt endleſs. After the words, "for debt became an outlaw," the Sloane MS. adds: "then joyninge to him many ſtout fellowes of lyke diſpoſition, amongſt whom one called *Little John* was principal or next to him, they haunted about Barnſdale forreſt, &c." See notes (KK) (LL).

With reſpect to *frier Tuck*, "thogh ſome ſay he was an other kynd of religious man, for that the order of freyrs was not yet ſprung up," *(MS. Sloan.)* yet as the Dominican friers (or friers preachers) came into England in the year 1221, upward of 20 years before the death of Robin Hood, and ſeveral orders of theſe religious had flouriſhed abroad for ſome time, there does not ſeem much weight in that objection: nor in fact, can one pay much regard to the term *frier*, as it ſeems to have been the common title given by the vulgar (more eſpecially after the reformation) to all the regular clergy, of which the friers were at once the loweſt and moſt numerous. If *frier Tuck* be the ſame perſon who, in one of the oldeſt ſongs, is called *The curtal frier of Fountaindale*, he muſt neceſſaryly have been one of the monks of that abbey, which was of the Ciſtertian order. However this may be, *frier Tuck* is frequently no iced, by old writers, as one of the companions of Robin Hood, and as ſuch was an eſſential character in the morris-dance, (ſee note (H). He is thus mentioned by Skelton, laureat, in his "goodly interlude" of *Magnificence*, written about the year 1500, and with an evident alluſion to ſome game or practice now totally forgotten and inexplicable,

> " Another bade ſhave halfe my berde,
> And boyes to the pylery gan me plucke,
> And wolde have made me *freer Tucke*,
> To preche oute of the pylery hole."

In the year 1417, as Stow relates, " one by his counterfeite name, called *frier Tucke*, with manie other malefactors, committed many robberies in the counties of Surrey & Suſſex, whereupon the king ſent out his writs for their apprehenſion." (*Annales*, 1592.)

George a Green is *George o'the Green*, meaning perhaps the *town-green*, in which the *pound* or *pinfold* ſtood of which he had the care. He has been particularly celebrated, and " As good as George a Green" is ſtill a common ſaying. Drayton, deſcribing the progreſs of the river Calder, in the weſt-riding of Yorkſhire, has the following lines:

> " It chanc'd ſhe in her courſe on ' Kirkley' caſt her eye,
> Where merry Robin Hood, that honeſt thief, doth lie;
> Beholding fitly too before how Wakefield ſtood,
> She doth not only think of luſty Robin Hood,
> But of his merry man, the pindar of the town
> Of Wakefield, George a Green, whoſe fames ſo far are blown
> For their ſo valiant fight, that every freemans ſong
> Can tell you of the ſame, quoth ſhe, be talk'd on long
> For ye were merry lads, and thoſe were merry days."

Thus, too, Richard Brathwayte, in his poetical epiſtle " to all true-bred northerne ſparks of the generous ſociety of the Cottoneers" (*Strappado for the divell*, 1615):

> " But haſte, my muſe, in colours to diſplay
> Some auncient cuſtomes in their high-roade way,
>
> . . . .
>
> At leaſt ſuch places labour to make knowne
> As former times have honour'd with renowne.
>
> . . . .
>
> The firſt whereof that I intend to ſhow
> Is merry Wakefield, and her pindar too,

Which fame hath blaz'd with all that did belong,
Unto that towne in many gladſome ſong,
The pindars valour, and how firme he ſtood
In th' townes defence 'gainſt th' rebel Robin Hood,
How ſtoutly he behav'd himſelfe, and would,
In ſpite of Robin, bring his horſe to th' fold,
His many May-games which were to be ſeene
Yearly preſented *upon Wakefield greene*,
Where lovely Jugge and luſtie Tib would go,
To ſee Tom-lively turne upon the toe;
Hob, Lob, and Crowde the fidler would be there,
And many more I will not ſpeake of here.
Good god! how glad hath been this hart of mine,
To ſee that towne, which hath, in former time,
So flouriſh'd and ſo gloried in her name,
Famous by th' pindar who firſt rais'd the ſame!
Yea, I have paced ore *that greene* and ore
And th' more I ſaw't I tooke delight the more,
" For where we take contentment in a place,
" A whole daies walke ſeemes as a cinquepace.
Yet as there is no ſolace upon earth,
Which is attended evermore with mirth,
But when we are tranſported moſt with gladneſſe,
Then ſuddenly our joy's reduc'd to ſadneſſe;
So far'd with me to ſee the pindar gone,
And of thoſe jolly laddes that were not one
Left to ſurvive: I griev'd more then Ile ſay:—
(But now for Bradford I muſt haſt away.)

. . . . . .

Unto thy taſk, my muſe, and now make knowne,
The jolly ſhoo-maker of Bradford towne,
His gentle-craft ſo rais'd in former time
By princely journey-men his diſcipline,
" Where he was wont with paſſengers to quaffe,
" But ſuffer none to carry up their ſtaffe
Upon their ſhoulders, whilſt they paſt through town,
For if they did he ſoon would beat them downe;
(So valiant was the ſouter) and from hence
Twixt Robin Hood and him grew th' difference;
Which, cauſe it is by moſt ſtage-poets writ,
For brevity I thought good to omit."

In the latter part of this extract, honeſt Richard evidently alludes to " A pleaſant conceyted comedie of George a Greene, the pinner of Wakefield; as it was ſundry times acted by the ſervants of the right honourable the earle of Suſſex," 1599, 4to. which has been erroneously aſcribed to Heywood the epigrammatiſt, and is reprinted, with other traſh, in the late edition of Dodſleys *Old plays*; only it unluckily happens that *Robin Hood* is almoſt the only perſon who has NO difference with the *ſouter* (or ſhoe-maker) *of Bradford*. The play in ſhort, (or at leaſt that part of it which we have any concern with) is founded on the ballad of *Robin Hood and the pinder of Wakefield*, (ſee part II. ſong 3,) which it directly quotes, and is in fact a moſt deſpicable performance. King Edward *(the fourth)* having taken king James of Scotland priſoner, after a moſt bloody battle near Middleham-caſtle, from which of 30,000 Scots not 5000 had eſcaped, comes with his royal captive in diſguiſe to Bradford, where they meet *Robin Hood* and *George a Green*, who have juſt had a ſtout affray: and, after having read this, and a great deal more ſuch nonſenſical ſtuff, captain Groſe ſagaciously "ſuppoſes, that this play has little or no foundation in hiſtory;" and very gravely ſits down, and debates his opinion in form.

"The hiſtory of George a Green, pindar of the town of Wakefield", 4to. no date, is a modern production, chiefly founded on the old play juſt mentioned, of neither authority nor merit.

Our gallant pinder is thus facetiously commemorated by *Drunken Barnaby*:

"*Hinc diverſo curſo, ſero*
Quod audiſſem de pindero
Wakefeeldenſi; *gloria mundi*,
Ubi ſocii ſunt jucundi,
Mecum ſtatui peragrare
Georgii fuſtem *viſitare*.'

"Turning thence, none could me hinder
To ſalute the *Wakefield pindar*;
Who indeed is the world's glory,
With his comrades never ſorry.
This was the cauſe, leſt you ſhould miſs it,
George's club I meant to viſit.

"*Veni* Wakefield *peramœnum*,
Ubi quærens Georgium Greenum,
Non inveni, ſed in lignum
Fixum reperi Georgii *ſignum*,
Ubi allam bibi feram
Donce Georgio *fortior eram.*"

"Strait at Wakefield I was ſeen a,
Where I ſought for *George a Green a*;
But could find not ſuch a creature,
Yet on a ſign I ſaw his feature,
Where ſtrength of ale had ſo much ſtir'd me,
That I grew ſtouter far than *Jordie*."

Beſides the companions of our hero enumerated in the text, and whoſe names are moſt celebrated and familiar, we find thoſe of *William of Goldsbrough*, (mentioned by Grafton,) *Right-hitting Brand,* (by Mundy,) and *Gilbert with the white hand*, who is thrice named in the *Lytell geſte of Robyn Hode*, (I. 52. 71.) and is likewiſe noticed by biſhop Gawin Douglas, in his *Palice of Honour*, printed at Edinburgh in 1579, but written before 1518:

"Thair ſaw I Maitlaind upon auld Beird Gray,
Robene Hude, and *Gilbert with the quhite* '*hand*,'
How Hay of Nauchton flew, in Madin land."*

As no mention is made of Adam Bell, Clim of the Clough and William of Cloudeſlie, either in the ancient legend, or in more than one of the numerous ſongs of Robin Hood, nor does the name of the latter once occur in the old metrical hiſtory of thoſe famous archers, reprinted in Percys *Reliques*, and among *Pieces of ancient popular poetry*, it is to be concluded that they flouriſhed at different periods, or at leaſt had no connection with each other. In a poem, however, intitled "Adam Bell, Clim of the Clough, and YOUNG William of

* *Scotiſh poems*, i. 122. The laſt verſe is undoubtedly ſenſe as it now ſtands; but a collation of MSS. would probably authoriſe us to read:

"*Quhom* Hay of Nauchton *ſlew* in Madin land."

Cloudesley, the second part," 1616. 4to. b. l. (*Bib. Bod. Art. L.* 71. being a more modern copy than that in *Selden C.* 39, which wants the title, but was probably printed with the first part, which it there accompanies, in 1605; differing considerably therefrom in several places; and containing many additional verses;) are the following lines (not in the former copy):

" Now beare thy fathers heart, my boy,
  Said William of Cloudesley then,
When i was young i car'd not for
  The brags of sturdiest men.
The pinder of Wakefield, George a Green,
  I try'd a sommers day,
Yet he nor i were victors made
  Nor victor'd went away.
Old Robin Hood, nor Little John,
  Amongst their merry men all,
Nor fryer Tuck, so stout and young,
  My courage could appall."

(H) "MARIAN".] Who or whatever this lady was, it is observable that no mention of her occurs either in the *Lytell geste of Robyn Hode*, or in any other poem or song concerning him, except a comparatively modern one of of no merit (see part II. song 24). She is an important character, however, in the two old plays of *The death* and *downfall of Robert earl of Huntington*, written before 1600, and is frequently mentioned by dramatic or other writers about that period. The morris dance, so famous of old time, was (as is elsewhere noticed) composed of the following constituent characters: *Robin Hood, Little John, frier Tuck,* and *maid Marian.*

In the *First part of K. Henry IV.* Falstaff says to the hostess,—" There's no more faith in thee than in a stew'd prune; nor no more truth in thee than in a drawn fox; and for womanhood, *maid Marian* may be the deputy's wife of the ward to thee:" upon which Dr. Johnson observes, that " *Maid Marian* is a man dressed like a woman, who attends the dancers of the morris." " In the *ancient songs of Robin Hood,*" says Percy,, " frequent mention is made of *maid Marian*, who appears to have been his concubine." I could quote," adds he, "many paſſages IN MY OLD MS. to this purpoſe, but ſhall produce only one :*

"Good Robin Hood was living then,
Which now is quite forgot,
And ſo was fayre *maid Marian*, &c."

Mr. Steevens, too, after citing the old play of *The downfall of Robert earl of Huntington*, 1601, to prove "that *maid Marian* was originally a name aſſumed by *Matilda*, the daughter of *Robert lord Fitzwater*, while *Robin Hood* remained in a ſtate of outlawry," obſerves, that "Shakſpeare ſpeaks of *maid Marian* in her degraded ſtate, when ſhe was repreſented by a ſtrumpet or a clown": and refers to figure 2 in the plate at the end of the play, with Mr. Tollets obſervations on it. The widow, in ſir W. Davenants *Love and honour*, ſays: "I have been *miſtreſs Marian* in a *maurice* ere now;" and Mr. Warton quotes an old piece, intitled "Old Meg of Herefordſhire for a *maid Marian*, and Hereford town for a morris-dance: or 12 morris-dancers in Herefordſhire of 1200 years old," London, 1609, quarto: which is dedicated, he ſays, to one Hall, a celebrated tabourer in that country. See note (FF).

* Without "the ancient ſongs," to which the doctor refers, are confined to his "old MS." he evidently aſſerts what he would probably find it difficult to prove. As for the paſſage he produces, it ſeems nothing to the purpoſe; as, in the firſt place, it is apparently not "ancient"; and, in the ſecond, it is apparently not from a "ſong of Robin Hood."

† Mr. Warton, having obſerved that "The play of ROBIN and MARIAN is ſaid to have been performed by the ſchool-boys of Angiers, according to annual cuſtom, in the year 1392: The boys were *deguiſiez*, ſays the old French record; und they had among them UN FILLETTE *deſguiſee*; (*Carpent. Du Cange, v.* ROBINET-PENTECOSTE.)" adds "Our old character of *Mayd Marian* may be hence illuſtrated." (*His. En. po.* i. 245.) This, indeed, ſeems ſufficiently plauſible; but unfortunately the *Robin* and *Marian* of *Angiers* are not the *Robin* and *Marian* of *Sherwood*. The play is ſtill extant. See *Fabliaux ou contes*, Paris, 1781, ii. 144.

(I) "His company, &c."] See the entire paſſage quoted from Major in a ſubſequent note. "By ſuch boo-tyes as he could get," ſays the writer of the Sloane MS. "his company encreaſt to an hundred and a halfe."

(J)—"the words of an old writer."] The author of the Sloane manuſcript; which adds: "after ſuch maner he procured the pynner of Wakefeyld to become one of his company, and a freyr called Muchel [r. Tuck]... Scarlock he induced upon this occaſion: one day meeting him as he walket ſolitary & like to a man forlorne, be-cauſe a mayd to whom he was affyanced was taken from [him] by the violence of her frends, & given to ano-ther that was old & welthy, whereupon Robin, under-ſtanding when the maryage-day ſhould be, came to the church as a *begger*, & having his own company not far of, which came in ſo ſoone as they hard the ſound of his horne, he tooke the bryde perforce from him that [bare] in hand to have marryed her, & cauſed the preiſt to wed her & Scarlocke togeyther." (See part II. ſong 8.) This MS. of which great part is merely the old legend or *Lytell geſte of Robyn Hode* turned into proſe, appears to have been written before the year 1600.

(K) "In ſhooting, &c."] *MS. Sloan.* Grafton alſo ſpeaks of our heros "excellyng principally in archery or ſhooting, his manly courage agreeyng thereunto."

Their archery, indeed, was unparalleled, as both Ro-bin Hood and Little John have frequently ſhot an arrow a meaſured mile, or 1760 yards, which, it is ſuppoſed, no one, either before or ſince, was ever able to do. "Tradi-tion," ſays maſter Charlton, "informs us that in one of 'Robin Hoods' peregrinations, he, attended by his truſty mate Little John, went to dine [at Whitby-abbey] with the abbot Richard, who, having heard them often famed for their great dexterity in ſhooting with the long bow, begged them after dinner to ſhew him a ſpecimen thereof; when, to oblige the abbot, they went up to the top of the abbey, whence each of them ſhot an arrow, which fell not far from Whitby-laths, but on the contrary ſide of the lane; and in memorial thereof, a pillar was ſet up by the abbot in the place where each of the arrows was found, which are yet ſtanding in theſe our days; that field where the pillar for Robin Hood's arrow ſtands being ſtill called *Robin Hood's field*, and the other where the pillar for Little John's arrow is placed, ſtill preſerving the name of *John's field*. Their diſtance from Whitby abbey is MORE THAN A MEASURED MILE, which ſeems very far for the flight of an arrow, and is a circumſtance that will ſtagger the faith of many; but as to the credibility of the ſtory, every reader may judge thereof as he thinks proper; only I muſt here beg leave to obſerve that theſe very pillars are mentioned, and the fields called by the aforeſaid names, in the old deeds for that ground, now in the poſſeſſion of Mr. Thomas Watſon." (*Hiſtory of Whitby*, York, 1779. p. 146.)*

* "The quarry from whence king Wolfere fetched ſtones for his royal ſtructure [*i. e.* Peterborough] was undoubtedly that of Bernach near unto Stamford....And I find in the charter of K. Edward the Confeſſor, which he granted to the abbot of Ramſey, that the abbot of Ramſey ſhould give to the abbot and convent of Peterburgh 4000 eeles in the time of Lent, and in conſideration thereof the abbot of Peterburgh ſhould give to the abbot of Ramſey as much freeſtone from his pitts in Bernack, and as much ragſtone from his pitts in Peterburgh as he ſhould need. Nor did the abbot of Peterburgh from theſe pits furniſh only that but other abbies alſo, as that of St. Edmunds-Bury: in memory whereof there are two long ſtones yet ſtanding upon a balk in Caſtor-field, near unto Gunwade ferry; which erroneous tradition hath given out to be draughts of arrows from Alwalton church-yard thither; the one of Robin Hood, and the other of Little John; but the truth is, they were ſet up for witneſſes, that the carriages of ſtone from Bernack to Gunwade-ferry, to be conveyed to S. Edmunds-Bury, might paſs that way without paying toll; and in ſome old terrars they are called S. Edmunds ſtones. Theſe ſtones are nicked in their tops after the manner of arrows, probably enough in memory of S. Edmund, who was ſhot to death with arrows by the Danes." Guntons *Hiſtory of the church of Peterburgh*, 1686, p. 4.

Dr. Meredith Hanmer, in his *Chronicle of Ireland*, (p. 179.) ſpeaking of Little John, ſays, " There are memorable acts reported of him, which I hold not for truth, that he would ſhoot an arrow A MILE OFF, and a great deale more; but them," adds he, " I leave among the lyes of the land."*

(L) " An outlaw, in thoſe times, being deprived of protection, owed no allegiance, &c."] Such a character was, doubtleſs, at the period treated of, in a very critical ſituation; it being equally as legal and meritorious to hunt down and diſpatch him as it was to kill a wolf, the head of which animal he was ſaid to bear. " *Item forisfacit*," ſays Bracton, (who wrote about the time,) *omnia que pacis ſunt, quia a tempore quo utlagatus eſt* CAPUT GERIT LUPINUM, *ita ut impune ab omnibus interfici poſſit. (l. 2. c. 35.)* In the great roll of the Exchequer, in the 7th year of king Richard I. is an allowance by writ, of two marks, to Thomas de Preſtwude, for bringing to Weſtminſter the head of William de Elleford an

* " In this relation," Mr. Walker obſerves, " the doctor not only evinces his credulity, but diſplays his ignorance of archery; for the ingenious and learned Mr. Barrington, than whom no man can be better informed on the ſubject, thinks that eleven ſcore and ſeven yards is the utmoſt extent that an arrow can be ſhot from a long bow." (*Archæologia*, vol. VII.) According to tradition, he adds, Little John ſhot an arrow from the Old-bridge, Dublin, to the preſent ſite of St. Michaels church, a diſtance not exceeding, he believes, that mentioned by Mr. Barrington. (*Hiſtorical eſſay on the dreſs of the ancient and modern Iriſh*, p. 129.)

What Mr. Barrington " thinks" may be true enough, perhaps, of the Toxopholite-ſociety and other modern archers; but people ſhould not talk of ROBIN HOOD *who never ſhot in his bow*. The above ingenious writers cenſure of Dr. Hanmers *credulity* and *ignorance*, ſeems to be miſapplyed; ſince he cannot be ſuppoſed to believe what he *holds not for truth*, and actually *leaves among the lyes of the land*.

See alſo the old ſong, printed in the appendix, p. 207. Drayton, a well-informed and intelligent man, who wrote before archery had fallen into complete diſuſe, ſays—

" At marks full *forty ſcore* they us'd to prick and rove."

outlaw. (See Madoxes *Hiſtory of the Exchequer*, 136.) Thoſe who received or conſorted with a perſon outlawed were ſubject to the ſame puniſhment. Such was the humane policy of our enlightened anceſtors!

(M)

" —— how,
. . . . they could diſcourſe
The freezing hours away!"]

(*Cymbeline*, act 3, ſcene 3.) The chief ſubjects of our heros converſation are ſuppoſed, by a poetical genius of the 16th century, to have been the commendation of a foreſt-life, and the ingratitude of mankind.

" I have no tales of Robin Hood, though mal-content was he
In better daies, firſt Richards daies, and liv'd in woods as we
A Tymon of the world; but not devoutly was he ſoe,
And therefore praiſe I not the man: but for from him did groe
Words worth the note, a word or twaine of him ere hence we goe,
Thoſe daies begot ſome mal-contents, the principall of whome
A county was, that with a troope of yomandry did rome,
Brave archers and deliver men, ſince nor before ſo good,
Thoſe took from rich to give the poore, and manned Robin Hood.
He fed them well, and lodg'd them ſafe in pleaſant caves and bowers,
Oft ſaying to his merry men, What juſter life than ours?
Here uſe we tallents that abroad the churles abuſe or hide,
Their coffers excrements, and yeat for common wants denide.
We might have ſterved for their ſtore, & they have dyc'ſt our bones,
Whoſe tongues, driftes, harts, intice, meane, melt, as ſyrens, foxes, ſtones,
Yea even the beſt that betterd them heard but aloofe our mones.
And redily the churles could prie and prate of our amis,
Forgetfull of their owne. . . .
I did amis, not miſſing friends that wiſht me to amend:
I did amend, but miſſed friends when mine amis had end:
My friends therefore ſhall finde me true, but I will truſt no frend.
Not one I knewe that wiſht me ill, nor any workt me well,
To loſe, lacke, live, time, frends, in yncke, an hell, an hell, an hell!
Then happie we (quoth Robin Hood) in merry Sherwood that dwell.*

* Warners *Albions England*, 1602, p. 132. It is part of the hermits ſpeech to the earl of Lancaſter.

It has been conjectured, however, that, in the winter-ſeaſon, our hero and his companions ſeverally quartered themſelves in villages or country-houſes more or leſs remote, with perſons of whoſe fidelity they were aſſured. It is not improbable, at the ſame time, that they might have tolerably comfortable habitations erected in the woods.

Archery, which our hero and his companions appear to have carryed to a ſtate of perfection, continued to be cultivated for ſome ages after their time, down, indeed, to that of Henry VIII. or about the year 1540, when, owing to the introduction of artillery and matchlock-guns, it became neglected, and the bowmen of Creſſy and Agincourt utterly extinct: though it may be ſtill a queſtion whether a body of expert archers would not, even at this day be ſuperior to an equal number armed with muſkets. The loſs ſuſtained from this change by the people at large ſeems irreparable. Anciently, the uſe of the bow or bill qualified every man for a ſoldier; and a body of peaſants, led on by a Tyler or a Cade, was not leſs formidable than any military force that could be raiſed to oppoſe them: by which means the people from time to time preſerved the very little liberty they had, and which their tyrants were conſtantly endeavouring to wreſt from them: See how the caſe ſtands at preſent: the ſovereign, let him be who or what he will, (kings have been tyrants and may be ſo again,) has a ſtanding army, well diſciplined and accoutred, while the ſubjects or people are abſolutely defenceleſs: as much care having been taken, particularly ſince "the glorious revolution," to deprive them of arms as was formerly beſtowed to enforce their uſe and practice. The following extract from Hales *Hiſtoria placitorum coronæ* (i. 118.) will ſerve to ſhew how familiar the bow and arrow was in the 14th century. "*M.* 22. *E.* 3. *Rot.* 117. *coram rege Ebor.* This was the caſe of Henry Veſcy, who had been indicted before the ſheriff *in turno ſuo* . . . of divers felonies, whereupon the ſheriff *mandavit commiſſionem ſuam Henrico de Clyderawe & aliis* *ad capiendum prædictum* H. Vescy, & *salvo ducendum usque castrum de Ebor.*' Vescy would not submit to an arrest, but fled, & *inter fugiendum* shot with his bow and arrows at his pursuers, but in the end was kild by Clyderawe :" to which may be added a remarkable passage in Harisons "Description of England," (prefixed to Holinsheds chronicle, 1587,) to prove how much it had declined in the 16th. "In times past," says he, "the cheefe force of England consisted in their long bowes. But now we have in maner generallie given over that kind of artillerie, and for long bowes in deed doo practise to shoot compasse for our pastime; which kind of shooting can never yeeld anie smart stroke, nor beat down our enemies, as our countriemen were woont to doo at everie time of need. Certes the Frenchmen and Rutters* deriding our new archerie in respect of their corslets, will not let, in open skirmish, if anie leisure serve, to turne up their tailes, and crie, Shoote, English; and all because our strong shooting is decaied and laid in bed. But if some of our Englishmen now lived that served king Edward the third in his warres with France, the breech† of such a varlet should have beene nailed to his bum with one arrow, and an other fethered in his bowels, before he should have turned about to see who shot the first." (p. 198.) Bishop Latimer, in his sixth sermon before K. Edward VI. gives an interesting account how the sons of yeomen were, in his infancy, trained up to the bow.

(N)

"All clad in Lincoln green—"]

This species of cloth is mentioned by Spenser (*Faerie queene*, VI. ii. 5.)

"All in a woodmans jacket he was clad
Of *Lincolne greene*, belay'd with silver lace;
And on his head an hood with aglets sprad,
And by his side his hunters horne he hanging had."

* Flemings. † Breeches.

It is likwife noticed by our poet himfelf, in another place:

"Swains in fhepherds gray, and gyrles in *Lincolne greene*."*

See *Polyolbion*, fong XXV. where the marginal note fays, "*Lincolne* anciently dyed the beft *green* in England." Thus *Coventry* had formerly the reputation of dying the beft *blue*. See Rays *Proverbs*, p. 178. *Kendal green* is equally famous, and appears to have been cloth of a fimilar quality. This colour was adopted by forefters to prevent their being too readyly difcovered by the deer. See Sir John Wynnes *Hiftory of the Guedir family*, (Barringtons *Mifcellanies*,) p. 419. Thus the Scotifh highlanders ufed to wear brown plaids to prevent their being diftinguifhed among the heath. It is needlefs to obferve that *green* has ever been the favourite drefs of an *archer*, *hunter*, &c. See note (DD). † We now call it a Saxon or grafs green:

"His coat is of a *Saxon green*, his waiftcoat's of a plaid." *O. fong.*

Lincoln green was well known in France in or before the thirteenth century. Thus, in an old *fabliau*, transprofed by M. Le Grand (*Fabliaux ou contes*, iv. 12.) "*Il mit donc fon furcot fourré d'écureuil, & fa belle robe* d'ESTANFORT teinte en verd." *Eftanfort* is Stamford, in Lincolnfhire. This cloth is, likewife, often mentioned by the old Scotifh poets, under the names of *Lincum licht*, *Lincum twyne*, &c. and appears to have been in

* Thus alfo in part II. ballad 1.

"She got on her holyday kirtle and gown,
They were of a light *Lincolne green*."

† In the fign of *The* green man *and* ftill, we perceive a *huntfman*, in a *green coat*, ftanding by the fide of a *ftill*; in allufion, as it has been facetiously conjectured, to the partiality fhewn by that defcription of gentry to a morning dram. The genuine reprefentation, however, fhould be the *green-man*, (or *man who deals in green herbs*,) with a bundle of *pepper-mint*, or *penny-royal*, under his arm, which he brings to have *diftilled*.

universal request: and yet, notwithstanding this cloud of evidence, mister John Pinkerton has had the confidence to assert that "no particular cloth was ever made at Lincoln." (See *Ancient Scotish poems*, ii. 430.) But, indeed, this worthy gentleman, as Johnson said of Goldsmith, only stumbles upon truth by accident.

(O)

"From wealthy abbots chests, &c."]

"But who," exclaims Dr. Fuller, having cited this passage, "made him a judge? or gave him a commission to take where it might be best spared, and give where it was most wanted?" That same power, one may answer, which authorises kings to take where it can be *worst* spared, and give it where it is *least* wanted. Our hero, in this respect, was a knight-errant; and wanted no other commission than that of Justice, whose cause he militated. His power, compared with that of the king of England, was, by no means, either equally usurped, or equally abused: the one reigned over subjects (or slaves) as a master (or tyrant), the other possessed no authority but what was delegated to him by the free suffrage of his adherents, for their general good: and, as for the rest, it would be absurd to blame in Robin what we should praise in Richard. The latter, too, warred in remote parts of the world against nations from which neither he nor his subjects had sustained any injury; the former at home against those to whose wealth, avarice, or ambition, he might fairly attribute not only his own misfortunes, but the misery of the oppressed and enslaved society he had quitted. In a word, every man who has the power has also the authority to pursue the ends of justice; to regulate the gifts of fortune, by transfering the superfluities of the rich to the necessities of the poor; by relieving the oppressed, and even, when necessary, destroying the oppressor. These are the objects of the social union; and every individual may, and to the utmost of his power should, endeavour to promote them. Had our Robin Hood been, like Mc Donald of Barrisdale, a reader of Virgil, he, as well as that gallant chief, might have inſcribed on his baldric,

> " *Hæ tibi erunt artes; pacis componere mores,*
> *Parcere ſubjectis, et debellare ſuperbos.*" *

(*O) " But it is to be remembered," *&c.*] The paſſage, from Majors work, which has been already quoted, is here given entire (except as to a ſingle ſentence introduced in another place). *Circa hæc tempora* [*ſ. Ricardi I.*] *ut auguror, Robertus Hudus & Parvus Joannes latrones famatiſſimi, in nemoribus latuerunt, ſolum opulentum virorum bona diripientes. Nullum niſi eos invadentem vel reſiſtentem pro ſuarum rerum tuitione occiderunt. Centum ſagittarios ad pugnam aptiſſimos Robertus latrociniis aluit quos* 400 *viri fortiſſimi invadere non audebant. Fæminam nullam opprimi permiſit, nec pauperum bona ſurripuit, verum eos ex abbatum bonis ablatis opipare pavit. Viri rapinam improbo, ſed latronum omnium humaniſſimus & princeps erat.*" (*Majoris Britanniæ hiſtoria. Edin.* 1740. p. 128.)

Stowe, in his *Annales*, 1592, p. 227. gives an almoſt

* See Pennants *Tour in Scotland MDCCLXXII.* part I p. 404. The original reading, whether altered by miſtake or deſign, is—

" —— *paciſ*que imponere morem."

One might, to the ſame purpoſe, addreſs our hero in the words of Plautus: (*Trinummus*, Act IV. ſcene i.)

" *Atque hanc tuam gloriam jam ante auribus acceperam, & nobiles apud homines,*
Pauperibus te parcere ſolitum, divites damnare atque domare.
Abi, laudo. ſcis ordine, ut æquom'ſt,
Tractare homines, hoc dîs dignum'ſt, ſemper mendicis modeſti ſint."

> " —— I've head before
> This commendation of you, and from great ones,
> That you were wont to ſpare the indigent,
> And cruſh the wealthy.—I applaud your juſtice
> In treating men according to their merits,—
> 'Tis worthy of the gods to have reſpect
> Unto the poor."

literal verſion of the above paſſage; Richard Robinſon verſifies it *; and Camden ſlightly refers to it.

(P)—"has had the honour to be compared to the illuſtrious Wallace, *&c.*"] In the firſt volume of Pecks intended ſupplement to the *Monaſticon*, conſiſting of collections for the hiſtory of Præmonſtratenſian monaſteries, now in the Britiſh Muſeum, is a very curious riming Latin poem, with the following title: "*Prioris Alnwicenſis de bello Scotico apud Dnmbarr, tempore rigis Edwardi I. dictamen ſive rithmus Latinus, quo de* WILLIELMO WALLACE, Scotico illo ROBIN WHOOD, *plura ſed invidioſe canit:*" and in the margin are the following date and reference: 22. *Julii* 1304. 32. *E.* 1. *Regiſt. Prem. fol.* 59. a." This, it may be obſerved, is the firſt known inſtance of our heros name being mentioned by any writer whatever; and affords a ſtrong and reſpectable proof of his early popularity.

(Q)—"ſupported in pampered luxury."] A well-drawn character of a lordly prelate of our own days may be found in *The adventures of Hugh Trevor*, a novel, by Thomas Holcroft (one of the perſons who had the honour to be indicted for high-treaſon in 1794). The ſacred functions of theſe auguſt dignitaries ſeem pretty accurately delineated in the following *jeu d'eſprit*, inſcribed, many years ago, on the epiſcopal ſeat in a certain cathedral:

* "Richard Cœur de Lyon cald a king and conquerour was,
With Phillip king of France who did unto Jeruſalemm paſſe:

. . . .

In this kings time was Robyn Hood, that archer and outlawe,
And little John his partener eke, unto them which did drawe
One hondred tall and good archers, on whom foure hondred men,
Were their power never ſo ſtrong, could not give onſet then;
The abbots, monkes, and carles rich theſe onely did moleſt,
And reſkewd woemen when they ſaw of theeves them ſo oppreſt;
Reſtoring poore mens goods, and eke abundantly releeved
Poore travellers which wanted food, or were with ſicknes greeved."

(*Third aſſertion*, &c. (quoted elſewhere).

"This is the throne of the biſhop of Durham;
Who has fifteen thouſand a year, and odd,
For eating and drinking,
And farting and ſtinking,
And ſaying *The peace of god.*"

This inſcription, though calculated for the meridian of Durham, may ſerve as well for Canterbury, or Winchеſter. Mr. Hutchinſon, the induſtrious hiſtorian of the northern palatinate, who has unfortunately omitted ſo intereſting an anecdote in the life of biſhop Talbot, will be eager, no doubt, to avail himſelf of it, in a future edition of his equally voluminous and important labours.

(R)—" the abbot of St. Marys in York"] " In the year 1088 Alan earl of Richmond founded here a ſtately abbey for black monks to the honour of St. Olave; but it was afterwards dedicated to the bleſſed virgin by the command of king William Rufus. Its yearly revenues at the ſuppreſſion amounted to 1550*l.* 7*ſ.* 9*d.* *Dugd.* 2850*l.* 1*ſ.* 5*d.* *Speed.*" Willis's *Mitred abbeys*, i. 214. The abbots in our heros time were—

Robert de Harpſham (el. 1184) *ob.* 1198.
Robert de Longo Campo. *ob.* 1239.
William Rondele. *ob.* 1244.
Tho. de Wharterhille. *ob.* 1258.

(S)—" the ſherif of Nottinghamſhire"] Ralph Murdach was ſherif of Derby and Nottinghamſhires in the 1ſt year of king Richard I. and for the 7 years preceding, and William Brewerre in his 6th year, between which and the 1ſt no name appears on the roll. See Fullers *Worthies*, &c.

(T)—" an anecdote preſerved by Fordun, *&c.*"] "*De quo eciam quædam commendabilia recitantur, ſicut patuit in hoc, quod cum ipſe quondam in Barniſdale iram* [f. *ob iram*] *regis & fremitum principis, miſſam, ut ſolitus erat, devotiſſime audiret, nec aliqua neceſſitate volebat interrumpere officium, quadam die cum audiret miſſam, à quodam vicecomite & miniſtris regis, ſæpius per prius ipſum infeſtantibus, in illo ſecretiſſimo loco nemorali, ubi miſſæ interfuit,* *exploratus, venientes ad eum qui de suis hoc perceperunt, ut omni annisu fugeret suggesserunt, qui, ob reverentiam sacramenti, quod tunc devotissime venerabatur, omnino facere recusavit. Sed ceteris suis, ob metum mortis trepidantibus, Robertus tantum confisus in eum, quem coluit reveritus, cum paucissimis, qui tunc forte ei affuerunt, inimicos congressus & eos de facili devicit, & de eorum spoliis ac redemptione ditatus, ministros ecclesiæ & missas semper in majori veneratione semper & de post habere præelegit, attendens quod vulgariter dictum est:*

Hoc deus exaudit, qui missam sæpius audit."

(J. De Fordun Scotichronicon, à Hearne. Ox. 1722. p. 774.)

This passage is found in no other copy of Forduns chronicle than one in the Harleian library. Its suppression in all the rest may be fairly accounted for on the principle which is presumed to have influenced the conduct of the ancient English historians. See note (a).

(U)—"a proclamation was published, *&c.*"] "The king att last," says the Harleian MS. "sett furth a proclamation to have him apprehended, *&c.*" Grafton, after having told us that he "practised robberyes, *&c.*" adds, "The which beyng certefyed to the king, and he beyng greatly offended therewith, caused his proclamation to be made that whosoever would bryng him quicke or dead, the king would geve him a great summe of money, as by the recordes in the Exchequer is to be seene: But of this promise no man enjoyed any benefite. For the sayd Robert Hood, being afterwardes troubled with sicknesse, *&c.*" (p. 85.) See note (L).

(V) "At length, the infirmities of old age increasing upon him, *&c.*"] Thus Grafton: "The sayd Robert Hood, beyng troubled with sicknesse, came to a certain nonry in Yorkshire called Bircklies [r. Kircklies], where desiryng to be let blood, he was betrayed and bled to death." The Sloane MS. says that "[Being] dystempered with could and age, he had great payne in his lymmes, his bloud being corrupted, therfore, to be eased of his payne by letting bloud, he repayred to the priores of Kyrkeſly, which ſome ſay was his aunt, a woman very ſkylful in phyſique & ſurgery; who, perceyving him to be Robyn Hood, & waying howe fel an enimy he was to religious perſons, toke reveng of him for her owne howſe and all others by letting him bleed to death. It is alſo ſayd that one ſir Roger of Doncaſter, bearing grudge to Robyn for ſome injury, incyted the priores, with whome he was very familiar, in ſuch a maner to diſpatch him." See the *Lytell geſte of Robyn Hode*, ad finem. The Harleian MS. after mentioning the proclamation "ſett furth to have him apprehended" adds, "at which time it happened he fell ſick at a nunnery in Yorkſhire called Birkleys [r. Kirkleys]; & deſiring there to be let blood, hee was beytrayed & made bleed to death."

Kirkleys, Kirklees or Kirkleghes, formerly Kuthale, in the deanry of Pontefract, and archdeaconry of the weſt riding of Yorkſhire, was a Ciſtercian, or, as ſome ſay, a Benedictine nunnery, founded, in honour of the virgin Mary and St. James, by Reynerus Flandrenſis in the reign of king Henry II. Its revenues at the diſſolution were ſomewhat about £.20 and the ſite was granted (36 Hen. 8.) to John Taſburgh and Henry Savill, from whom it came to one of the anceſtors of Sir George Armytage bart. the preſent poſſeſſor. The remains of the building (if any) are very inconſiderable, and its regiſter has been ſearched after in vain. See Tanners *Notitia*, p. 674. Thoreſbys *Ducatus Leodienſis*, p. 91. Hearnes "Account of ſeveral antiquities in and about the univerſity of Oxford," at the end of Lelands *Itinerary*, vol. ii. p. 128.

In 1706 was diſcovered, among the ruins of the nunnery, the monument of *Eliſabeth de Stayntοn* prioreſs; but it is not certain that this was the lady from whom our hero experienced ſuch kind aſſiſtance. See Thoreſby and Hearne *ubi ſupra*.

"One may wonder," ſays Dr. Fuller, "how he eſcaped the hand of juſtice, dying in his bed, for ought is found to the contrary: but it was becaufe he was rather a *merry* than a *mifchievous* thief (complementing paffengers out of their purfes) never murdering any but *deer*, and . . . . 'feafting' the vicinage with his venifon." (*Worthies*, p. 320.) See the following note.

(W) "He was interred under fome trees at a fhort diftance from the houfe; a ftone being placed over his grave with an infcription to his memory. "*Kirkley monafterium monialium*, ubi Ro: Hood nobilis ille exlex fepultus." Lelands *Collectanea*, i. 54. "Kirkleys Nunnery, in the woods whereof Robin Hoods grave is, is between Halifax and Wakefield upon Calder." *Letter from* Jo. Savile *to* W. Camden, *Illuf. viro epis.* 1691.

> "———————— as Caldor comes along,
> It chanc'd fhe in her courfe on 'Kirkley' caft her eye,
> Where merry Robin Hood, that honeft thief, doth lie."
> (Poly-Olbion, Song 28.)

See alfo Camdens *Britannia*, 1695, p. 709.

In the fecond volume of Dr. Stukeleys *Itinerarium curiofum* is an engraving of "The profpect of Kirkley's abby, where Robin Hood dyed, from the footway leading to Heartishead church, at a quarter of a mile diftance. A. The New Hall. B. The Gatehoufe of the Nunnery. C. *The trees among which Robin Hood was buryed.* D. The way up the Hill were this was drawn. E. Bradley wood. F. Almondbury hill. G. Caftle field. Drawn by Dr. Johnfton among his Yorkfhire antiquitys. p. 54. of the drawings. E. Kirkall, fculp." It makes plate 99 of the above work, but is unnoticed in the letter prefs.

According to the Sloane MS. the priorefs, after "letting him bleed to death, buryed him under a great ftone by the hywayes fyde:" which is agreeable to the account in Graftons chronicle, where it is faid that, after his death, "the prioreffe of the fame place caufed him to be buried by the highway fide, where he had ufed to rob and fpoyle thofe that paffed that way. And vpon his grave the fayde prioreffe did lay a very fayre ftone, wherein the names of *Robert Hood*, *William of Goldeſborough*, and others were graven. And the cauſe why ſhe buryed him there was, for that the common paſſengers and travailers, knowyng and ſeeyng him there buryed, might more ſafely and without feare take their jorneys that way, which they durſt not do in the life of the ſayd outlawes. And at eyther ende of the ſayde tombe was erected a croſſe of ſtone, which is to be ſeene there at this preſent."

"Near unto '*Kirklees*' the noted *Robin Hood* lies buri under a grave-ſtone that yet remains near the park, but the inſcription ſcarce legible." Thoresbys *Ducatus Leodienſis*, p. 91. In the *Appendix*, p. 576. is the following note, with a reference to "page 91:"

"Amongſt the papers of the learned Dr. Gale, late dean of Yorke, was found this epitaph of Robin Hood:

hear undernead dis laitl ſtean
laiz robert earl of huntingtun
near arcir ver az hie ſa geud
an pipl kauld im robin heud
ſick utlawz az hi an iz men
vil england nivr ſi agen.

obiit 24 [r. 14] kal dekembris 1247.

The genuineneſs of this epitaph has been queſtioned. Dr. Percy, in the firſt edition of his "Reliques of ancient Engliſh poetry," (1765,) ſays "It muſt be confeſſed this epitaph is ſuſpicious, becauſe in the moſt ancient poems of Robin Hood, there is no mention of this imaginary earldom." This reaſon, however, is by no means concluſive, the moſt ancient poem now extant having no pretenſion to the antiquity claimed by the epitaph: and indeed the doctor himſelf ſhould ſeem to have afterward had leſs confidence in it, as, in both the ſubſequent editions, thoſe words are omitted, and the learned critic merely obſerves that the epitaph *appears* to him *ſuſpicious*. It will be admitted that the bare ſuſpicion of this ingenious writer, whoſe knowlege and judgment of ancient poetry are ſo conſpicuous and eminent, ought to have conſiderable weight. As for the preſent editors part, though he does not pretend to ſay that the language of this epitaph is that of Henry the thirds time, nor indeed to determine of what age it is, he can perceive nothing in it from whence one ſhould be led to pronounce it ſpurious, *i. e.* that it was never inſcribed on the grave-ſtone of Robin Hood. That there actually was ſome inſcription upon it in Mr. Thoreſbys time, though then ſcarce legible, is evident from his own words: and it ſhould be remembered, as well that the laſt century was not the æra of impoſition, as that Dr. Gale was both too good and too learned a man either to be capable of it himſelf or to be liable to it from others.*

That induſtrious chronologiſt and topographer, as well as reſpectable artiſt and citizen, maſter Thomas Gent, of York, in his " Liſt of religious houſes," annexed to " The ancient and modern ſtate of" that famous city, 1730, 12mo. p. 234, informs us that he had been told, " That his [Robin Hoods] tombſtone, having his effigy thereon, was order'd, not many years ago, by a certain knight to be placed as a harth-ſtone in his great hall. When it was laid over-night, the next morning it was 'ſurprizingly' removed [on or to] one ſide; and ſo three times it was laid, and as ſucceſſively turned aſide. The knight, thinking he had done wrong to have brought it thither, order'd it ſhould be drawn back again; which was performed by a pair of oxen and four horſes, when twice the number could ſcarce do it before. But as this," adds the ſagacious writer, " is a ſtory only, it is left to the reader, to judge at pleaſure." *N. B.* This is the ſecond inſtance of a miracle wrought in favor of our hero!

In Goughs *Sepulchral monuments*, p. cviii. is " the fi-

* That dates, about this period, were frequently by *ides* and *kalends*, ſee Madoxes *Formulare Anglicanum*, (Diſſertation) p. xxx.

gure of the ſtone over the grave of Robin Hood [in Kirklees park, being a plain ſtone with a ſort of croſs fleuree thereon] now broken and much defaced, the inſcription illegible. That printed in Thoreſby *Ducat. Leod.* 576, from Dr. Gale's papers, was never on it.* The late ſir Samuel Armitage, owner of the premiſes, cauſed the ground under it to be dug a yard deep, and found it had never been diſturbed; ſo that it was probably brought from ſome other place, and by vulgar tradition aſcribed to Robin Hood" (refers to "Mr. Watſons letter in Antiquary ſociety minutes"). This is probably the tomb-ſtone of Eliſabeth de Staynton, mentioned in the preceding note.

The old epitaph is, by ſome anonymous hand, in a work entitled "*Sepulchrorum inſcriptiones:* or a curious collection of 900 of the moſt remarkable epitaphs," Weſtminſter, 1727, (vol. ii p. 73.) thus not inelegantly paraphraſed:

"Here, underneath this little ſtone,
Thro' Death's aſſaults, now lieth one,
Known by the name of Robin Hood,
Who was a thief, and archer good;
Full thirteen (r. thirty) years, and ſomething more,
He robb'd the rich to feed the poor:
Therefore, his grave bedew with tears,
And offer for his ſoul your prayers."

* That this epitaph had been printed, or was well known, at leaſt, long before the publication of Mr. Thoreſbys book, if not before either he or Dr. Gale was born, appears from the "true tale of Robin Hood" by Martin Parker, written, if not printed, as early as 1631. (See volume I. p. 127.) The Arabic figures muſt have been inſerted by the copyiſt for the Roman numerals; otherwiſe there will be an end of its pretenſion to authenticity. (N. B. *The note in the preceding page was detached from the preſent by miſtake.)*

† In "The travels of Tom Thumb over England and Wales' [by Mr. Robert Dodſley], p. 106. is another though inferior verſion

"Here, under this memorial ſtone,
Lies Robert earl of Huntingdon:

(X) "Various dramatic exhibitions."] The earlyest of these performances now extant is, "The playe of Robyn Hode, very proper to be played in Maye games," which is inserted in the appendix to this work, and may probably be as old as the 15th century. That a different play, however, on the same subject has formerly existed, seems pretty certain from a somewhat curious passage in "The famous chronicle of king Edward the first, sirnamed Edward Longshankes, &c." by George Peele, printed in 1593.

" *Lluellen* . . . . . weele get the next daie from Brecknocke the BOOKE OF ROBIN HOOD, the frier he shall instruct us in his cause, and weele even here . . . wander like irregulers up and down the wildernesse, ile be *maister of misrule*, ile be *Robin Hood* that once, cousin 'Rice', thou shalt be *little John*, and hers frier David, as fit as a die for *frier Tucke*. Now, my sweet Nel, if you will make up the messe with a good heart for *maide Marian*, and doe well with Lluellen under the green-woode trees, with as good a wil as in the good townes, why *plena est curia*. *Exeunt*.

Enter Mortimor, solus.

Mortimor . . . . . Maisters, have after gentle Robin Hood,
You are not so well accompanied I hope,
But if a *potter* come to plaie his part,
Youle give him stripes or welcome good or worse. *Exit*.

Enter Lluellen, Meredith, frier, Elinor, and their traine. They are all clad in greene, &c. *sing*, &c. Blyth and bonny, *the song ended, Lluellen speaketh*.

Luellen. Why so, I see, my mates of olde,
All were not lies that Bedlams [beldams] told;
Of Robin Hood and little John,
Frier Tucke and maide Marian."

Mortimer, as a *potter*, afterwards fights the frier with "flailes."

As he, no archer e'er was good,
And people call'd him Robin Hood:
Such outlaws as his men and he
Again may England never see."

2. "The downfall of Robert earle of Huntington, afterward called Robin Hood of merrie Sherwodde: with his love to chaste Matilda, the lord Fitzwaters daughter, afterwardes his faire maide Marian. Acted by the right honourable, the earle of Notingham, lord high admirall of England, his servants. ¶ Imprinted at London, for William Leake, 1601." 4to. b. l.

3. "The death of Robert, earle of Huntington, otherwise called Robin Hood of merrie Sherwodde: with the lamentable tragedie of chaste Matilda, his faire maid Marian, poysoned at Dunmowe, by king John. Acted, &c. ¶ Imprinted, &c. [as above] 1601." 4to. b. l.

These two plays, usually called *the first* and *second part of Robin Hood*, were always, on the authority of Kirkman, falsely ascribed to Thomas Heywood, till Mr. Malone fortunately retrieved the names of the true authors, Anthony Mundy and Henry Chettle.* As they seem partly founded on traditions long since forgotten, and refer occasionally to documents not now to be found, at any rate, as they are much older than most of the common ballads upon the subject, and contain some curious and possibly authentic particulars not elsewhere to be met with, the reader will excuse the particularity of the account and length of the extracts here given.

* In "a large folio volume of accounts kept by Mr. Philip Henslowe, who appears to have been proprietor of the Rose theatre near the Bankside in Southwark," he has entered—

"Feb. 1597-8. "The first part of Robin Hood, by Anthony Mundy.

The second part of the downfall of earl Huntington, sirnamed Robinhood, by Anthony Mundy and Henry Chettle."

In a subsequent page is the following entry: "Lent unto Robarte Shawe, the 18 of Novemb. 1598, to lend unto Mr. Cheattle, upon the mending of *the first part of Robart Hoode*, the sum of x s." and afterwards—"For mending of *Robin Hood* for the corte." See Malones edition of "The plays and poems of William Shakspeare," 1790. vol. I. part II. (Emendations and additions.)

The *first part*, or *downfall of Robert earle of Huntington*, is supposed to be performed at the court and command of Henry the 8th; the poet Skelton being the dramatist, and acting the part of *chorus*. The introductory scene commences thus:

" *Enter sir John Eltam, and knocke at Skeltons doore.*

Sir John. Howe, maister Skelton! what, at studie hard?
opens the doore.

Skelt. Welcome and wisht for, honest sir John Eltam,—
Twill trouble you after your great affairs,

(i. e. *the surveying of certain maps which his majesty had employed him in*;)

To take the paine that I intended to intreate you to,
About rehearsall of your promis'd play.
Elt. Nay, master Skelton; for the king himselfe,
As wee were parting, bid mee take great heede
Wee faile not of our day: therefore I pray
Sende for the rest, that now we may rehearse,
Skel. O they are readie all, and drest to play.
What part play you?
Elt. Why, I play little John,
And came of purpose with this greene sute.
Skel. Holla, my masters, little John is come.

At every doore all the players runne out; some crying where? where? *others* Welcome, sir John: *among other the boyes and clowne.*

Skel. Faith, little Tracy, you are somewhat forward.
What, our maid Marian leaping like a lad!
If you remember, Robin is your love,
Sir Thomas Mantle yonder, not sir John.
Clow. But, master, sir John is my fellowe, for I am Much the millers sonne. Am I not?
Skel. I know yee are sir:—
And, gentlemen, since you are thus prepar'd,
Goe in, and bring your dumbe scene on the stage,
And I, as prologue, purpose to expresse
The ground whereon our historie is laied.

Exeunt, manet Skelton.

Trumpets sounde, [1] *enter first king Richard with drum and auncient, giving Ely a purse and scepter, his mother and brother John, Chester, Lester, Lacie, others at the kings appointment, doing reverence. The king goes in: presently Ely ascends the chaire, Chester, John, and the queene part displeasantly.* [2] *Enter* ROBERT, EARLE OF HUNTINGTON, *leading Marian; followes him Warman, and after Warman, the prior; Warman ever flattering and making curtsie, taking gifts of the prior behinde and his master before. Prince John enters, offereth to take Marian; Queen Elinor enters, offering to pull Robin from her; but they infolde each other, and sit downe within the curteines.* [3] *Warman with the prior, sir Hugh Lacy, lord Sentloe, and sir Gilbert Broghton folde hands, and drawing the curteins, all (but the prior) enter, and are kindely received by* Robin Hoode."

During the exhibition of the second part of the dumb-shew, Skelton instructs the audience as follows:

" This youth that leads yon virgin by the hand
Is *our earle Robert*, or *your Robin Hoode*,
That in those daies, was *earle of Huntington*;
The ill-fac't miser, brib'd in either hand,
Is Warman, once the steward of his house,
Who, Judas like, betraies his liberall lord,
Into the hands of that relentlesse prior,
Calde Gilbert Hoode, uncle to Huntingtor.
Those two that seeke to part these lovely friends,
Are Elenor the queene, and John the prince,
She loves earle Robert, he maide Marian,
But vainely; for their deare affect is such,
As only death can sunder their true loves.
Long had they lov'd, and now it is agreed,
This day they must be troth-plight, after wed:
At Huntingtons faire house a feast is helde,
But envie turnes it to a house of teares.
For those false guestes, conspiring with the prior;
To whom earle Robert greatly is in debt,
Meane at the banquet to betray the earle,
Unto a heavie writ of outlawry:
The manner and escape you all shall see.

. . . .

Looke to your entrance, get you in, sir John.
My shift is long, for I play frier Tucke;
Wherein, if Skelton hath but any lucke,
Heele thanke his hearers oft with many a ducke.

For many talk of Robin Hood that never ſhot in his bowe,
But Skelton writes of Robin Hood what he doth truly knowe."

After ſome Skeltonical rimes, and a ſcene betwixt the prior, the ſherif, and juſtice Warman, concerning the outlawry, which appears to be proclaimed, and the taking of earl Huntington at dinner, "*Enter Robin Hoode, little John following him; Robin having his napkin on his ſhoulder, as if hee were ſodainly raiſed from dinner.*" He is in a violent rage at being outlawed, and Little John endeavours to pacify him. Marian being diſtreſſed at his apparent diſorder, he diſſembles with her. After ſhe is gone, John thus addreſſes him:

" Now muſt your honour leave theſe mourning tunes,
And thus by my areede you ſhall provide:
Your plate and jewels ile ſtraight packe up,
And toward Notingham convey them hence.
At Rowford, Sowtham, Wortley, Hothersfield,
Of all your cattell mony ſhall be made,
And I at Mansfield will attend your comming;
Where weele determine which waie's beſt to take.
Rob. Well, be it ſo, a gods name, let it be;
And if I can, Marian ſhall come with mee.
John. Elſe care will kill her; therefore if you pleaſe,
At th'utmoſt corner of the garden wall,
Soone in the evening waite for Marian,
And as I goe ile tell her of the place.
Your horſes at the Bell ſhall readie bee,
I meane Belſavage,* whence, as citizens
That 'meane' to ride for pleaſure ſome ſmall way,
You ſhall ſet foorth."

The company now enters, and Robin charges them with the conſpiracy, and rates their treacherous proceed-

* That is, the inn ſo called, upon Ludgate-hill. The modern ſign, which however ſeems to have been the ſame 200 years ago, is *a bell* and *a wild man*; but the original is ſuppoſed to have been *a beautiful Indian*; and the inſcription, *La belle ſauvage*. Some, indeed, aſſert that the inn once belonged to a lady *Arabella Savage*; and others, that its name, originally *The* bell *and* ſavage, aroſe (like *The George and blue boar*) from the junction of two inns, with thoſe reſpective ſigns. *Non noſtrûm eſt tantas componere lites.*

ing. Little John in attempting to remove the goods is ſet upon by Warman and the ſherif; and during the fray "*Enter prince John, Ely and the prior, and others.*" Little John tells the prince, he but defends the box containing his own gettings; upon which his royal highneſs obſerves,

> " You do the ſellow wrong; his goods are his:
> You only muſt extend upon the earles.
> *Prior.* That was, my lord, but nowe is Robert Hood,
> A ſimple yeoman as his ſervants were."

Ely gives the prior his commiſſion, with directions to make ſpeed, leſt " in his country-houſes all his heards be ſolde;" and gives Warman a patent " for the high ſheriffewick of Nottingham." After this, " Enter Robin like a citizen;" and then the queen and Marian diſguiſed for each other. Robin takes Marian, and leaves the queen to prince John, who is ſo much enraged at the deception that he breaks the head of Elys meſſenger. Sir Hugh, brother to lord Lacy, and ſteward to Ely, who had been deeply concerned in Huntingtons ruin is killed in a brawl, by prince John, whom Ely orders to be arreſted; but the prince, producing letters from the king, revoking Elys appointment, " lifts up his drawne ſworde" and " *Exit, cum Leſter and Lacy,*" in triumph. Then, " *Enter Robin Hoode, Matilda, at one door, little John, and Much the millers ſonne at another doore.*" After mutual congratulations, Robin aſks if it be

> " —— poſſible that Warmans ſpite
> Should ſtretch ſo farre, that he doth hunt the lives
> Of bonnie Scarlet, and his brother Scathlock.
> *Much.* O, I, ſir. Warman came but yeſterday to take charge of the jaile at Notingham, and this daie, he saies, he will hang the two outlawes. . . .
> *Rob.* Now, by my honours hope, . . .
> He is too blame: ſay, John, where muſt they die?
> *John.* Yonder's their mothers houſe, and here the tree,
> Whereon, poore men, they muſt forgoe their lives;
> And yonder comes a lazy lozell frier,
> That is appointed for their confeſſor,

Who, when we brought your monie to their mothers,
Was wiſhing her to patience for their deaths."

Here "*Enter frier Tucke;*" ſome converſation paſſes, and the frier ſkeltonizes; after which he departs, ſaying,

" —— let us goe our way,
Unto this hanging buſineſſe; would for mee
Some reſcue or repreeve might ſet them free.
Rob. Heardſt thou not, little John, the friers ſpeach?
John. He ſeemes like a good fellow, my good lord.
Rob. He's a good ſellowe, John, upon my word.
Lend me thy horne, and get thee in to Much,
And when I blowe this horne, come both and helpe mee.
John. Take heed, my lord: the villane Warman knows [you,
And ten to one, he hath a writ againſt you.
Rob. Fear not: below the bridge a poor blind man doth [dwell,
With him I will change my habit, and diſguiſe,
Only be readie when I call for yee,
For I will ſave their lives, if it may bee. . . .

Enter Warman, Scarlet and Seathlock bounde, frier Tuck as their confeſſor, officers with halberts.

War. Maſter frier, be briefe, delay no time.
Scarlet and Scatlock, never hope for life;
Here is the place of execution,
And you muſt anſwer lawe for what is done.
Scar. Well, if there be no remedie, we muſt:
Though it ill ſeemeth, Warman, thou ſhouldſt bee,
So bloodie to purſue our lives thus cruellie.
Scat. Our mother ſav'd thee from the gallows, Warman,
His father did preferre thee to thy lord:
One mother had wee both, and both our fathers
To thee and to thy father were kinde friends. . . .
War. Ye were firſt outlaws, then ye prooved theeves. . . .
Both of your fathers were good honeſt men;
Your mother lives their widowe in good fame:*
But you are ſcapethrifts, unthrifts, villanes, knaves,
And as ye liv'd by ſhifts, ſhall die with ſhame."

To them enters Ralph, the ſherifs man, to acquaint

* She is called the widow Scarlet; ſo that Scathlocke was the elder brother. In fact, however, it was mere ignorance in the author to ſuppoſe the Scathlocke and Scarlet of the ſtory diſtinct perſons, the latter name being an evident corruption of the former; *Scathlock, Scadlock, Scarlock, Scarlet.*

him that the *carnifex*, or executor of the law, had fallen off his "curtall" and was "cripplefied" and rendered incapable of performing his office; ſo that the ſherif was to become his deputy. The ſherif inſiſts that Ralph ſhall ſerve the turn, which he refuſes. In the midſt of the altercation, "*Enter Robin Hoode, like an old man*," who tells the ſherif that the two outlaws had murdered his young ſon, and undone himſelf; ſo that for revenge ſake he deſires they may be delivered to him. They denying the charge, "Robin whiſpers with them," and with the ſherifs leave, and his mans help, unbinds them: then, ſounds his horn; and "*Enter little John, Much . . . Fight; the frier, making as if he helpt the ſheriffe, knockes down his men, crying*, Keepe the kings peace. *Sheriffe* [perceiving that it is "the outlawed earle of Huntington"] *runnes away, and his men*." (See the ballad of "Robin Hood reſcuing the widows ſons," part II. num. xxiii.)

"*Fri.* Farewell, earle Robert, as I am true frier,
I had rather be thy clarke, then ſerve the prior.
Rob. A jolly ſellowe! Scarlet, knoweſt thou him?
Scar. Hee is of Yorke, and of Saint Maries cloiſter;
There where your greedie uncle is lord prior. . . .
Rob. Here is no biding, maſters; get yee in. . . .
John, on a ſudaine thus I am reſolv'd,
To keepe in Sherewoodde tille the kings returne,
And being outlawed, leade an outlawes life. . . .
John. I like your honours purpoſe exceeding well.
Rob. Nay, no more honour, I pray thee, little John;
Henceforth I will be called Robin Hoode,
Matilda ſhall be my maid Marian."

Then follows a ſcene betwixt old Fitzwater and prince John, in the courſe of which the prince, as a reaſon to induce Fitzwater to recall his daughter Matilda, tells him that ſhe is living in an adulterous ſtate, for that

"—Huntington is excommunicate,
And till his debts be paid, by Romes decree,
It is agreed, abſolv'd he cannot be;
And that can never be.—So never wife, &c."

Fitzwater, on this, flies into a paſſion, and accuſes the

prince of being already marryed to "earle Chepstowes daughter." They "*fight*; *John falles.*" Then enter the queen, *&c.* and John sentences Fitzwater to banishment: after which, "*Enter Scathlocke and Scarlet, winding their hornes, at severall doores. To them enter Robin Hoode, Matilda, all in greene, . . . Much, little John; all the men with bowes and arrowes.**

. . . .

Rob. Wind once more, jolly huntsmen, all your horns,
Whose shrill sound, with the ecchoing wods assist,
Shall ring a sad knell for the fearefull deere,
Before our feathered shafts, deaths winged darts,
Bring sodaine summons for their fatall ends.
Scar. Its ful seaven years since we were outlawed first,
And wealthy Sherewood was our heritage:
For all those yeares we raigned uncontrolde,
From Barnsdale shrogs to Notinghams red cliffes.
At Blithe and Tickhill were we welcome guests;
Good George a Greene at Bradford was our friend,
And wanton Wakefields pinner lov'd us well.†
At Barnsley dwels a potter, tough and strong,
That never brookt we brethren should have wrong.
The nunnes of Farnsfield (pretty nunnes they bee)
Gave napkins, shirts, and bands to him and mee.
Bateman of Kendall gave us Kendall greene;
And Sharpe of Leedes sharpe arrows for us made.
At Rotherham dwelt our bowyer, god him blisse,
Jackson he hight, his bowes did never misse.
This for our goode, our scathe let Scathlocke tell,
In merry Mansfield how it once befell.
Scath. In merry Mansfield, on a wrestling day,
Prizes there were, and yeomen came to play,
My brother Scarlet and myselfe were twaine;

* In "The booke of the inventary of the goods of my lord admeralles men tacken the 10 of Marche in the yeare 1598," are the following properties for Robin Hood and his retinue, in this identical play:

"*Item*, vi grene cottes for Roben Hoode, and iiii knaves sewtes.
Item, i hatte for Robin Hoode, i hobihorse.
Item, Roben Hoodes sewte.
Item, the fryers trusse in *Roben Hoode*."

Malones *Shak.* II. ii. (Emen. & ad.)

† *George a Greene* and *Wakefields pinner*, were one and the same person. The *shoemaker of Bradford* is anonymous.

Many refifted, but it was in vaine,
For of them all we wonne the maftery,
And the gilt wreathes were given to him and me.
There by fir Doncafter of 'Hothersfield,'
We were bewraid, befet, and forft to yield;
And fo borne bound, from thence to Notingham,
Where we lay doom'd to death till Warman came."

Some cordial expreffions pafs between Robin and Matilda. He commands all the yeomen to be cheerful; and orders little John to read the articles.

" *Joh.* Firft, no man muft prefume to call our mafter,
By name of earle, lorde, baron, knight, or fquire:
But fimply by the name of Robin Hoode.—
That faire Matilda henceforth change her name,
'And' by maid Marians name, be only cald.
Thirdly, no yeoman following Robin Hoode
In Sherewod, fhall ufe widowe, wife, or maid,
But by true labour, luftfull thoughts expell.
Fourthly, no paffenger with whom ye meete,
Shall yee let paffe till hee with Robin feafte:
Except a poaft, a carrier, or fuch folke,
As ufe with foode to ferve the market townes.
Fiftly, you never fhall the poore men wrong.
Nor fpare a prieft, a ufurer, or a clarke.
Laftly, you fhall defend with all your power
Maids, widowes, orphants, and diftreffed men.
All. All thefe we vowe to keepe, as we are men.
Rob. Then wend ye to the greenewod merrily,
And let the light roes bootleffe from yee runne,
Marian and I, as foveraigns of your toyles,
Will wait, within our bower, your bent bowes fpoiles.
Exeunt winding their hornes."

In the next fcene, we find frier Tucke feignedly entering into a confpiracy with the prior and fir Doncafter, to ferve an execution on Robin, in difguife. Jinny, the widow Scarlets daughter, coming in, on her way to Sherwood, is perfuaded by the frier to accompany him, " difguifed in habit like a pedlers mort." Fitzwater enters like an old man:—fees Robin fleeping on a green bank, Marian ftrewing flowers on him; pretends to be blind and hungry, and is regaled by them. In anfwer to a queftion why the fair Matilda (Fitzwaters daughter) had changed her name, Robin tells him it is

" Becaufe fhe lives a fpotleffe maiden life:
And fhall, till Robins outlawe life have ende.
That he may lawfully take her to wife;
Which, if king Richard come, will not be long."

" Enter frier Tucke and Jinny like pedlers finging," and afterward " Sir Doncafter and others weaponed."— The frier difcovers the plot, and a fray enfues. The fcene then changes to the court, where the prior is informed of fix of his barns being deftroyed by fire, and of the different execrations of all ranks upon him, as the undoer of " the good lord Robert, earle of Huntington;" that the convent of St. Marys had elected " Olde father Jerome" prior in his place; and laftly a herald brings his fentence of banifhment, which is confirmed by the entrance of the prior. Lefter brings an account of the imprifonment of his gallant fovereign, king Richard, by the duke of Auftria, and requires his ranfom to be fent. He then introduces a defcription of his matchlefs valour in the holy land. John not only refufes the ranfom money, but ufurps the ftile of king: upon which Lefter grows furious, and rates the whole company. The following is part of the dialogue:

" *Joh.* (*to Lefter*) Dareft thou attempt thus proudly in [our fight?
Left. What is't a fubject dares, that I dare not?
Salf. Dare fubjects dare, their foveraigne being by?
Left. O god, that my true foveraigne were ny!
Qu. Lefter, he is.
Left. Madam, by god, you ly.
Cheft. Unmanner'd man.
Left. A plague of reverence!"

After this, and more on the fame fubject, the fcene returns to the foreft; where Ely, being taken by Much, " like a countryman with a bafket", is examined and detected by Robin, who promifes him protection and fervice. On their departure:

" *Joh.* Skelton, a worde or two befide the play.
Fri. Now, fir John Eltam, what ift you would fay.

Jhon. Methinks I fee no *jeasts of Robin Hoode,*
No *merry morices of frier Tuck,*
No *pleafant fkippings up and downe the wodde,*
No *hunting fongs,* no *courfing of the bucke:*
Pray god this play of ours may have good lucke,
And the king's majeftie mislike it not!
Fri. And if he doe, what can we doe to that?
I promis'd him a play of Robin Hoode,
His honorable life, in merry Sherewod;
His majeftie himfelfe furvaid the plot,
And bad me boldly write it, it was good.
For *merry jeafts, they have bene fhowne before:*
As *how the frier fell into the well,*
For love of Jinny, that faire bonny bell:
How Greeneleafe rob'd the fhrieve of Notingham,
And other mirthful matter, full of game."

"*Enter Warman banifhed.*" He laments his fall, and applies to a coufin, on whom he had beftowed large poffeffions, for relief; but receives nothing, except reproaches for his treachery to his noble mafter. The jailor of Notingham, who was indebted to him for his place, refufes him even a fcrap of his dogs meat, and reviles him in the fevereft terms. Good-wife Tomfon, whofe hufband he had delivered from death, to his great joy, promifes him a caudle, but fetches him a halter; in which he is about to hang himfelf, upon fome tree in the foreft, but is prevented by Fitzwater, and fome of Robin Hoods men, who crack a number of jokes upon him: Robin puts an end to their mockery, and proffers him comfort and favour. Then enters frier Tucke, with an account of fir Doncafter and the prior being ftriped and wounded in their way to Bawtrey: Robin out of love to his uncle haftens to the place. After this, "*Enter prince John, folus, in green, bowe and arrowes.*

John. Why this is fomewhat like, now may I fing,
As did the Wakefield pinder in his note;
At Michaelmas commeth my covenant out,
My mafter gives me my fee:
Then Robin Ile weare thy Kendall greene,
And wend to the greenewodde with thee."*

* See the ballad of "The jolly pinder of Wakefield," Part II. Num. III.

He aſſumes the name of Woodnet, and is detected by Scathlocke and frier Tucke. The prince and Scathlocke fight, Scathelocke grows weary, and the frier takes his place. Marian enters, and perceiving the frier, parts the combatants. Robin enters, and John ſubmits to him. Much enters, running, with information of the approach of "the king and twelve and twenty ſcore of horſes." Robin places his people in order. The trumpets ſound, the king and his train enter, a general pardon enſues, and the king confirms the love of Robin and Matilda. Thus the play concludes, Skelton promiſing *the ſecond part*, and acquainting the audience of what it ſhould conſiſt.

The *ſecond part*, or *death of Robert earle of Huntington*, is a purſuit of the ſame ſtory. The ſcene, ſo far as our hero is concerned, lyes in Sherwood. A few extracts may not be unacceptable.

"*Sc. iiii. Winde hornes. Enter king, queene, &c. Frier Tuck carrying a ſtags head, dauncing.*" The frier has been ſent for to read the following inſcription upon a copper ring round the ſtags neck:

"When Harold Hare-foote raigned king,
About my necke he put this ring."

The king orders "head, ring and all" to be ſent to Nottingham caſtle, to be kept for monuments. Fitzwater tells him, he has heard "an olde tale,"

"That Harold, being Goodwins ſonne of Kent,*
Hunted for pleaſure once within this wood,
And ſingled out a faire and ſtately ſtagge,
Which, foote to foote, the king in running caught;
And ſure this was the ſtagge.
King. It was no doubt.
Cheſter. But ſome, my lord, affirme,
That Julius Cæſar, many years before,
Tooke ſuch a ſtagge, and ſuch a poeſie writ:"†

* Fitzwater confounds one man with another; Harold Harefoot was the ſon and ſucceſſor of Canute the great.

† This tradition is refered to, and the inſcription given in Mr. Rays *Itineraries*, 1760. p. 153.—"We rode through a buſhet

Upon which his majesty very sagaciously remarks,

> " It should not be in Julius Cæsars time:
> There was no English used in this land

or common called Rodwell-hake, two miles from Leeds, where (according to the vulgar tradition) was once found a stag, with a ring of brass about its neck, having this inscription:

> When Julius Cæsar here was king,
> About my neck he put this ring:
> Whosoever doth me take,
> Let me go for Cæsar's sake."

In *The midwife*, or *Old woman's magazine*, (vol. i. p. 250.) Mrs. Midnight, in a letter " To the venerable society of antiquarians," containing a description of Cæsars camp, on Windsor forest, has the following passage: " There have been many extraordinary things discovered about this camp. One thing, I particularly remember, was a deer of about sixteen hundred years old . . . . . . This deer it seems was a favourite of Cæsar's, and on that account he bedecked her neck with a golden collar and an inscription, which I shall by and by take notice of; she had been frequently taken, but when the hunters, the peasants and poor people saw the golden collar on her neck, they readily let her go again. However, as she continually increased in strength and in bulk, as well as in age, after the course of about fifteen or sixteen centuries, the flesh and skin were entirely grown over this collar, so that it could not be discover'd till after she was kill'd, and then to the surprize of the virtuosi, it appear'd with this inscription:

> When Julius Cæsar reigned here,
> Then was I a little deer;
> If any man should me take,
> Let me go for Cæsar's sake.

" This collar, which is of pure gold, I am told weighs thirty ounces, and as the blood of the creature still appears fresh upon it, I believe it may be as valuable as any of your *gimcracks*; however, there will be no harm in my sending of it to you; and if I can procure it, you may depend on my taking the utmost care of it." As no notice is announced of this wonderful piece of antiquity in the voluminous and important lucubrations of the above learned body, it most probably never came into their possession; which is very much to be lamented, as it would have been an admirable companion for *Hardecnutes chamber-pot*, and other similar curiosities.

The original of all these stories is to be found in Pliny, who says: " It is generally held and confessed that the stagge or hind

Untill the Saxons came, and this is writ
In Saxon characters."

The next quotation may be of ſervice to Dr. Percy, who has been pleaſed to queſtion our heros nobility, becauſe "the moſt ancient poems make no mention of this *earldom*," and the old legend expreſsly aſſerts him "to have been a *yeoman*." It is very true; and we ſhall here not only find his title eſtabliſhed, but alſo diſcover the ſecret of his not being uſually diſtinguiſhed or deſigned by it.

"*Enter Roben Hoode.*

King. How now, *earle Robert!*
Fri. A forfet, a forfet, my liege lord,
My maſters lawes are on record,
The court-roll here your grace may ſee.
King. I pray thee. frier, read them mee.
Fri. One ſhall ſuffice, and this is hee.
No man that commeth in this wod,
To feaſt or dwell with Robin Hood,
Shall call him earle, lord, knight, or ſquire,
He no ſuch titles doth deſire,
But Robin Hood, plain Robin Hoode,
That honeſt YEOMAN, *ſtout and good,*
On paine of forfeiting a marke,
That muſt be paid to mee his clarke.
My liege, my liege, this lawe you broke,
Almoſt in the laſt word you ſpoke;
That crime may not acquitted bee,
Till frier Tuck receive his fee."

Now, the reaſon that "the moſt ancient poems make no mention of this earldom," and the old legend expreſsly aſſerts him "to have been a yeoman," appears, plainly enough, to be, that as, purſuant to his own injunction, he was never called, either by his followers, or in the vicinity, by any other name than *Robin Hood*, ſo particularly the minſtrels, who were always, no doubt, welcome to Sherwood,*

live long: for an hundred yeer after Alexander the great, ſome were taken with golden collars about their necks, overgrowne now with haire and growne within the ſkin: which collars the ſaid king had done upon them." *Naturall hiſtorie* (by Holland), 1601. (B. 8. c. 32.)

* Robin, in the old legend, expreſſes his regard for this order of men (concerning which the reader may conſult an ingenious "Eſſay"

and liberally entertained by him and his yeomanry, would take ſpecial care never to offend againſt the above law: which puts an end to the diſpute. *Q. E. D.*

Our hero is, at length, poiſoned by a drink which Doncaſter and the prior, his uncle, had prepared for him to give to the king. His departing ſcene, and laſt dying ſpeech are beautiful and pathetic.

" *Rob.* Inough, inough, Fitzwater, take your child.
My dying froſt, which no ſunnes heat can thawe,
Cloſes the powers of all my outward parts;
My freezing blood runnes back unto my heart,
Where it aſſiſts death, which it would reſiſt:
Only my love a little hinders death,
For he beholds her eyes, and cannot ſmite.
. . . .
Mat. O let mee looke for ever in thy eyes,
And lay my warme breath to thy bloodleſſe lips,
If my ſight can reſtraine deaths tyrannies,
Or keep lives breath within thy boſome lockt."

He deſires to be buryed

" At Wakefield, underneath the abbey-wall;

directs the manner of his funeral; and bids his yeomen,

" For holy dirges, ſing 'him' wodmens ſongs."

The king, upon the earls death, expreſſes his ſorrow for the tragical event; ratifies the will; repeats the directions for the funeral; and ſays,

" Fall to your wod-ſongs, therefore, yeomen bold,
And deck his herſe with flowers, that lov'd you deere."

The whole concludes with the following ſolemne dirge:

in the *Reliques of ancient Engliſh poetry*, (vol. I.) and ſome " Obſervations" in a collection of *Ancient ſongs*, printed in 1790):

" Whether he be meſſengere,
Or *a man that myrthes can*,
Or yf he be a pore man,
Of my good he ſhall have ſome."

" Weepe, weepe, ye wod-men waile,
Your hands with ſorrow wring;
Your maſter Robin Hood lies deade,
Therefore ſigh as you ſing.

Here lies his primer, and his beades,
His bent bowe, and his arrowes keene,
His good ſworde and his holy croſſe:
Now caſt on flowers freſh and greene.

And, as they fall, ſhed teares and ſay,
Well a, well a day, well a, well a day!
Thus caſt yee flowers and ſing,
And on to Wakefield take your way."

The poet then proſecutes the legend of Matilda, who is finally poiſoned, by the procurement of king John, in Dunmow-priory.

The ſtory of this lady, whom the author of theſe plays is ſuppoſed to have been the firſt that converted into the character of maid Marian, or connected in any ſhape with the hiſtory of Robin Hood, is thus related by Stow, under the year 1213: " The chronicle of Dunmow ſayth, this diſcord aroſe betwixt the king and his barons, becauſe of Mawd called the faire, daughter to Robert Fitzwalter, whome the king loved, but her father would not conſent; and thereupon enſued warre throughout England . . . . . Whilſt Mawd the faire remayned at Dunmow, there came a meſſenger unto her from king John about his ſuite in love, but becauſe ſhe would not agree, the meſſenger poyſoned a boyled or potched egge againſt ſhe was hungrie, whereof ſhe died." (*Annales*, 1592.) Two of Draytons *heroical epiſtles* paſs between king John and Matilda. He has alſo written her *legend*.

4. " Robin Hood's penn'orths, by Wm. Haughton."*

5. " Metropolis coronata, the triumphs of ancient drapery: or, rich cloathing of England, in a ſecond yeeres performance. In honour of the advancement of ſir John Jolles, knight, to the high office of lord maior of London, and taking his oath for the ſame authoritie, on

* This play is entered in maſter Henſlows account-book with the date of December 1600. See Malones *Shakſpeare*, Vol. II. Part II. (Emen. & ad.)

Monday being the 30. day of October, 1615. Performed in heartie affection to him, and at the bountifull charges of his worthy brethren the truely honourable society of drapers, the first that received such dignitie, in this citie. Devised and written by A. M. [Anthony Mundy] citizen and draper of London." 1615. 4to.

This is one of the pageants formerly usual on Lord-mayors-day, and of which several are extant, written as well by our author Mundy,* as by Middleton, Dekker, Heywood, and other hackney dramatists of that period. They were thought of such consequence that the city had for some time (though probably not till after the restoration) a professed laureat for their composition; an office which expired with Elkanah Settle in 1723-4. They consisted chiefly of machinery, allegorical or historical personages, songs and speeches.

" After all these shewes, thus ordered in their appointed places, followeth another device of huntsmen, all clad in greene, with their bowes, arrowes and bugles, and a new slaine deere, carried among them. It savoureth of *earle Robert de la Hude*, sometime the noble *earle of Huntington*, and sonne in law (by marriage) to old *Fitz-Alwine*,† raised by the muses all commanding power, to honour this triumph with his father. During the time of his out-lawed life in the forest of merry Shirwood, and elsewhere, while the cruel oppression of a most unnatural and covetous brother hung heavy upon him, Gilbert de la Hude lord abbot of Christall [r. Kirkstall] abbey, who had all or most of his lands in mortgage: he

* " The triumphes of reunited Britannia. A pageant in honour of sir Leonard Holliday lord mayor." 1605.

† Henry Fitz-Alwine Fitz-Liefstane, gold-smith, first mayor of London, was appointed to that office by K. Richard I. in 1189, and continued therein till the 15th of K. John, 1212, when he " deceased, and was buried in the priorie of the holy trinitie, neare unto Aldgate." (Stows *Survay*, 1598. p. 418.) His relationship with Robin Hood is merely poetical, and invented by Mundy " for the nonce;" though it is by no means improbable that they were acquainted, and that our hero might have occasionally dined at the mansion-house on a lord-mayors day.

was commonly called Robin Hood, and had a gallant company of men (out-lawed in the like manner) that followed his downecaſt fortunes; as *little John*, *Scathlocke*, *Much the millers ſon*, *Right-hitting Brand*, *fryar Tuck*, and many more. In which condition of life we make inſtant uſe of him, and part of his brave bowmen, fitted with bowes and arrowes, of the like ſtrength and length, as good records deliver teſtimonie, were then uſed by them in their killing of deere. . . . . . .

Afterward, [*viz.* after "Fitz-Alwines ſpeech to the lord maior at night,"] as occaſion beſt preſenteth itſelfe, when the heate of all other employments are calmly overpaſt, earle Robin Hood, with fryer Tuck, and his other brave huntes-men, attending (now at laſt) to diſcharge their duty to my lord, which the buſie turmoile of the whole day could not before affoord: they ſhewe themſelves to him in this order, and earle Robin himſelfe thus ſpeaketh.

The ſpeech ſpoken by earl Robert de la Hude, commonly called Robin Hood.

Since graves may not their dead containe,
Nor in their peacefull ſleepes remaine,
But triumphes and great ſhowes muſt uſe them,
And we unable to refuſe them;
It joyes me that earle Robert Hood,
Fetcht from the forreſt of merrie Shirwood,
With theſe my yeomen tight and tall,
Brave huntſmen and good archers all,
Muſt in this joviall day partake,
Prepared for your honours ſake.
No ſooner was i rayſde from reſt,
And of my former ſtate poſſeſt
As while i liv'd, but being alone,
And of my yeomen ſeeing not one,
I with my bugle gave a call,
Made all the woods to ring withall.
Immediately came little John,
And Scathlock followed him anon,
With Much the honeſt millers ſonne;
And ere ought elſe could be done,
The frollicke frier came tripping in,
His heart upon a merrie pinne.

Mafter (quoth he) in yonder brake,
A deere is hid for Marians fake,
Bid Scathlock, John, or honeft Brand,
That hath the happy hitting hand,
Shoote right and have him : and fee, my lord,
The deed performed with the word.
For Robin and his bow men bold,
Religiously did ever holde,
Not emptie-handed to be feene,
Were't but at feafting on a greene;
Much more then, when fo high a day
Calls our attendance : all we may
Is all too little, tis your grace
To winke at weakeneffe in this cafe,
So fearing to be over-long,
End all with our old hunting fong.

. . . .

The fong of Robin Hood and his huntes-men.

Now wend we together, my merry men all,
  Unto the forreft fide a :
And there to ftrike a buck or a doae,
  Let our cunning all be tride a.

Then goe we merrily, merrily on,
  To the green-wood to take up our ftand [a],
Where we will lye in waite for our game,
  With our beft bowes all in our hand [a].

What life is there like to bold Robin Hood?
  It is fo pleafant a thing a :
In merry Shirwood he fpends his dayes,
  As pleafantly as a king a.

No man may compare with bold Robin Hood,
  With Robin Hood, Scathlocke and John [a]:
Their like was never, nor never will be,
  If in cafe that they were gone [a].

They will not away from merry Shirwood,
  In any place elfe to dwell [a]:
For there is neither city nor towne,
  That likes them half fo well [a].

Our lives are wholly given to hunt,
  And haunt the merry greene-wood [a];
Where our beft fervice is daily fpent,
  For our mafter Robin Hood [a]."

6. "Robin Hood and his paſtoral May games." 1624.
7. "Robin Hood and his crew of ſoldiers." 1627.

Theſe two titles are inſerted among the plays mentioned by Chetwood, in his *Britiſh theatre*, (p. 67.) as written by anonymous authors in the 16th century to the reſtoration. But neither Langbaine, who mentions both, nor any other perſon, pretends to have ever ſeen either of them. The former, indeed, may poſſibly be "The playe of Robyn Hode," already noticed; and the other is probably a future article. Langbaine, it is to be obſerved, gives no date to either piece; ſo that, it may be fairly concluded, thoſe above ſpecifyed are of Chetwoods own invention, which appears to have been abundantly fertile in every ſpecies of forgery and impoſture.

8. "The ſad ſhepherd, or a tale of Robin Hood."

The ſtory of our renowned archer cannot be ſaid to have been wholely occupyed by bards without a name; ſince, not to mention Mundy or Drayton, the celebrated Ben Jonſon intended a paſtoral drama on this ſubject, under the above title; but dying, in the year 1637, before it was finiſhed, little more than the two firſt acts has deſcended down to us. His laſt editor (Mr. Whalley), while he regrets that it is but a fragment, ſpeaks of it in raptures, and, indeed, not without evident reaſon, many paſſages being eminently poetical and judicious.

"The perſons of the play," ſo far as concerns our immediate purpoſe, are: [1] "Robin Hood, the chief woodman [*i. e.* foreſter], maſter of the feaſt. [2] Marian, his lady, the miſtreſs. [3] Friar Tuck, the chaplain and ſteward. [4] Little John, bow-bearer. [5, 6] Scarlet, Scathlock,* two brothers, huntſmen. [7] George a Green, huiſher of the bower. [8] Much, Robin Hoods bailiff or acater." The reſt are, the gueſts invited, the witch of Paplewick, her daughter, the ſwin'ard her ſon, Puck Hairy or Robin Goodfellow, their hind, and laſtly a devout hermit. "The ſcene,

* Jonſon was led into this miſtake by the old play of Robin Hood. See before, p. lvii.

Sherwood, confifting of a landfcape of a foreft, hills, valleys, cottages, a caftle, a river, paftures, herds, flocks, all full of country fimplicity; *Robin Hoods bower, his well*, &c." "The argument of the firft act" is as follows: "Robin Hood, having invited all the fhepherds and fhepherdeffes of the vale of Be'voir to a feaft in the foreft of Sherwood, and trufting to his miftrefs, maid Marian, with her woodmen, to kill him venifon againft the day; having left the like charge with friar Tuck his chaplain and fteward, to command the reft of his merry men to fee the bower made ready, and all things in order for the entertainment: 'meets' with his guefts at their entrance into the wood, and conducts them to his bower: where, by the way, he receives the relation of the THE SAD SHEPHERD Æglamour, who is fallen into a deep melancholy for the lofs of his beloved Earine, reported to have been drowned in paffing over the Trent, fome few days before. . . . In the mean time Marian is come from hunting. . . . Robin Hood enquires if fhe hunted the deere at force, and what fport he made? how long he ftood? and what head he bore? all which is briefly anfwered, with a relation of breaking him up, and the raven, and her bone. The fufpect had of that raven to be Maudlin the witch of Paplewick, whom one of the huntfmen met i' the morning at the rouzing of the deer, and is confirmed by her being then in Robin Hoods kitchen, i' the chimney corner, broiling the fame bit which was thrown to the raven at the quarry or fall of the deer. Marian, being gone in to fhew the deer to fome of the fhepherdeffes, returns difcontented; fends away the venifon fhe had killed to her they call the witch; quarrels with her love Robin Hood, abufeth him, and his guefts the fhepherds; and fo departs, leaving them all in wonder and perplexity."

By "the argument of the fecond act" it appears that the witch had "taken the fhape of Marian to abufe Robin Hood, and perplex his guefts." However, upon an explanation of the matter with the true Marian, the trick is found out, the venifon recovered, and "Robin

Hood diſpatcheth out his woodmen to hunt and take her: which ends the act." The third act was deſigned to be taken up with the chace of the witch, her various ſchemes to elude the purſuers, and the diſcovery of Earine in the ſwineherds enchanted oak. Nothing more of the authors deſign appearing, we have only to regret the imperfect ſtate of a paſtoral drama, which, according to the above learned and ingenious editor, would have done honour to the nation.*

9. "Robin Hood and his crew of ſouldiers, a comedy acted at Nottingham on the day of his ſaCRed majeſties corronation. *Vivat rex.* The actors names: Robin Hood, commander; Little John, William Scadlocke, ſouldiers; meſſenger from the ſheriffe. London, printed for James Davis, 1661." 4to.

This is an interlude, of a few pages and no merit; alluding to the late rebellion, and the ſubject of the day. The outlaws, convinced by the reaſoning of the ſherifs meſſenger, become loyal ſubjects.

10. "Robin Hood. An opera, as it is perform'd at Lee's and Harpers great theatrical booth in Bartholomew-fair." 1730. 8vo.

11. "Robin Hood." 1751. 8vo.

This was a ballad-farce, acted at Drury-lane theatre; in which the following favourite ſong was originally ſung by Mr. Beard, in the character of Robin Hood.

As blithe as the linnet ſings in the green wood,
 So blithe we'll wake the morn;
And through the wide foreſt of merry Sherwood
 We'll wind the bugle-horn.

The ſheriff attempts to take bold Robin Hood,
 Bold Robin diſdains to fly;
Let him come when he will, we'll, in merry Sherwood,
 Or vanquiſh, boys, or die.

* This play appears to have been performed upon the ſtage after the reſtoration. The prologue and epilogue (ſpoken by Mr. Portlock) are to be found in num. 1009 of the Sloane MSS. It was republiſhed, with a continuation and notes, by Mr. Waldron, of Drury-lane theatre, in 1783.

Our hearts they are ftout, and our bows they are good,
As well their mafters know;
They're cull'd in the foreft of merry Sherwood,
And never will fpare a foe.

Our arrows fhall drink of the fallow deer's blood,
We'll hunt them all o'er the plain;
And through the wide foreft of merry Sherwood,
No fhaft fhall fly in vain.

Brave Scarlet, and John, who ne'er were fubdu'd,
Give each his hand fo bold;
We'll range through the foreft of merry Sherwood,
What fay my hearts of gold?

12. "Robin Hood; or, Sherwood foreft: a comic opera. As "performed at the theatre-royal in Covent-garden. By Leonard Mac Nally, efq." 1784. 8vo.

This otherwife infignificant performance was embellifhed with fome fine mufic by Mr. Shield. The melody of one fong, beginning,

"I've travers'd Judah's barren fands,"

is fingularly beautiful. It has been fince reduced to, and is ftill frequently acted as, an after-piece.

A drama on the fubject of Robin Hood, under the title of *The forefters*, has been long expected from the elegant author of *The fchool for fcandal*. The firft act, faid to have been written many years ago, is, by thofe who have feen or heard it, fpoken of with admiration.

(Y)—" innumerable poems, rimes, fongs and ballads."] The original and moft ancient pieces of this nature have all perifhed in the lapfe of time, during a period of between five and fix hundred years continuance; and all we now know of them is that fuch things once exifted. In the *Vifion of Pierce Plowman*, an allegorical poem, thought to have been compofed foon after the year 1360, and generally afcribed to Robert Langeland, the author introduces an ignorant, idle and drunken fecular prieft, the reprefentative, no doubt, of the parochial clergy of that age, in the character of Sloth, who makes the following confeffion:

"I cannot parfitli mi paternofter, as the preift it fingeth,
But I can RYMS OF ROBEN HODE, and '*Randolf*' *erl of Chefter*,
But of our lorde or our lady I lerne nothyng at all."*

Fordun, the Scotifh hiftorian, who wrote about 1340, fpeaking of Robin Hood and Little John, and their accomplices, fays, "of whom the foolifh vulgar in comedies and tragedies make lewd entertainment, and are delighted to hear the jefters and minftrels fing them above all other ballads:"† and Mair (or Major), whofe hif-

* 1ft edit. 1550, fo. xxvi, b. (*Randolf* is misprinted *Rand of.*) Subfequent editions, even of the fame year, reading only "*Randall of Chefter*," Mr. Warton (*Hiftory of Englifh poetry*, ii. 179.) makes this genius, whom he calls a *frier*, fay "that he is well acquainted with THE *rimes of Randall of Chefter*;" and thefe rimes he, whimfically enough, conjectures to be the old *Chefter Whitfun-plays*; which, upon very idle and nonfenfical evidence, he fuppofes to have been written by *Randal Higden*, the compiler of the *Polychronicon*. Of courfe, if this abfurd idea were at all founded, THE *rimes of Robin Hood* muft likewife allude to certain Yorkfhire or Nottinghamfhire plays, *written by himfelf*. The "Randolf erl of Chefter" here meant is Randal Blundevile, the laft earl of that name, who had been in the holy land, was a great warrior and patriot, and dyed in 1231.

The reading of the original edition is confirmed by a very old manufcript, in the Cotton library, (*Vefpafian*, B. XVI.) differing confiderably from the printed copies, which gives the paffage thus:

"I can nouzt perfiitli my pater-nofter as a preft hit fyngeth:
I can rymes of Robyn Hood, of RONDOLF ERL OF CHESTRE,
Ac of oure lorde ne of oure ladi the lefte that ever was maked."

(See alfo *Caligula*, A. XI.)

The fpeaker himfelf could have told Mr. Warton he was no *frier*:

"I have ben PRIESTE & PERSON paffynge thyrty winter,
Yet can I nether folfe, ne finge, ne fayntes lyves read;
But I can find in a fielde or in a furlong an hare,
Better than in *Beatus vir* or in *Beati omnes*
Conftrue one claufe well, & kenne it to my parifhens."

† "*De quibus ftolidum vulgus bianter in comœdiis & tragœdiis prurienter feftum faciunt, & fuper ceteras 'romancias' mimos & bardanos cantitare delectantur.*" Scotichronicon (*à Hearne*), p. 774. *Comedies* and *tragedies* are—not dramatic compofitions, but—poems of a comic or ferious caft. *Romancé* in Spanifh, and *ro-*

tory was publiſhed by himſelf in 1521, obſerves that "The exploits of this Robert are celebrated in ſongs throughout all Britain."* So, likewiſe, Hector Bois (or Boethius), who wrote about the ſame period, having mentioned "that waithman Robert Hode with his fallow litil Johne," adds, "of quhom ar mony fabillis and mery ſportis ſoung amang the vulgar pepyll."† Whatever may have been the nature of the compoſitions alluded to by the above writers, ſeveral of the pieces printed in the preſent collection are unqueſtionably of great antiquity; not leſs, that is, than between three and four hundred years old. The *Lytell geſte*, which is firſt inſerted, is probably the oldeſt thing upon the ſubject we now poſſeſs;‡ but a legend, apparently of the ſame ſpecies, was

mance, in French, ſignify—not a tale of chivalry, but—a vulgar ballad, at this day.

* "*Rebus hujus Roberti geſtis tota Britannia in cantibus utitur.*" Majoris Britanniæ hiſtoria, Edin. 1740. p. 128.

† *Hyſtory of Scotland*, tranſlated by maiſter Johne Bellendene, Edin. 1541. fo. The word "waithman" was probably ſuggeſted to the tranſlator by Andrew of Wyntowns "Orygynale cronykil," written about 1420, which, at the year 1283, has the following lines:

"Lytil Jhon and Robyne Hude
Wayth-men were commendyd gud:
In Yngil-wode and Barnyſdale
Thai oyſyd all this tyme thare trawale."

It ſeems equivalent to the Engliſh *vagabond*, or, perhaps, *outlaw*. *Waith* is *waif*; and it is to be remembered that, in the technical language of the Engliſh courts, a woman is ſaid to be *waived*, and not *outlawed*.

‡ Of this poem there have been, at leaſt, four editions, perhaps more. In "an old book in black letter in the advocates library [Edinburgh], ſent to the faculty by a gentleman from Ayrſhire in 1788," are "Fourteen leaves of fitts, &c. of Robyn Hood, with a print of him on horſeback; over which "¶ Here beginneth a geſt of Robyn Hode." See Ames's *Typographical antiquities*, by Herbert, p. 1815.) Moſt of the pieces in this volume appear to have been printed "be Walter Chepman and Andrew Millar in the South-gait of Edinburgh," in or about 1508. The above imperfect "geſte of Robyn Hode" is conjectured to be an edition of the old poem in queſtion; but all endeavours to procure a ſight of or

once extant, of, perhaps, a ſtill earlyer date, of which it is ſome little ſatisfaction to be able to give even the following fragment, from a ſingle leaf, fortunately preſerved in one of the volumes of old printed ballads in the Britiſh muſeum, in a hand-writing as old as Henry the 6ths time. It exhibits the characters of our hero and his *fidus Achates* in the nobleſt point of view.

" He ſay*d* Robyn Hod . . . . yne the preſon,
And owght off hit was g*on*.

The porter roſe a-non certeyn,
  As ſone as he hard Johan call;
Lytyll Johan was redy with a ſword,
  And bare hym throw to the wall.

Now will I be jayler, ſayd lytyll Johan,
  And toke the keys in hond;
He toke the way to Robyn Hod,
  And ſone he hyme unbond.

He gaffe hym a good ſwerd in his hond,
  His hed ther-with for to kepe;
And ther as the wallis wer loweſt,
  Anon down ther they lepe.

. . . .
. . . .
. . . .

  To Robyn . . . . . ſayd:

I have d*one* the a god torne for an . .
  Quit me when thow may;
I have done the a gode torne, ſayd lytyll [Johan],
  Forſothe as I the ſaye;

extract from it have proved unſucceſsful, though the editor even took a journey to Edinburgh chiefly for the purpoſe, and received every poſſible degree of attention and civility from the worthy librarian: the book having been now detained out of the library for ſome years. " Robene Hude and litil Jhone" occurs alſo among the tales enumerated in Wedderburns *Complainte of Scotland*, printed, at Saint-Andrews, in 1549. In a liſt of " bookes printed, and . . . ſold by Jane Bell, at the eaſt end of Chriſt-church [1655]," in company with *Frier Ruſh*, *The frier and the boy*, &c. is " a book of Robin Hood and Little John." Captain Cox of Coventry appears to have had a copy of ſome old edition: ſee Lanehams *Letter from Killingworth*, 1575.

I have browghte the under the gren wod . . .
  Farewell & have gode daye.

Nay, be my trowthe, ſayd Robyn,
  So ſchall it never bee;
I make the maſter, ſayd Robyn,
  Off all my men & me.
Nay, be my trowthe, ſayd lytyll Johan,
  So ſchall it never bee."

This, indeed, may be part of the "ſtory of Robin Hood and little John," which M. Wilhelm Bedwell found in the ancient MS. lent him by his much honoured good friend M. G. Withers, whence he extracted and publiſhed "The turnament of Tottenham," a poem of the ſame age, and which ſeemed to him to be done (perhaps but tranſcribed) by ſir Gilbert Pilkington, formerly, as ſome had thought, parſon of that pariſh.*

That poems and ſtories on the ſubject of our hero and his companions were extraordinarily popular and common before and during the ſixteenth century is evident from the teſtimony of divers writers. Thus, Alexander Barclay, prieſt, in his tranſlation of *The ſhyp of folys*, firſt printed by Pynſon in 1508, afterward by Wynken de Worde in 1517, and laſtly by John Cawood in 1570, ſays:

"I write no *jeſte* ne *tale* of ROBIN HOOD."

Again:

"For goodlie ſcripture is not worth an hawe,
But tales are loved ground of ribaudry;
And many are ſo blinded with their ſoly,
That no ſcriptur thinke they ſo true nor gode,
As is *a fooliſh jeſt* of ROBIN HODE."

Again:

"And of all *fables* and *jeſtes* of ROBIN HOOD,
Or other trifles."

The ſame Barclay, in the fourth of his *Egloges*, ſub-

* "Deſcription of the town of Tottenham-high-croſſe, &c." London, (1631, 4to.) 1718, 8vo.

joined to the laſt edition of *The ſhip of foles*, but originally printed ſoon after 1500, has the following paſſage:

> " Yet would I gladly heare ſome *mery fit*
> Of MAIDE MARION, or els of ROBIN HOOD,
> Or Benteleyes ale, which chafeth well the blood,
> Of Perte of Norwich, or Sauce of Wilberton,
> Or buckiſhe Joly * well ſtuffed as a ton."

Robert Braham, in his epiſtle to the reader, prefixed to Lydgates *Troy-book*, 1555, is of opinion that "Caxtons recueil" [of Troy] is "worthye to be numbred amongeſt the *trifelinge tales* and *barrayne luerdries* of ROBYN HODE and Bevys of Hampton." (See Ames's *Typographical antiquities*, by Herbert, p. 849.)

"For one that is ſand blynd," ſays ſir Thomas Chaloner, "woulde take an aſſe for a moyle, or another prayſe a *rime* of ROBYN HODE for as excellent a making as *Troylus* of Chaucer, yet ſhoulde they not ſtraight-waies be counted madde therefore? (Eraſmus's *Praiſe of folye*, ſig. h.)

"If good lyfe," obſerves biſhop Latimer, "do not inſue and folowe upon our readinge to the example of other, we myghte as well ſpende that tyme in reading of prophane hyſtories, of Canterburye tales, or *a fit of* ROBEN HODE." (*Sermons*, ſig. A. iiii.)

The following lines, from a poem in the Hyndford MS. compiled in 1568, afford an additional proof of our heros popularity in Scotland:

> " Thair is no *ſtory* that I of heir,
> Of *Johne* nor ROBENE HUDE,
> Nor zit of Wallace wicht but weir,
> That me thinkes half ſo gude,
> As of thre palmaris, *&c.*"

That the ſubject was not forgotten in the ſucceeding age, can be teſtifyed by Drayton, who is elſewhere quoted, and in his ſixth eclogue makes Gorbo thus addreſs "old Winken de Word:"

* Mr. Warton reads *Toby*; and ſo, perhaps, it may be in former editions.

"Come, ſit we down under this hawthorn-tree,
The morrows light ſhall lend us day enough,
And let us tell of Gawen, or ſir Guy,
Of ROBIN HOOD, or of old Clem a Clough."

Richard Johnſon, who wrote "The hiſtory of Tom Thumbe," in proſe, (London, 1621, 12mo. b. l.) thus prefaces his work: "My merry muſe begets no tales of Guy of Warwicke, &c. nor will I trouble my penne with the *pleaſant glee* of ROBIN HOOD, LITTLE JOHN, the FRYER, and his MARIAN; nor will I call to mind the luſty PINDER of WAKEFIELD, &c."

In "The Calidonian forreſt," a ſort of allegorical or myſtic tale, by John Hepwith, gentleman, printed in 1641, 4to. the author ſays,

"Let us talke of Robin Hoode,
And little John in merry Shirewoode, &c."*

Of one very ancient, and undoubtedly once very popular, ſong this ſingle line is all that is now known to exiſt:

"Robin Hood in Barnſdale ſtood."

However, though but a line, it is of the higheſt authority in Weſtminſter-hall, where, in order to the deciſion of a knotty point, it has been repeatedly cited, in the moſt ſolemn manner, by grave and learned judges.

* Honeſt Barnaby, who wrote or traveled about 1640, was well acquainted with our heros ſtory.

"*Veni* Nottingham, *tyrones*
Sherwoodenſes *ſunt* latrones,
Inſtar Robin Hood, & *ſervi*
Scarlet & Joannis Parvi;
Paſſim. ſparſim. peculantur,
Cellis. ſylvis deprædantur.

"Thence to Nottingham, where rovers,
Highway riders. Sherwood drovers,
Like old *Robin Hood*, and *Scarlet*,
Or like *Little John* his varlet;
Here and there they ſhew them doughty,
In cells and woods to get their booty."

M. 6 *Jac. B. R. Witham* v. *Barker*. Yelv. 147. *Trespass*, for breaking plaintifs close, *&c. Plea, Liberum tenementum* of sir John Tyndall, and justification as his servant and by his command. *Replication*, That it is true it is his freehold, but that long before the time when *&c.* he leased to plaintif at will, who entered and was possessed until, *&c. traversing*, that defendant entered, *&c.* by command of sir John. *Demurrer:* and adjudged against plaintif, on the ground of the replication being bad, as not setting forth any seisin or possession in sir John, out of which a lease at will could be derived. For a title made by the plea or replication should be certain to all intents, because it is traversable. Here, therefor, he should have stated sir Johns seisin, as well as the lease at will; which is not done here: "**mes tout un come il uſt replie** Robin Whood in Barnwood stood, absque hoc **q̃ def. p commandement sir** John. Quod nota. Per Fenner, Williams **et** Crook **justices sole en court. Et judgment done accordant.** Yelv. **p̃ def.**"

In the case of *Bush* v. *Leake*, *B. R. Trin.* 23 *G.* 3. Buller, justice, cited the case of *Coulthurst* v. *Coulthurst*, *C. B. Pasch.* 12 *G.* 3. (an action on bond) and observed "There, a case in Yelverton was alluded to, where the court said, you might as well say, by way of inducement to a traverse, *Robin Hood in Burnwood stood.*"

It is almost unnecessary to observe, because it will be shortly proved, that *Barnwood*, in the preceding quotations, ought to be *Barnsdale.** With respect to

* There is, in fact, such a place as *Barnwood forest*, in Buckinghamshire; but no one, except Mr. Hearne, has hitherto supposed that part of the country to have been frequented by our hero. *Barnwood*, in the case reported by Yelverton, has clearly arisen from a confusion of *Barn*sdale and green *wood*. "Robin Hood in the *greenwood* stood" was likewise the beginning of an old song now lost (see vol. II. p. 46): and it is not a little remarkable that Jefferies, serjeant, on the trial of Pilkington and others, for a riot, in 1683, by a similar confusion, quotes the line in question thus:

"Robin Hood upon *Greendale* stood." (*State-trials*, iii. 634.)

With reſpect to *Whood*, the reader will ſee, under note (P), a remarkable proof of the antiquity of that pronunciation, which actually prevails in the metropolis at this day. See alſo the word "whodes" in note (FF).

This celebrated and important line occurs as the firſt of a fooliſh mock-ſong, inſerted in an old morality, intitled "A new interlude and a mery of the nature of the iiii elementes," ſuppoſed to have been printed by John Raſtall about 1520; where it is thus introduced:

" *Hu*[*manyte*]. —— let us ſome luſty balet ſyng.
Yng[*norance*]. Nay, ſyr, by the hevyn kyng:
For me thynkyth it ſervyth for no thyng,
All ſuche pevyſh prykeryd ſong.
Hu. Pes, man, pryk-ſong may not be dyſpyſyd,
For therwith god is well pleſyd.

. . . .

Yng. Is god well pleaſyd, troweſt thou, therby?
Nay, nay, for there is no reaſon why.
For is it not as good to ſay playnly
Gyf me a ſpade,
As gyf me a ſpa ve va ve va ve vade?
But yf thou wylt have a ſong that is good,
I have one of ROBYN HODE,
The beſt that ever was made.
Hu. Then a feleſhyp, let us here it.
Yng. But there is a bordon, thou muſt bere it,
Or ellys it wyll not be.
Hu. Than begyn, and care not for . . .

Downe downe downe, &c.

Yng. Robyn Hode in Barnyſdale ſtode,
And lent hym tyl a mapyll thyſtyll;

The following moſt vulgar and indecent rime, current among the peaſantry in the north of England, may have been intended to ridicule the perpetual repetition of "Robin Hood in greenwood ſtood:"

Robin Hood
In green-wood ſtood,
With his back againſt a tree;
He fell flat
Into a cow-plat,
And all beſhitten was he.

Than cam our lady & swete saynt Andrewe;
Slepyst thou, wakyst thou, Geffrey Coke?*

A c. wynter the water was depe,
I can not tell you how brode;
He toke a gose nek in his hande,
And over the water he went.

He start up to a thystell top,
And cut hym downe a holyn clobbe;
He stroke the wren betwene the hornys,
That fyre sprange out of the pygges tayle.

Jak boy is thy bow i-broke,
Or hath any man done the wryguldy wrange?
He plukkyd muskyllys out of a wyllowe,
And put them in to his sachell.

Wylkyn was an archer good,
And well coude handell a spade;
He toke his bend bowe in his hand,
And set him downe by the fyre.

He toke with hym lx. bowes and ten,
A pese of bese, another of baken.
Of all the byrdes in mery Englond,
So merely pypys the mery botell."

All the entire poems and songs known to be extant will be found in the following collection; but many more may be traditionally preserved in different parts of the country which would have added considerably to its value.† That some of these identical pieces, or others of

* It is possible that, amid these absurdities, there may be other lines of the old song of Robin Hood, which is the only reason for reviving them.

"O sleepst thou, or wakst thou, Jeffery Cooke?"

occurs, likewise, in a medley of a similar description, in *Pammelia*, 1609.

† In *The gentleman's magazine*, for December, 1790, is the first verse of a song used by the inhabitants of Helston in Cornwall, on the celebration of an annual festivity on the eighth of May, called the *Furry-day*, supposed Floras day, not, it is imagined, "as many have thought, in remembrance of some festival instituted in honour of

the like nature, were great favourites with the common people in the time of queen Elizabeth, though not much

that goddeſs, but rather from the garlands commonly worn on that day." (See the ſame publication for June and October, 1790.) This verſe was the whole that Mr. Urbans correſpondent could then recollect, but he thought he might be afterward able "to ſend all that is known of it, for," he ſays, "it formerly was very long, but is now much forgotten." The ſtanza is as follows:

"Robin Hood and Little John
They are both gone to fair O;
And we will go to the merry green-wood,
To ſee what they do there O.
With hel an tow,
And rum-be-low,
And chearily we'll get up,
As ſoon as any day O,
All for to bring the ſummer home,
The ſummer and the May O."

"After which," he adds, "there is ſomething about the grey gooſe wing; from all which," he concludes, "the goddeſs Flora has nothing to ſay to it." She may have nothing to ſay to the ſong, indeed, and yet a good deal to do with the thing. But the fact is that the firſt *eight* days of May, or the *firſt* day and the *eighth*, ſeem to have been devoted by the Celtic nations to ſome great religious ceremony. Certain ſuperſtitious obſervances of this period ſtill exiſt in the highlands of Scotland, where it is called the *Bel-tein*; *Beltan*, in that country, being a common term for the beginning of May, as "between the Beltans" is a ſaying ſignificant of the *firſt* and *eighth* days of that month. The games of Robin Hood, as we ſhall elſewhere ſee, were, for whatever reaſon, always celebrated in May.—*N. B.* "*Hel-an-tow,*" in the above ſtanza, ſhould be *heave and how*. . *Heave and how*, and *Rumbelow*, was an ordinary chorus to old ballads; and is at leaſt as ancient as the reign of Edward II. ſince it occurs in the ſtanza of a Scotiſh ſong, preſerved by ſome of our old hiſtorians, on the battle of Bannock-burn.

To lengthen this long note: Among the Harleian MSS. (num. 367.) is the fragment of "a tale of Robin Hood dialouge-wiſe beetweene Watt and Jeffry. The morall is the overthrowe of the abbyes; the like being attempted by the Puritane, which is the wolfe, and the politician, which is the fox, agaynſt the buſhops. Robin Hood, buſhop; Adam Bell, abbot; Little John, colleauges or the univerſity." This ſeems to have been a common mode of ſatyrizing both the old church and the reformers. In another MS. of the

esteemed, it would seem, by the refined critic, may, in addition to the testimonies already cited, be infered from a passage in Webbes *Discourse of English poetrie*, printed in 1586. "If I lette passe," says he, "the unaccountable rabble of ryming ballet-makers, and compylers of sencelesse sonets, who be most busy to stuffe every stall full of grosse devises and unlearned pamphlets, I trust I shall with the best sort be held excused. For though many such can frame an *alehouse-song* of five or sixe score verses, hobbling uppon some tune of a *northern jygge*, or ROBYN HOODE, or *La lubber*, &c. and perhappes observe just number of sillables, eyght in one line, sixe in an other, and therewithall an A to make a jercke in the ende, yet if these might be accounted poets (as it is sayde some of them make meanes to be promoted to the lawrell) surely we shall shortly have whole swarmes of poets; and every one that can frame a booke in ryme, though, for want of matter, it be but in commendations of copper noses or bottle ale, wyll catch at the garlande due to poets: whose potticall (poeticall, I should say) heades, I woulde wyshe, at their worshipfull comencements, might, in steede of lawrell, be gorgiously garnished with fayre greene barley, in token of their good affection to our Englishe malt." The chief object of this satire seems to be William Elderton, the drunken ballad-maker, of whose compositions all but one or two have unfortunately perished.*

same collection, (N. 207) written about 1532, is a tract intitled "The banckett of John the reve, unto Peirs Ploughman, Laurens Laborer, Thomlyn Tailyor, and Hobb of the Hille, with others:" being, as Mr. Wanley says, a dispute concerning transubstantiation by a Roman catholic. The other, indeed, is much more modern: it alludes to the indolence of the abbots, and their falling off from the original purity in which they were placed by the bishops, whom it inclines to praise. The object of its satire seems to be the Puritans; but here it is imperfect, though the lines preserved are not wholly destitute of poetical merit.—"Robin Hood and the duke of Lancaster, a ballad, to the tune of *The abbot of Canterbury*, 1727, is a satire on sir Robert Walpole.

* Chatterton, in his "Memoirs of a sad dog," represents "baron

Moſt of the ſongs inſerted in the ſecond of theſe volumes were common broad-ſheet ballads, printed in the black letter, with wood cuts, between the reſtoration and the revolution; though copies of ſome few have been found of an earlyer date. "Who was the author of the collection, intitled *Robin Hood's garland*, no one," ſays ſir John Hawkins, "has yet pretended to gueſs. As ſome of the ſongs have in them more of the ſpirit of poetry than others, it is probable." he thinks, "it is the work of various hands: that it has from time to time been varied and adapted to the phraſe of the times," he ſays, "is certain." None of theſe ſongs, it is believed, were ever collected into a *garland* till ſome time after the reſtoration; as the earlyeſt that has been met with, a copy of which is preſerved in the ſtudy of Anthony à Wood, was printed by W. Thackeray, a noted balladmonger, in 1689. This, however, contains no more than *ſixteen* ſongs, ſome of which, very falſely as it ſeems, are ſaid to have been "never before printed." "The lateſt edition of any worth," according to ſir John Hawkins, "is that of 1719." None of the old editions of this *garland* have any ſort of preface: that prefixed to

Otranto" (meaning, the honorable Horace Walpole, now earl of Orford) when on a viſit to "ſir Stentor," as highly pleaſed with *Robin Hoods ramble*, "melodiously chaunted by the knight's groom and dairy-maid, to the excellent muſic of a two ſtringed violin and bag-pipe," which tranſported him back "to the age of his favourite hero, Richard the third;" whereas, ſays he, "the ſongs of Robin Rood were not in being till the reign of queen Elizabeth." This, indeed, may be in a great meaſure true of thoſe which we now have, but there is ſufficient evidence of the exiſtence and popularity of ſuch-like ſongs for ages preceding; and ſome of theſe, no doubt, were occaſionally moderniſed or new-written, though moſt of them muſt be allowed to have periſhed.

The late Dr. Johnſon, in controverting the authenticity of *Fingal*, a compoſition in which the author, Mr. Macpherſon, has made great uſe of ſome unqueſtionably ancient Iriſh ballads, ſaid, "He would undertake to write an epick poem on the ſtory of *Robin Hood*, and half England, to whom the names and places he ſhould mention in it are familiar, would believe and declare they had heard it from their earlieſt years." (Boſwells *Journal*, p. 486.)

the modern ones, of Bow or Aldermary church-yard, being taken from the collection of old ballads, 1723, where it is placed at the head of *Robin Hoods birth and breeding*. The full title of the last London edition of any note is—"Robin Hood's garland: being a complete history of all the notable and merry exploits performed by him and his men on many occasions: To which is *added* a *preface*, [*i. e.* the one already mentioned] giving a more full and particular account of his birth, &c. than any hitherto published. [*Cut of archers shooting at a target.*]

I'll send this arrow from my bow,
  And in a wager will be bound
To hit the mark aright, although
  It were for fifteen hundred pound.
Doubt not I'll make the wager good,
Or ne'er believe bold Robin Hood.'

Adorned with twenty-seven neat and curious cuts adapted to the subject of each song. London, Printed and sold by R. Marshall, in Aldermary church-yard, Bow-lane." 12mo. On the back of the title-page is the following Grub-street address:

"To all gentlemen archers."

"This garland has been long out of repair,
  Some songs being wanting, of which we give account;
For now at last, by true industrious care,
  The *sixteen* songs to twenty-seven we mount;
Which large addition needs must please, I know,
All the ingenious 'yeomen' of the bow.
To read how Robin Hood and Little John,
  Brave Scarlet, Stutely, valiant, bold and free,
Each of them bravely, fairly play'd the man,
  While they did reign beneath the green-wood tree;
Bishops, friars, likewise many more,
Parted with their gold, for to increase their store,
But never would they rob or wrong the poor."

The last seven lines are not by the author of the first six, but were added afterward; perhaps when the *twenty-four* songs were increased to *twenty-seven*.*

* The following note is inserted in the fourth edition of the

(Y)—" has given rise to divers proverbs:"] Proverbs, in all countries, are, generally speaking, of very great antiquity; and therfor it will not be contended that those concerning our hero are the oldest we have. It is highly probable, however, that they originated in or near his own time, and of course have existed for upward of 500 years, which is no modern date. They are here arranged, not, perhaps, according to their exact chronological order, but by the age of the authorities they are taken from.

1. *Good even, good Robin Hood.*

The allusion is to *civility* extorted by *fear*. It is preserved by Skelton, in that most biting satire, against cardinal Wolsey, *Why come ye not to court?* (Works, 1736, p. 147.)

" He is set so hye,
In his hierarchy,

Reliques of ancient English poetry, published in July 1795 (vol. I. p. xcvii):

" Of the 24 songs in what is now called " Robin Hood's garland," many are so modern as not to be found in Pepys's collection completed only in 1700. In the [editors] folio MS. are ancient fragments of the following, *viz.*—Robin Hood and the beggar.—Robin Hood and the butcher.—Robin Hood and fryer Tucke.—Robin Hood and the pindar.—Robin Hood and queen Catharine, in two parts.—Little John and the four beggars, and " Robine Hood his death." This last, which is very curious, has no resemblance to any that have yet been published; [it is probably num. XXVIII. of part I.] and the others are extremely different from the printed copies; but they unfortunately are in the beginning of the MS. where half of every leaf hath been torn away."

As this MS. " contains several songs relating to the civil war in the last century," the mere circumstance of its comprising fragments of the above ballads is no proof of a higher antiquity; any more than its not containing " one that alludes to the restoration" proves its having been compiled before that period; or than, because some of these 24 songs are not to be found in Pepys's collection, they are more modern than 1700. If the MS. could be collated, it would probably turn out that many of its contents have been inaccurately and unfaithfully transcribed, by some illiterate person, from printed copies still extant, and, consequently, tha it is, so far, of no authority. See the advertisement prefixed.

. . . .
That in the chambre of ſtars
All matters there he mars;
Clapping his rod on the borde,
No man dare ſpeake a word;
For he hath all the ſaying,
Without any renaying:
He rolleth in his recordes,
He ſaith, How ſay ye my lordes?
Is not my reaſon good?
Good even, good Robin Hood."*

2. *Many men talk of Robin Hood that never ſhot in his bow.*

"That is, many diſcourſe (or prate rather) of matters wherein they have no ſkill or experience. This proverb is now extended all over England, though originally of *Nottinghamſhire* extraction, where *Robin Hood* did principally reſide in *Sherwood* forreſt. He was an arch robber, and withal an excellent archer; though ſurely the poet † gives a *twang* to the *looſe of his arrow*, making him ſhoot one a *cloth-yard long, at full forty ſcore mark, for compaſs never higher than the breaſt*, and *within leſs than a foot of the mark*. But herein our author hath verified the proverb, talking at large of Robin Hood, in whoſe bow he never ſhot. Fullers *Worthies*, p. 315.

"One may juſtly wonder," adds the facetious writer, "this archer did not at laſt hit the mark, I mean, *come to the gallows* for his many robberies."

The proverb is mentioned, and given as above, by ſir Edward Coke in his 3d Inſtitute, p. 197. See alſo note (X). It is thus noticed by Jonſon, in "The king's entertainment at Walbeck in Nottinghamſhire, 1633:"

"This is . . . father Fitz-Ale, herald of Derby, &c.
He can fly o'er hills and dales,

* Mr. Warton has mistaken and misprinted this line ſo as to make it abſolute nonſenſe.

"Is not my reaſon good?
Good—even good—Robin Hood."

(*Hiſ En. po.* vol. ii.)

† *Draytons Poly-Olbion*, ſong 26, p. 122. (*Supra* p. viii.)

And report you more odd tales
Of our out law Robin Hood,
That revell'd here in Sherewood,
And more ftories of him fhow,
(Though he *ne'er fhot in his bow*)
Than au' men or believe, or know.

We likewife meet with it in *Epigrams*, &c. 1654:

" *In Virtutem.*

" Vertue we praife, but practice not her good,
(Athenian-like) we act not what we know;
So *many men* doe *talk of Robin Hood*,
Who never yet *fhot* arrow *in his bow*."

On the back of a ballad, in Anthony a Woods collection, he has written,

" There be fome that prate
Of Robin Hood, and of his bow,
Which never fhot therein, I trow."

Ray gives it thus:

" Many talk of Robin Hood, that never fhot in his bow,
And many talk of little John, that never did him know:"

which Kelly has varyed, but without authority.

Camdens printer has feparated the lines, as diftinct proverbs (*Remains*, 1674):

" Many fpeak of Robin Hood that never fhot in his bow.
" Many a man talks of little John that never did him know."

This proverb likewife occurs in *The downfall of Robert earle of Huntington*, 1600, and feems alluded to in a fcarce and curious old tract intitled " The contention betwyxte Churchyeard and Camell, upon David Dycers Dreame &c." 1560. 4to. b. l.

" Your fodain ftormes and thundre claps, your boafts and braggs fo loude: [cloud.
Hath doone no harme thogh Robin Hood fpake with you in a
Go learne againe of litell Jhon, *to fhute in Robyn Hods bowe*,
Or Dicars dreame fhall be unhit, and all his whens, I trowe."*

* In Churchyards " Replication onto Camels objection," he tells the latter:

The Italians appear to have a ſimilar ſaying.

Molti parlan di Orlando
Chi non viddero mai ſuo brando.

3. *To overſhoot Robin Hood.*

"And laſtly and chiefly, they cry out with open mouth *as if they had overſhot Robin Hood*, that Plato baniſhed them [*i. e.* poets] out of his commonwealth." Sir P. Sidneys *Defence of poeſie.*

4. *Tales of Robin Hood are good* [*enough*] *for fools.*

This proverb is inſerted in Camdens *Remains*, printed originally in 1605; but the word in brackets is ſupplyed from Ray.

5. *To ſell Robin Hoods pennyworths.*

"It is ſpoken of things ſold under half their value; or if you will, *half ſold half given.* Robin Hood came lightly by his ware, and lightly parted therewith; ſo that he could afford *the length of his bow* for a *yard* of velvet. Whitherſoever he came, he carried a *fair* along with him; chapmen crowding to buy his ſtollen commodities. But ſeeing *The receiver is as bad as the thief*, and ſuch *buyers* are as bad as *receivers*, the cheap pennyworths of plundered goods may *in fine* prove dear enough to their conſciences." Fullers *Worthies.* p. 315.

This ſaying is alluded to in the old north-country ſong of *Randal a Barnaby:*

"All men ſaid, it became me well,
And *Robin Hoods pennyworths I did ſell.*"

6. *Come, turn about, Robin Hood.*

Implying that to challenge or defy our hero muſt have been the *ne plus ultra* of courage. It occurs in *Wit and drollery*, 1661.

"Your knowledge is great, your judgement is good,
The moſt of your ſtudy hath ben of *Robyn Hood*;
And Bevys of Hampton, and ſyr Launcelot de Lake,
Hath taught you full oft your verſes to make."

" Oh Love, whofe power and might,
No creature ere withftood,
Thou forceft me to write,
Come turn about Robin-hood."

7. *As crook'd as Robin Hoods bow.*

That is, we are to conceive, when bent by himfelf. The following ftanza of a modern Irifh fong is the only authority for this proverb that has been met with.

" The next with whom I did engage,
It was an old woman worn with age,
Her teeth were like tobacco pegs,
Befides fhe had two bandy legs,
Her back more crook'd than Robin Hoods bow,
Purblind and decrepid, unable to go;
Altho' her years were fixty three,
She fmil'd at the humours of *Socfhe Bue.*"

(AA)—" to fwear by him, or fome of his companions, appears to have been a ufual practice."] The earlyeft inftance of this practice occurs in a pleafant ftory among " Certaine merry tales of the mad men of Gottam," compiled in the reign of Henry VIII. by Dr. Andrew Borde, an eminent phyfician of that period, which here follows *verbatim*, as taken from an old edition in black letter, without date, (in the Bodleian library,) being the firft tale in the book.

" There was two men of Gottam, and the one of them was going to the market to Nottingham to buy fheepe, and the other came from the market; and both met together upon Nottingham bridge. Well met, faid the one to the other. Whither be yee going? faid he that came from Nottingham. Marry, faid he that was going thither, I goe to the market to buy fheepe. Buy fheepe! faid the other, and which way wilt thou bring them home? Marry, faid the other, I will bring them over this bridge. By Robin Hood, faid he that came from Nottingham, but thou fhalt not. By maid Marrion, faid he that was going thitherward, but I will. Thou fhalt not, faid the one. I will, faid the other. Ter here! ſaid the one. Shue there! ſaid the other. Then they beate their ſtaves againſt the ground, one againſt the other, as there had beene an hundred ſheepe betwixt them. Hold in, ſaid the one. Beware the leaping over the bridge of my ſheepe, ſaid the other. I care not, ſaid the other. They ſhall not come this way, ſaid the one. But they ſhall, ſaid the other. Then ſaid the other, & if that thou make much to doe, I will put my finger in thy mouth. A turd thou wilt, ſaid the other. And as they were at their contention, another man of Gottam came from the market, with a ſacke of meale upon a horſe, and ſeeing and hearing his neighbours at ſtrife for ſheepe, and none betwixt them, ſaid, Ah fooles, will you never learn wit? Helpe me, ſaid he that had the meale, and lay my ſack upon my ſhoulder. They did ſo; and he went to the one ſide of the bridge, and unlooſed the mouth of the ſacke, and did ſhake out all his meale into the river. Now, neighbours, ſaid the man, how much meale is there in my ſacke now? Marry, there is none at all, ſaid they. Now, by my faith, ſaid he, even as much wit is in your two heads, to ſtrive for that thing you have not. Which was the wiſeſt of all theſe three perſons, judge you."*

"By the bare ſcalp of Robin Hoods fat frier,"

is an oath put by Shakſpeare into the mouth of one of his outlaws in the *Two gentlemen of Verona*, act 4. ſcene 1. "Robin Hoods fat frier" is frier Tuck; a circumſtance of which doctor Johnſon, who ſet about explaining that author with a very inadequate ſtock of information, was perfectly ignorant.

(BB)—"his ſongs have been prefered not only, on the moſt ſolemn occaſion, to the pſalms of David, but in

* See the original ſtory, in which two brothers, of whom one had wiſhed for as many oxen as he ſaw ſtars, the other for a paſture as wide as the firmament, kill each other about the paſturage of the oxen, (from *Camer. oper. ſubſciſ. cent.* 1. *c.* 92. *p.* 429) in Wanleys *Little world of man*, edition of 1774, p. 426.

fact to the new testament."] "[On Friday, March 9th. 1733] was executed at Northampton William Alcock for the murder of his wife. He never own'd the fact, nor was at all concern'd at his approaching death, refusing the prayers and assistance of any persons. In the morning he drank more than was sufficient, yet sent and paid for a pint of wine, which being deny'd him, he would not enter the cart before he had his money return'd. On his way to the gallows he sung part of an OLD SONG OF ROBIN HOOD, with the chorus, *Derry, derry, down,** &c. and swore, kick'd and spurn'd at every person that laid hold of the cart; and before he was turn'd off, took off his shoes, to avoid a well known proverb; and being told by a person in the cart with him, it was more proper for him to read, or hear some body read to him, than so vilely to swear and sing, he struck the book out of the persons hands, and went on damning the spectators, and calling for wine. Whilst psalms and prayers were performing at the tree, he did little but talk to one or other, desiring some to remember him, others to drink to his good journey; and to the last moment declared the injustice of his case." (*Gentleman's magazine*, volume III. page 154.)

To this may be added, that at Edinburgh, in 1565, "Sandy Stevin menstrall" [*i. e.* musician] was convinced of blasphemy, alledging, That he would give no moir credit to *The new testament*, then to *a tale of Robin-Hood,* except it wer confirmed be the doctours of the church." (Knox's *Historie of the reformation in Scotland.* Edin. 1732, p. 368.)

William Roy, in a bitter satire against cardinal Wolsey,

* "*Derry down* is the burden of the old songs of the Druids sung by their Bards and Vaids, to call the people to their religious assemblys in the groves. *Doire* in Irish (the old Punic) is a grove: corrupted into *derry*. A famous Druid grove and academy at the place since called *Londonderry* from thence." *MS. note by Dr. Stukely, in his copy of Robin Hoods garland.*

intitled, "Rede me and be nott wrothe For I ſaye nothynge but ſothe," printed abroad, about 1525, ſpeaking of the biſhops, ſays,—

> "Their frantyke foly is ſo pevisſhe,
> That they contempne in Englisſhe,
>   To have *the new teſtament*;
> But as for *tales of Robyn Hode*,
> With wother jeſtes nether honeſt nor goode,
>   They have none impediment."

To the ſame effect is the following paſſage in another old libel upon the prieſts, intitled "I playne Piers which can not flatter, a plowe-man men me call, *&c.*" b. l. n. d. printed in the original as proſe:

> "No Chriſten booke
> Maye thou on looke,
>   Yf thou be an Engliſhe ſtrunt,
> Thus dothe alyens us loutte,
> By that ye ſpreade aboute,
>   After that old ſorte and wonte.
> You allowe they ſaye,
> *Legenda aurea*,
>   *Roben Hoode*, Bevys, & Gower,
> And all bagage be ſyd,
> But *gods word* ye may not abyde,
>   Theſe lyeſe are your churche 'dower.'*

See, alſo, before, p. lxxvii.

(CC) "His ſervice to the word of god."] "I came once myſelfe," ſays biſhop Latimer, (in his ſixth ſermon before king Edward VI.) "to a place, riding on a journey homeward from London, and I ſent word over night into the town that I would preach there in the morning, becauſe it was a holy day, and methought it was an holidayes worke; the churche ſtode in my way; and I toke my horſſe and my companye and went thither;

* Theſe two ſingular articles, with others here quoted, are in the equally curious and extenſive library of George Steevens eſquire, whoſe liberality in the communication of his literary treaſures increaſes, if poſſible, with their rarity and value.

I thought I ſhould have found a great companye in the churche, and when I came there the churche dore was faſte locked. I tarried there half an houre and more, and at laſt the keye was founde; and one of the pariſhe commes to me, and ſayes, Syr, thys ys a buſye day with us, we cannot heare you; it is ROBYN HOODES DAYE. The pariſhe are gone abroad to gather for ROBYN HOODE, I pray you let them not. I was fayne there to geve place to ROBYN HOODE. I thought my rochet ſhould have been regarded, thoughe I were not; but it woulde not ſerve, it was fayne to geve place to ROBYN HOODES MEN.

"It is no laughying matter, my friendes, it is a wepynge matter, a heavy matter, under the pretence for gatherynge for ROBYN HOODE, a traytoure * and a thefe, to put out a preacher, to have his office leſſe eſtemed, to prefer ROBYN HOD before the mynyſtration of GODS word; and all thys hath come of unpreachynge prelates. Thys realme hath been il provided, for that it hath had ſuche corrupte judgementes in it, to prefer ROBYN HODE to GODDES WORDE. Yf the byſshoppes had bene preachers, there ſholde never have bene any ſuch thynge, *&c.*"

(DD)—"may be called the patron of archery."] The bow and arrow makers, in particular, have always held his memory in the utmoſt reverence. Thus, in the old ballad of *Londons ordinary:*

> "The hoſiers will dine at the Leg,
> The drapers at the ſign of the Bruſh,
> The *fletchers* to *Robin Hood* will go,
> And the ſpendthrift to Beggars-buſh."†

* The biſhop grows ſcurrilous. "I never heard," ſays Coke, attorney-general, "that *Robin Hood* was a *traitor*; they ſay he was an *outlaw*." (*State-trials*, i. 218.—Raleigh had ſaid, "Is it not ſtrange for me to make myſelf a *Robin Hood*, a Kett, or a Cade?")

† This ballad ſeems to have been written in imitation of a ſong in Heywoods *Rape of Lucrece*, 1630, beginning—

> "The gentry to the Kings-head,
> The nobles to the crown, *&c.*"

The picture of our hero is yet a common ſign in the country, and, before hanging-ſigns were aboliſhed in London, muſt have been ſtill more ſo in the city; there being at preſent no leſs than a dozen alleys, courts, lanes, &c. to which he or it has given a name. (See Baldwins *New complete guide*, 1770.) *The Robin-Hood-ſociety*, a club or aſſembly for public debate, or ſchool for oratory, is well known. It was held at a public houſe, which had once born the ſign, and ſtill retained the name of this great man, in Butcher-row, near Temple-bar.

It is very uſual, in the north of England, for a publican, whoſe name fortunately happens to be *John Little*, to have the ſign of Robin Hood and his conſtant attendant, with this quibbling ſubſcription:

> You gentlemen, and yeomen good,
> Come in and drink with Robin Hood;
> If Robin Hood be not at home,
> Come in and drink with *Little John*.*

An honeſt countryman, admiring the conceit, adopted the lines, with a ſlight, but, as he thought, neceſſary alteration, *viz.*

> If Robin Hood be not at home,
> Come in and drink with—*Simon Webſter.*

Drayton, deſcribing the various enſigns or devices of the Engliſh counties, at the battle of Agincourt, gives to

> " Old NOTTINGHAM, *an archer clad in green*,
> Under a tree with his drawn bow that ſtood,
> Which in a chequer'd flag far off was ſeen;
> *It was the picture of* OLD ROBIN HOOD."

(EE)—" the ſupernatural powers he is, in ſome parts, ſuppoſed to have poſſeſſed."] " In the pariſh of

* In Arnolds *Eſſex harmony*, (ii. 98.) he gives the inſcription, as a catch for three voices, of his own compoſition, thus:

> " My beer is ſtout, my ale is good,
> Pray ſtay and drink with Robin Hood;
> If Robin Hood abroad is gone,
> Pray ſtay and drink with little John."

Halifax is an immenſe ſtone or rock, ſuppoſed to be a druidical monument, there called *Robin Hood's penny-ſtone*, which he is ſaid to have uſed to pitch with at a mark for his amuſement. There is likewiſe another of theſe ſtones, of ſeveral tons weight, which the country-people will tell you he threw off an adjoining hill with a ſpade as he was digging. Every thing of the marvellous kind being here attributed to Robin Hood, as it is in Cornwall to K. Arthur." (Watſons *Hiſtory of Halifax*, p. 27.)

At Bitchover, ſix miles ſouth of Bakewell, and four from Haddon, in Derbyſhire, among ſeveral ſingular groupes of rocks, are ſome ſtones called *Robin Hoods ſtride*, being two of the higheſt and moſt remarkable. The people ſay Robin Hood lived here.

(FF)—" having a feſtival allotted to him, and ſolemn games inſtituted in honour of his memory, *&c.*"] Theſe games, which were of great antiquity, and different kinds, appear to have been ſolemnized on the firſt and ſucceeding days of May; and to owe their original eſtabliſhment to the cultivation and improvement of the manly exerciſe of archery, which was not, in former times, practiſed merely for the ſake of amuſement.

" I find," ſays Stow, " that in the moneth of May, the citizens of London, of all eſtates, lightlie in every pariſh, or ſometimes two or three pariſhes joyning together, had their ſeverall *mayinges*, and did fetch in Maypoles, with divers *warlike ſhewes*, with good *archers*, *morrice-dancers*, and other devices for paſtime all the day long: and towards the evening they had ſtage-playes and bonefires in the ſtreetes. . . . . . Theſe greate Mayinges and Maygames, made by the governors and maſters of this citie, with the triumphant ſetting up of the greate ſhafte, (a principall Maypole in Cornhill, before the pariſh church of S. Andrew, therefore called Underſhafte) by meane of an inſurrection of youthes againſt alianes on Mayday, 1517, the ninth of Henry the eight, have not beene ſo freely uſed as afore." (*Survay of London*, 1598. p. 72.)

The diſuſe of theſe ancient paſtimes, and the conſequent "neglect of archerie," are thus pathetically lamented by Richard Niccolls, in his *Londons artillery*, 1616:

"How is it that our London hath laid downe
This worthy practiſe, which was once the crowne
Of all her paſtime, when her *Robin Hood*
Had wont each yeare when *May* did clad the wood.
With luſtie greene, to lead his yong men out,
Whoſe brave demeanour, oft when they did ſhoot,
Invited royall princes from their courts,
Into the wilde woods to behold their ſports!
Who thought it then a manly ſight and trim,
To ſee a youth of cleane compacted lim,
Who, with a comely grace, in his left hand
Holding his bow, did take his ſtedfaſt ſtand,
Setting his left leg ſomewhat foorth before,
His arrow with his right hand nocking ſure,
Not ſtooping, nor yet ſtanding ſtreight upright,
Then, with his left hand little 'bove his ſight,
Stretching his arm out, with an eaſie ſtrength,
To draw an arrow of a yard in length."*

A deſcription of one drawing a bow.

The lines,

"Invited royall princes from their courts
Into the wild woods to behold their ſports,"

may be reaſonably ſuppoſed to allude to Henry VIII. who appears to have been particularly attached, as well to the exerciſe of archery, as to the obſervance of May. Some ſhort time after his coronation, ſays Hall, he "came to Weſtminſter, with the quene, and all their traine: and on a tyme being there, his grace, therles of Eſſex, Wilſhire, and other noble menne, to the numbre of twelve, came ſodainly in a mornyng into the quenes chambre, all appareled in ſhort cotes of Kentiſh Kendal, with hodes on

* This deſcription is finely illuſtrated by an excellent wood cut at the head of one of Anthony à Woods old ballads in the Aſhmoleian muſeum. The frontiſpiece to Gervas Markhams *Archerie*, 16 . . is, likewiſe, a man drawing a bow.

their heddes, and hofen of the fame, every one of them his bowe and arrowes, and a fworde and a bucklar, like outlawes, or ‘ Robyn’ Hodes men; wherof the quene, the ladies, and al other there, were abafhed, afwell for the ftraunge fight, as alfo for their fodain commyng: and after certayn daunces and paftime made thei departed.” (*Hen. VIII.* fo. 6, b.) The fame author gives the following curious account of “ A maiynge” in the 7th year of this monarch (1516): “ The kyng & the quene, accompanied with many lordes & ladies, roade to the high grouude on Shoters hil to take the open ayre, and as they paffed by the way they efpied a company of tall yomen, clothed all in grene, with grene whodes & bowes & arrowes, to the number of ii.C. Then one of them whiche called hymfelfe *Robyn Hood,* came to the kyng, defyring hym to fe his men fhote, & the kyng was content. Then he whifteled, & all the ii.C. archers fhot & lofed at once; & then he whifteled again, and they likewyfe fhot agayne; their arrowes whifteled by craft of the head, fo that the noyes was ftraunge and great, and muche pleafed the kyng, the quene, and all the company. All thefe archers were of the kynges garde, and had thus appareled themfelves to make folace to the kynge. Then Robyn Hood defyred the kyng and quene to come into the grene wood, and to fe how the outlawes lyve. The kyng demaunded of the quene and her ladyes, if they durft adventure to go into the wood with fo many outlawes. Then the quene faid, if it pleafed hym, fhe was content. Then the hornes blewe tyll they came to the wood under Shoters-hill, and there was an arber made of bowes, with a hal, and a great chamber, and an inner chamber, very well made and covered with floures and fwete herbes, whiche the kyng muche praifed. Then fayd Robyn Hood, Sir, outlawes brekefaftes is venyfon, and therefore you muft be content with fuch fare as we ufe. Then the kyng and quene fate doune, and were ferved with venyfon and vyne by Robyn Hood and his men, to their great contentacion. Then the kyng departed and his company, and Robyn Hood and his men them conduicted; and as they were returnyng, there met with them two ladyes in a ryche chariot drawen with v. horſes, and every horſe had his name on his head, and on every horſe ſat a lady with her name written . . . . and in the chayre ſate the lady May, accompanied with lady Flora, richely appareled; and they ſaluted the kyng with diverſe goodly ſonges, and ſo brought hym to Grenewyche. At this maiyng was a greate number of people to beholde, to their great ſolace and confort." (fo. lvi, b.)

That this ſort of May-games was not peculiar to London, appears from a paſſage in Richard Robinſons "Third aſſertion Engliſhe hiſtoricall, frendly in favour and furtherance of Engliſh archery:"*

" And, heare becauſe of archery I do by penne explane
The uſe, the proffet, and the praiſe, to England by the ſame,
Myſelfe remembreth of a childe in contreye native mine, (1553)
A *May-game* was of Robyn Hood, and of his traine that time, (7. E. 6.)
To traine up young men, ſtripplings and, eche other younger childe,
In ſhooting, yearely this with ſolempne feaſt was by the guylde
Or brotherhood of townsmen done, with ſport, with joy, and love,
To proffet which in preſent tyme, and afterward did prove."

* See " The auncient order ſocietie and unitie laudable of prince Arthure and his knightly armory of the round table . . . Tranſlated and collected by R. R. London, Imprinted by John Wolfe dwelling in Diſtaffe-lane neere the ſigne of the Caſtle. 1583." 4to. b. l. It appears from this publication that on the revival of London archery in queen Elizabeths time, " the worſhipfull ſocyety of archers," inſtead of calling themſelves after Robin Hood and his companions, took the names of " the magnificent prince Arthure and his knightly traine of the round table." It is, probably, to one of the annual meetings of this identical ſociety, that maſter Shallow alludes, in *The ſecond part of K. Henry IV.* " I remember," ſays he, " at Mile-end green, [their uſual place of exerciſe,]—I was then Sir Dagonet in *Arthur's ſhew*," &c. (See alſo Steevens's *Shakſpeare*, 1793. ix. 142.) The ſucceſſors of the above " friendly and frank fellowſhip" aſſumed the ridiculous appellations of duke of Shoreditch marquis of Clarkenwell, earl of Pancridge, &c. See Woods *Bowmans glory*, 1682.

The games of Robin Hood ſeem to have been occaſionally of a dramatic caſt. Sir John Paſton, in the time of K. Edward IV. complaining of the ingratitude of his ſervants, mentions one who had promiſed never to deſert him, "and ther uppon," ſays he, "I have kepyd hym thys iii yer *to pleye ſeynt Jorge*, and *Robyn Hod and the ſhryf off Notyngham*,* and now when I wolde have good horſe he is goon into *Bernyſdale*, and I withowt a keeper."

In ſome old accounts of the church-wardens of Saint Helens at Abingdon, Berks, for the year 1556, there is an entry *For ſetting up* ROBINS HOODES BOWER; I ſuppoſe, ſays Warton, for a pariſh interlude. (See *Hiſtory of Engliſh poetry*, ii. 175.) †

* Meaning that his ſole or chief employment had been in Chriſtmas or May-games, Whitſun-ales, and ſuch like idle diverſions. See *Original letters*, &c. ii. 134.

† The preciſe purpoſe or meaning of *ſetting up Robin Hoods bower* has not been ſatisfactorily aſcertained. Mr. Hearne, in an attempt to derive the name of "The Chiltern country" (ciltern, Saxon) from *ſilex*, a flint, has the following words: "*Certe Silceſtriam*, &c. *i e.* Certainly Silcheſter, in Hampſhire, ſignifies nothing but *the city of flints* (that is, *a city compoſed or built of flint-ſtones*). And what is more, in that very Chiltern country you may frequently ſee houſes built of flints, in erecting which, in ancient times, I ſuppoſe that many perſons involved themſelves deeply in debt, and that, in order to extricate themſelves, they took up money at intereſt of I know not what great men, which ſo far diſturbed their minds that they would become thieves, and do many things in no wiſe agreeable to the Engliſh government. Hence, the nobility ordered that large woods in the Chiltern country ſhould, in a great meaſure, be cut down, leſt they ſhould conceal any conſiderable body of robbers, who were wont to convert the ſame into lurking places. It concerns this matter to call to mind, that of this ſort of robbers was that *Robin* or *Robert Hood*, of whom the vulgar dayly ſing ſo many wonderful things. He (being now made an outlaw) before he retired into the north parts, frequently robing in the Chiltern country, lurked in the thickets thereof on purpoſe that he ſhould not be taken. Thence it was, that to us boys, (exhilarating, according to cuſtom, the mind with ſports) certain countrymen, with whom we

In ſome places theſe games were nothing more than a morris-dance, in which *Robin Hood*, *Little John*, *Maid Marian*, and *frier Tuck* were the principal perſonages; the others being a clown or fool, the hobby-horſe, (which appears, for ſome reaſon or other, to have been frequently forgot,*) the taborer, and the dancers, who were more or leſs numerous. Thus Warner:

"At Paſke began our *morriſe*, and ere penticoſt our *May*,
Tho *Roben Hood*, *liell John*, *frier Tucke*, and *Marian* deftly play,
And lard and ladie gang till kirke with lads and laſſes gay."†

Perhaps the cleareſt idea of theſe laſt-mentioned games, about the beginning of the 16th century, will be derived from ſome curious extracts given by Mr. Lyſons, in his valuable work intitled "The environs of London," (Vol. I. 1792. p. 226) from the contempora-

had accidentally ſome converſation, ſhewed us that ſort of den or retreat (vulgarly called *Robin Hoods bower*) in Maydenhead-thicket: which thicket is the ſame that Leland in his Itinerary, called *Frith*, by which name the Anglo-Saxons themſelves ſpoke of thickets. For although ꝼꞃıð in reality ſignifys *peace*, yet ſince numerous groves with them (as well as before with the Britons) were deemed ſacred, it is by no means to be wondered at that a great wood (becauſe manifeſtly an aſylum) ſhould in the judgment of the Anglo-Saxons be called by no other name than ꝼꞃıðeꞅ: and that Maydenhead-thicket was eſteemed among the greater woods Leland himſelf is a witneſs. Rightly therefor did Robin Hood (as ꝼꞃıð-bena) reckon himſelf to abide there in ſecurity. (*Chronicon de Dunſtaple*, p. 387.) What he means by all this is, doubtleſs, ſufficiently obſcure: the mere name, however, of *Robin Hoods bower* ſeems a very feeble authority for concluding that gallant outlaw to have robed or ſkulked in the Chiltern hundreds.

* See Steevenses *Shakſpeare*, 1793. x. 186.

† *Albions England*, 1602, p. 121. It is part of the "Northerne mans ſpeech againſt the friers." He adds;

"At Baptis-day with ale and cakes bout bonfires neighbours ſtood,
At Martle maſſe wa turnd a crabbe, thilke tolde of *Robin Hood*,
Till after long time myrke."

ry accounts of the "church-wardens of the pariſh of Kingſton upon Thames."

"Robin Hood and May-game.

"23 Hen. 7.	To the menſtorell upon May-day	0	0	4
——	For paynting of the mores garments and for ſarten gret leveres [57]	0	2	4
——	For paynting of a bannar for Robin Hode	0	0	3
——	For 2 M. & ½ pynnys —	0	0	10
——	For 4 plyts and ½ of laun for the mores garments — —	0	2	11
——	For orſeden [58] for the ſame —	0	0	10
——	For a goun for the lady —	0	0	8
——	For bellys for the dawnſars —	0	0	12
24 Hen. 7.	For little John's cote —	0	8	0
1 Hen. 8.	For ſilver paper for the mores dawnſars — —	0	0	7
——	For Kendall for Robyn Hode's cote	0	1	3

"[57] The word livery was formerly uſed to ſignify any thing delivered; ſee the Northumberland houſehold book, p. 60. If it ever bore ſuch an acceptation at that time, one might be induced to ſuppoſe, from the following entries, that it here meant a badge, or ſomething of that kind:

15 C. of leveres for Robin Hode — —	0	5	0
For leveres, paper and ſateyn — — —	0	0	20
For pynnes and leveres — — — —	0	6	5
For 13 C. of leverys — — — —	0	4	4
For 24 great lyvereys — — — —	0	0	4

We are told that formerly, in the celebration of May-games, the youth divided themſelves into two troops, the one in winter *livery*, the other in the habit of the ſpring. See Brands Popular antiquities, p. 261." This quotation is miſapplied. *Liveries*, in the preſent inſtance, are pieces of *paper* or *ſateyn* with ſome device thereon, which were diſtributed among the ſpectators. So in a paſſage which will be ſhortly quoted from *Jacke Drums entertainment*: "Well ſaid, my boyes, I muſt have my lords *livory*: what is't? a *May-pole?*" See alſo *Don Quixote*, part 2. chap. 22.

"[58] Though it varies conſiderably from that word, this may be a corruption of *orpiment*, which was much in uſe for colouring the morris garments." How *orſeden* can be a corruption of *orpi-*

—— For 3 yerds of white for the frere's [59] cote — —	o	3	o
—— For 4 yerds of kendall for mayde Marian's [60] huke [61] —	o	3	4
—— For saten of sypers for the same huke	o	o	6
—— For 2 payre of glovys for Robin Hode and mayde Maryan —	o	o	3
—— For 6 brode arovys —	o	o	6
—— To mayde Maryan for her labour for two years — —	o	2	o
—— To Fygge the taborer —	o	6	o
—— Rec[d] for Robyn Hod's gaderyng 4 marks [62]			

ment is not very easy to conceive: it may as well be supposed to mean *worsted* or *buckram*.

" 59 The friar's coat was generally of russet, as it appears by the following extracts. . . ." The coat of this mock frier would, doubtless, be made of the same stuff as that of a real one.

" 60 Marian was the assumed name of the beloved mistress of Robert earl of Huntingdon, whilst he was in a state of outlawry, as Robin Hood was his. See Mr Steeven's note to a passage in Shakspere's Henry IV. This character in the morris dances was generally represented by a boy. See Strutt's view of customs and manners, vol. iii. p. 150. It appears by one of the extracts, given above, that at Kingston it was performed by a woman, who was paid a shilling each year for her trouble."

" 61 Mr. Steevens suggests, with great probability, " that this word may have the same meaning as *howve* or *houve*, used by Chaucer for a head-dress; maid Marian's head-dress was always very fine: indeed some persons have derived her name from the Italian word *morione*, a head-d ess." Mr. Steevens was never less happy than he is in this *very probable* conjecture. The word *howve* or *houve*, in Chaucer, is a mere variation of *hood*: and maid Marians head-dress must, to be sure, have been " very fine" when made of 4 yards of broad cloath! A *huke* is a womans gown or habit (Huke. *palla*, *toga*, *pallium Belgicis feminis usitatum*. Skin) *Morione*. in Italian, signifies a murrion or scull-cap; and, it must be confessed, that they (if any there ever were) who thence derived the proper name of *Marian (Mary)* must have been blockheads of the first water.

" 62 It appears that this, as well as other games, was made a parish concern."

5 Hen. 8. Rec[d] for Robin Hood's gaderyng at Croydon — —	0	9	4
11 Hen. 8. Paid for three broad yerds of rosett for makyng the frer's cote	0	3	6
—— Shoes for the mores daunsars, the frere and mayde Maryan at 7[d] a payre	0	5	4
13 Hen. 8. Eight yerds of fustyan for the mores daunsars coats —	0	16	0
A dosyn of gold skynnes for the morres [63]	0	0	10
15 Hen. 8. Hire of hats for Robynhode	0	0	16
—— Paid for the hat that was lost —	0	0	10
16 Hen. 8. Rec[d] at the church-ale and Robynhode all things deducted —	3	10	6
—— Paid for 6 yerds $\frac{1}{4}$ of satyn for Robyn Hode's cotys — —	0	12	6
—— For makyng the same —	0	2	0
—— For 3 ells of locram [64] —	0	1	6
21 Hen. 8. For spunging and brushing Robynhode's cotys —	0	0	2
28 Hen. 8. Five hats and 4 porses for the daunsars — —	0	0	4$\frac{1}{2}$
—— 4 yerds of cloth for the fole's cote	0	2	0
—— 2 ells of worstede for mayde Maryans kyrtle — —	0	6	8
—— For 6 payre of double sollyd showne	0	4	6
—— To the mynstrele —	0	10	8
—— To the fryer and the piper for to go to Croydon — —	0	0	8

29 Hen. 8. Mem. Lefte in the keping of the wardens nowe beinge.

A fryers cote of russet and a kyrtele of a worstyde weltyd with red cloth, a mowren's [65] cote of buckram, and 4 morres daunsars cotes of white fustian spangelyd and

" 63 Probably gilt leather, the pliability of which was particularly accommodated to the motion of the dancers."

" 64 A sort of coarse linen.

" 65 Probably a Moor's coat; the word Morion is sometimes

two gryne ſaten cotes and a dyſardd's [66] cote of cotton and 6 payre of garters with bells."

Theſe games appear to have been diſcontinued at Kingſton, as a parochial undertaking at leaſt, after the above period .as the induſtrious enquirer found no further entries relating to them.

In an old circular wood cut, preſerved on the title of a penny-hiſtory, (*Adam Bell*, &c.) printed at Newcaſtle in 1772, is the apparent repreſentation of a morris-dance, conſiſting of the following perſonages: 1. A biſhop. 2. Robin Hood. 3. The potter (or begger). 4. Little John. 5. Frier Tuck. 6. Maid Marian. Figures 2 and 4 are diſtinguiſhed by their bows, and different ſize. The frier holds out a croſs; and Marian has flowing hair, and wears a ſort of coronet. But the execution of the whole is too rude to merit a copy.

Some of the principal characters of the Morris ſeem to have gradually diſappeared, ſo that at length it conſiſted only of the dancers, the piper, and the fool. In Mr. Tollets window we find neither Robin Hood nor Little John, though Marian and the frier are there diſtinguiſhed performers. But in the ſcene of one, introduced in the old play of *Jacke Drums entertainment*, firſt printed in 1601, there is not the leaſt ſymptom of any of the four.* "*The taber and pipe ſtrike up a morrice. A ſhoute within:* A lord, a lord, a lord, who!†

uſed to expreſs a Moor.—The morris dance is by ſome ſuppoſed to have been originally derived from Mooriſh-dance. Black buckram appears to have been much uſed for the dreſſes of the ancient mummers. One of the figures in Mr. Tollet's window, is ſuppoſed to be a moriſco."

" 66 Diſard is an old word for a fool."

* Neither is any notice taken of them, where the characters of the morris dance are mentioned, in *The two noble kinſmen*, by Shakſpeare and Fletcher.

† This was a uſual cry on occaſions of mirth and jollity. Thus, in the celebration of St. Stephens day, in the Inner-Temple hall, as we find it deſcribed in Dugdales *Origines juridiciales*: " Supper

Ed. Oh, a morrice is come, obſerve our country ſports,
'Tis Whitſon tyde, and we muſt frolick it.

Enter the morrice.

The ſong.

Skip it, and trip it, nimbly, nimbly,
Tickle it, tickle it luſtily,
Strike up the taber, for the wenches favour,
Tickle it, tickle it luſtily.
Let us be ſeen, on Hygate greene,
To dance for the honour of Holloway.
Since we are come hither, let's ſpare for no leather,
To dance for the honour of Holloway.

Ed. Well ſaid, my boyes, I muſt have my lords livory: what is't? a maypole? Troth, 'twere a good body for a courtiers impreza, if it had but this life, *Fruſtra floreſcit.* Hold couſin, hold.

He gives the fool money.

Foole. Thankes, couſin, when the lord my fathers audit comes, wee'l repay you againe. Your benevolence too, ſir.

Mam. What! a lords ſonne become a begger!

Foole. Why not? when beggers are become lords ſons. Come, 'tis but a trifle.

Mam. Oh, ſir, many a ſmall make a great.

Foole. No, ſir, a few great make a many ſmall. Come, my lords, poore and neede hath no law.

S. Ed. Nor neceſſitie no right. Drum, downe with them into the celler. Reſt content, reſt content; one bout more, and then away.

Foole. 'Spoke' like a true heart: I kiſſe thy foot, ſweet knight. *The morrice ſing and dance and* exeunt."

Much curious matter on the ſubject of the morris-dance is to be found in "Mr. Tollet's opinion concerning the morris-dancers upon his window." (See Steevens's *Shakſpeare*, v. 425. (edition, 1778) or viii. 596. (edition, 1793). See alſo Mr. Waldrons notes upon the *Sad ſhepherd*, 1783, p. 255. Morris-dancers are ſaid to be

ended, the conſtable-marſhall 'preſenteth' himſelf with drums afore him, mounted upon a ſcaffold, born by four men; and goeth three times round about the harthe, crying out aloud, *A lord, a lord, &c.* Then he deſcendeth and goeth to dance, &c." (p. 156.)

yet annually ſeen in Norfolk,* and make their conſtant appearance in Lancaſhire.†

In Scotland, "*The game of Robin Hood* was celebrated in the month of May. The populace aſſembled previous to the celebration of this feſtival, and choſe ſome reſpectable ‡ member of the corporation to officiate in the character of *Robin Hood*, and another in that of *Little John* his ſquire. Upon the day appointed, which was a Sunday or holyday, the people aſſembled in military array, and went to ſome adjoining field, where, either as actors or ſpectators, the whole inhabitants of the reſpective towns were convened. In this field they probably amuſed themſelves with a repreſentation of Robin Hood's predatory exploits, or of his encounters with the officers of juſtice [rather, perhaps, in feats of archery or military exerciſes].

"As numerous meetings for diſorderly mirth are apt to engender tumult, when the minds of the people came to be agitated with religious controverſy, it was found neceſſary to repreſs the game § of Robin Hood by public

* This county would ſeem to have been famous for their exertions a couple of centuries ago. Will Kemp the player was a celebrated morris dancer; and in the Bodleian library is the following ſcarce and curious tract by him: "Kemps nine daies wonder performed in a daunce from London to Norwich. Containing the pleaſure, paines and kind entertainment of William Kemp betweeen London and that city in his late morrice. Wherein is ſomewhat ſet downe worth note; to reproove the ſlaunders ſpred of him, many things merry, nothing hurtfull. Written by himſelf to ſatisfie his friends London, printed by E. A. for Nicholas Ling. 1600. 4to. b. l. On the title-page is a wooden cut-figure of Kemp as a morris dancer, preceded by a fellow with a pipe and drum, whom he, in the book, calls Thomas Slye his taberer.—See, in Richard Brathwaytes *Remains after death*, 1618, ſome lines "upon Kempe and his morice with his epitaph."

† "On Monday [July 30] the morris-dancers of Pendleton paid their annual viſit in Salford. They were adorned with all the variety of colours that a profuſion of ribbons could give them, and had a very ſhowy garland." *Star*. Aug. 9. 1792.

‡ "Council regiſter, v. 2. p. 30."

§ "Mary, parliament 6. c. 61. A. D. 1555." "Anentis *Robert*

ftatute. The populace were by no means willing to relinquifh their favourite amufement. Year after year the magiftrates of Edinburgh were obliged to exert their authority * in repreffing this game; often ineffectually. In the year 1561, the mob were fo enraged at being difappointed in *making a Robin Hood,* that they rofe in mutiny, feized on the city-gates, committed robberies upon ftrangers; and one of the ringleaders being condemned by the magiftrates to be hanged, the mob forced open the jail, fet at liberty the criminal and all the prifoners, and broke in pieces the gibbet erected at the crofs for executing the malefactor. They next affaulted the magiftrates, who were † fitting in the council-chamber, and who fled to the tolbooth for fhelter, where the mob attacked them, battering the doors, and pouring ftones thro' the windows. Application was made to the deacons of the corporations to appeafe the tumult. Remaining, however, unconcerned fpectators, they made this anfwer: "They will be magiftrates alone; let them rule the people alone." The magiftrates were kept in confinement till they made proclamation be publifhed,

Hude, and abbot of Unreafon. *Item*, It is ftatute and ordained, that in all times cumming, na maner of perfon be chofen *Robert Hude*, nor *Little John, abbot of unreafon, queenis of Maij*, nor utherwife, nouther in burgh, nor to landwart, in onie time to cum: and gif ony proveft, baillies, councell, and communitie, chufe fik ane perfonage as *Robert Hude, Little John, abbotis of unreafon*, or *queenis of Maij*, within burgh, the chufers of fik fall tine their freedome for the fpace of five zeires; and utherwife falbe punifhed at the queenis grace will; and the acceptar of fik like office fall be banifhed foorth of the realme: and gif ony fik perfones . . . . beis chofen out-with burgh, and uthers landward townes, the chufers fall pay to our foveraine ladie ten poundes, and their perfones [be] put in waird there to remaine during the queenis grace pleafure." *Abbot of unreafon* is the character better known in England by the title of abbot or lord of mifrule, "who," fays Percy, "in the houfes of our nobility prefided over the Chriftmas gambols, and promoted mirth and jolity at that feftive feafon." Northumberland houfehold book, (notes,) p. 441.

* "Council regifter, v. 4. p. 4. 30." † "Knox's hiftory, p. 270."

offering indemnity to the rioters upon laying down their arms. Still, however, ſo late as the year 1592, we find the general aſſembly complaining of the profanation of the ſabbath, by making * of *Robin Hood plays*." (Arnots *Hiſtory of Edinburgh*, p. 77.)

Notwithſtanding the above repreſentation, it is certain that theſe amuſements were conſiderably upon the decline before the year 1568. This appears from a poem by Alexander Scot, preſerved in the Hyndford MS. (in the advocates library, compiled and written in that identical year,) and inaccurately printed in *The ever green:*

> "In *May* quhen men zeid everichone
> With *Robene Hoid* and *Littill Johne*,
> To bring in bowis and birkin bobbynis;
> Now all ſic game is faſtlingis gone,
> Bot gif it be amangis clovin Robbynis."

(GG)—"His bow, and one of his arrows, his chair, his cap, and one of his ſlippers were preſerved till within the preſent century."] "We omitted," ſays Ray, "the ſight of Fountain's abbey, where *Robin Hood's* BOW is kept." (*Itineraries*, 1760. p. 161.)

"Having pleaſed ourſelves with the antiquities of 'Notingham,' we took horſe and went to viſit the *well* and ancient CHAIR of Robin Hood, which is not far from hence, within the foreſt of Sherwood. Being placed in the CHAIR, we had a CAP, which they ſay was his, very formally put upon our heads, and having performed the uſual ceremonies befitting ſo great a ſolemnity, we receiv'd the freedom of the chair, and were incorporated into the ſociety of that renowned brotherhood." (Bromes *Travels over England*, &c. 1700, p. 85.)

"On one ſide of this foreſt [*ſci.* of Sherwood] towards Nottingham," ſays the author of "The travels of Tom Thumb over England and Wales," (*i. e.* Robert Dod-

* "Book of univerſal kirk, p. 414." See alſo Keiths *Hiſtory of Scotland*, p. 216.

ſley,) " I was ſhewn a CHAIR, a BOW, and ARROW, all ſaid to have been his [Robin Hoods] property." (p. 82.)

" I was pleaſed with a SLIPPER, belonging to the famous Robin Hood, ſhewn me, fifty years ago, at *St. Anns well*, near Nottingham, a place upon the borders of Sherwood foreſt, to which he reſorted." (*Journey from Birmingham to London, by W. Hutton.* Bir. 1785, p. 174.)

(HH)—" not only places which afforded him ſecurity or amuſement, but even the well at which he quenched his thirſt, ſtill retain his name."] *Robin-Hoods-bay* is both a bay and a village, on the coaſt or Yorkſhire, between Whitby and Scarborough. It is mentioned by Leland as " a fiſcher tounlet of 20. bootes caullid *Robyn Huddes bay*, a dok or boſom of a mile vn length." (*Itinerary*, i. 53.) " When his robberies," ſays maſter Charlton, " became ſo numerous, and the outcries againſt him ſo loud, as almoſt to alarm the whole nation parties of ſoldiers were ſent down from London to apprehend him: and then it was, that fearing for his ſafety, he found it neceſſary to deſert his uſual haunts, and, retreating northward, to croſs the moors that ſurrounded Whitby, [one ſide whereof happens, a little unfortunately, to lye open to the ſea,] where, gaining the ſea-coaſt, he always had in readineſs near at hand ſome ſmall fiſhing veſſels, to which he could have refuge, if he found himſelf purſued; for in theſe, putting off to ſea, he looked upon himſelf as quite ſecure, and held the whole power of the Engliſh nation at defiance. The chief place of his reſort at theſe times, where his boats were generally laid up, was about ſix miles from Whitby, to which he communicated his name, and which is ſtill called *Robin Hoods bay*. There he frequently went a fiſhing in the ſummer ſeaſon, even when no enemy appeared to annoy him, and not far from that place he had butts or marks ſet up, where he used to exercise his men in shooting with the long-bow."*

Near Gloucester is "a famous hill," called "*Robin Hoods hill*;" concerning which there is a very foolish modern song. Another hill of the same name exists in the neighbourhood of Castleton, Derbyshire.

"Over a spring call'd ROBIN HOODS WELL, (3 or 4 miles [on] this side [*i. e.* north] of Doncaster, and but a quarter of a mile only from 2 towns call'd Skelbrough and Bourwallis) is a very handsome stone arch, erected by the lord Carlisle, where passengers from the coach frequently drink of the fair water, and give their charity to two people who attend there." (Gents *History of York*. York, 1730, p. 234.)†

* *History of Whitby*. York, 1779, p. 146. "It was always believed," adds the worthy pedagogue, "that these butts had been erected by him for that very purpose, till the year 1771, when this popular notion was discovered to be a mistake; they being no more than the barrows or *tumuli* thrown up by our pagan predecessors on interring their leaders or the other persons of distinction amongst them. However, notwithstanding this discovery, there is no doubt but Robin Hood made use of those houes or butts when he was disposed to exercise his men, and wanted to train them up in hitting a mark." Be that as it may, there are a few hillocks of a similar nature not far from Guisbrough, which likewise bear the name of *Robin Hoods buts*; and others, it is imagined, may be met with in other parts.

† Epigram on Robin Hoods well, "a fine spring on the road, ornamented by sir John Vanbrugh;" By Roger Gale, esq. (*Bib. Topo. Britan.* N°. II. part III. p. 427.)

"*Nympha fui quondam latronibus hospita sylvæ*
Heu nimium sociis nota Robine, tuis.
Me pudet innocuos latices fudisse scelestis,
Jamque viatori pocula tuta fero,
En pietatis honos! Comes hanc mihi Carliolensis
Ædem sacravit quâ bibis, hospes, aquas."

The same author (Gent), in his "long and pathetick prologue," setting forth "the contingencies, vicissitudes or changes of this transitory life," "spoken, for the most part, on Wednesday and Friday on the 18th and 20th of February, 1761, at the deep tragedy of beautiful, eloquent, tender-hearted, but unfortunate Jane Shore, ... uttered and performed at his benefit" ... (being then

Though there is no attendance at preſent, nor is the water altogether ſo *fair* as it might and ſhould be, the caſe was otherwiſe in the days of honeſt Barnaby.

" *Veni Doncaſter, &c.*
Neſcit ſitus artem modi,
Puteum Roberti Hoodi
Veni, & liquente vena
Vincto * *catino catena,*
Tollens ſitim, parcum odi,
Solvens obolum cuſtodi.

" Thence to Doncaſter, &c.
Thirſt knows neither mean nor meaſure,
Robin Hood's well was my treaſure;
In a † common diſh enchained,
I my furious thirſt reſtrained:
And becauſe I drank the deeper,
I paid two farthings to the keeper."

ætatis 70, and far declined into the vale of ſorrow,* has very artfully contrived to introduce our hero and his famous well.

" The concave-hall, 'mongſt ſources never view'd,
Nor heard the goddeſſes in merry mood,
At their choice viands ſing bold *Robin Hood*:†
Whoſe tomb at Kirkleys nunnery diſplay'd,
A falſe, hard-hearted, irreligious maid,
Who bled, and to cold death that earl betray'd.
But fame ſtill laſts, while country folks diſplay
His *limpid fountain*, and loud-ſurging bay."

* " *Viventes venæ, ſpinæ, catinuſque catenæ,*
Sunt Robin Hoodi *nota trophæa ſui.*"
† " A well, thorn, diſh, hung in an iron chain,
For monuments of Robin Hood remain."

* He dyed in 1778, aged 87.

† " *Omnes agnovere deam; lætique receptant*
Alcæum muſæ comitem, ponuntur Iacchi
Crateres; flaveatque ſcyphis Cerealia vina,
Accedunt vultus hilares; feſtique lepores,
Et jocus, et riſus: dulci teſtudine Naias
Pulchra modos variat; furtiſque inſignis et arcu
Hodi *latronis, fluvios bene nota per iſtos,*
Ludicra geſta cæni: reſonant laquearia plauſu."

He mentions it again:

> " *Nunc longinquos locos odi,*
> *Vale* fons Roberti Hoodi.
>
> " Now I hate all foreign places
> *Robin Hoods well*, and his chaces."

A different well, ſacred either to Robin Hood, or to St. Ann, has been already mentioned.

(II)—" confered as an honorable diſtinction upon the prime miniſter to the king of Madagaſcar."] The natives of this iland, who have dealings with our people, pride themſelves, it ſeems, in Engliſh names, which are beſtowed upon them at the diſcretion or caprice of the ſailers: and thus a venerable miniſter of ſtate, who ſhould have been called ſir Robert Walpole or cardinal Fleury, acquired the name of Robin Hood. Mr. Ives, by whom he is frequently mentioned, relates the following anecdote: " The reader will excuſe my giving him another inſtance . . . which ſtill more ſtrikingly diſplays the extreme ſenſibility of theſe iſlanders, in reſpect to their kings dignity. ROBIN HOOD (who ſeemed to act as *prime miniſter*, and negotiated moſt of the king's concerns with our agent-victualler) was one day tranſacting buſineſs with another gentleman of the ſquadron, and they happened to differ ſo much about the value of a certain commodity, that high words aroſe, and at length *Robin Hood* in the greateſt agitation ſtarted from the ground where he was ſitting, and ſwore that he would immediately acquaint the king of Baba with what had paſſed. Our Engliſh gentleman, too much heated with this threat, and the violent altercation which had preceded it, unguardedly replied, " D—n the king of Baba."—The eyes of *Robin Hood* flaſhed like lightning, and in the moſt violent wrath he retorted, " D—n king George." At the ſame inſtant he left the ſpot, hurrying away towards the Madagaſcarian cottages. Our countryman was ſoon ſtruck with the impropriety of his behaviour, followed and overtook the diſputant, and having made all proper conceſſions, the affair was happily terminated."*

(JJ) "After his death his company was diſperſed."] They, and their ſucceſſors, diſciples or followers, are ſuppoſed to have been afterward diſtinguiſhed, from the name of their gallant leader, by the title of *Roberdſmen.* Lord Coke, who is ſomewhat ſingular in accuſing him of living "by robbery, burning of houſes, felony, waſte and ſpoil, and principally by and with vagabonds, idle wanderers, night-walkers, and draw-latches," ſays that "albeit he lived in Yorkſhire, yet men of his quality took their denomination of him, and were called *Roberdſmen* throughout all England. Againſt theſe men," continues he, "was the ſtatute of Wincheſter made in 13 E. 1. [c. 14.] for preventing of robbery, murders, burning of houſes, &c. Alſo the ſtatute of 5 E. 3. [c. 14.] which 'recites' the ſtatute of Wincheſter, and that there had been divers manſlaughters, felonies, and robberies done in times paſt, by people that be called *Roberdſmen,* waſters and draw-latches; and remedy [is] provided by that act for the arreſting of them. At the parliament holden 50 E. 3." he adds, "it was petitioned to the king that ribauds and ſturdy beggars might be baniſhed out of every town. The anſwer of the king in parliament was, touching ribauds: The ſtatute of Wincheſter and the declaration of the ſame with other ſtatutes of *Roberdſmen,* and for ſuch as make themſelves gentlemen, and men of armes, and *archers,* if they cannot ſo prove theirſelves, let them be driven to their occupation or ſervice, or to the place from whence they came." He likewiſe notices the ſtatute of 7 R. 2. [c. 5.] by which it is provided "that the ſtatutes of *roberdſmen* and draw-latches, be firmly holden and kept:" (3 *Inſt.* 197.)

* *Voyage from England to India.* 1773, p. 8. In a ſubſequent page, this great man is employed in a commerce of a more delicate, indeed, but, according to European notions, leſs honorable nature, which he manages with conſummate addreſs.

Theſe *Roberdſmen* are mentioned in *Pierce the ploughmans crede*, written about 1400:

"And right as *Robarteſmen* raken aboute."*

Mr. Warton, who had once thought that the *friers Robertines* were here meant, obſerves that "the expreſſion of *Robin hoodes men*, in biſhop Latimers ſermon, [*ſupra*, p. xcv,] is not without an alluſion to the *bad* ſenſe of *Roberdſmen*." (*H. E. P.* ii. additions, ſig. d. 4.) It does not, however, appear that the latter word has been ever uſed in a *good* one; nor is there, after all, ſufficient ground for concluding that theſe people were ſo named after *Robin Hood*.

(KK)—"the honour of little Johns death and burial is contended for by rival nations."] I. By England. At the village of Hatherſage, about 6 miles from Caſtleton, in Derbyſhire, is Little Johns grave. A few years ago ſome curious perſon cauſed it to be opened, when there were found ſeveral bones of an uncommon ſize which he preſerved; but, meeting afterward with many unlucky accidents, he carefully replaced them; partly at the interceſſion of the ſexton, who had taken them up for him, and who had in like manner been viſited with misfortunes: upon reſtoring the bones all theſe troubles ceaſed. Such is the tradition at Caſtleton. E. Hargrove, in his "Anecdotes of archery," York, 1792, aſſerts, that "the grave is diſtinguiſhed by a large ſtone placed at the head, and another at the feet; on each of which are yet ſome remains of the letters I. L." (p. 26)† II. By Scotland. "In Murray land" according to that moſt

* They likewiſe ſeem alluded to in the *Viſion*, fo. 1, b.

"And ryſe wyth ribaudy as *Robertes knaves*."

† "On a looſe paper, in Mr. Aſhmole's hand writing, in the muſeum at Oxford, is the following little anecdote:

"The famous Little John (Robin Hood's companion) lyes buried in Fetherſedge church-yard, in the peak of Derbyſhire, one ſtone at his head, another at his feet, and part of his bow hangs up in the chancell. *Anno* 1652." H. E[llis]." *European magazine*, October 1794. p. 295.

veracious hiſtorian, maiſter Hector Boece, " is the kirke of Pette, quhare the banis of lytill Johne remanis in gret admiratioun of pepill. He hes bene fourtene fut of hycht with ſquare membris effering thairto. Vi. zeris," continues he, " afore the cumyng of this werk to lycht we ſaw his hanche-bane, als mekill as the haill bane of ane man: for we ſchot our arme in the mouth thairof. Be quhilk apperis how ſtrang and ſquare pepill grew in our regioun afore thay were effeminat with luſt and intemperance of mouth."* III. By Ireland. " There ſtandeth," as Stanihurſt relates, " in Oſtmantowne greene an hillocke, named little John his ſhot. The occaſion," he ſays, " proceeded of this.

" In the yeere one thouſand one hundred foure ſcore and nine, there ranged three robbers and outlaws in England, among which Robert Hood and little John weere cheefeteins, of all theeves doubtleſſe the moſt courteous. Robert Hood being betrayed at a nunrie in Scotland called Bricklies, the remnant of the crue was ſcattered, and everie man forced to ſhift for himſelfe. Whereupon little John was faine to flee the realme by ſailing into Ireland, where he ſojornied for a few daies at Dublin. The citizens being doone to underſtand the wandering outcaſt to be an excellent archer, requeſted him hartilie to trie how far he could ſhoot at randon; who yeelding to their beheſt, ſtood on the bridge of Dublin, and ſhot to that mole hill, leaving behind him a monument, rather by his poſteritie to be woondered, than poſſiblie by anie man living to be counterſcored. But as the repaire of ſo notorious a champion to anie countrie would ſoone publiſhed, ſo his abode could not be long concealed: and therefore to eſchew the danger

* *Hiſtorie of Scotland, tranſlatit be maiſter Johne Bellenden*, Edin. 1541. ſo. The luxury of his countrymen will appear a ſtrange complaint, in the mouth of a Scotiſhman of the 16th century, to ſuch as believe, with the late Dr. Johnſon, that they learned to plant kail from Cromwells ſoldiers, and that " when they had not kail they probably had nothing." (*Journey to the Weſtern iſlands*, p. 55.) See alſo Boiſes original work.

of [the] lawes, he fled into Scotland, where he died at a towne or village called Moravie."* Thus Stanihurſt, who is quoted by Dr. Hanmer in his *Chronicle of Ireland*, p. 179. but Mr. Walker, after obſerving that "poor Little John's great practical ſkill in archery could not ſave him from an ignominious fate," ſays, "it appeared, from ſome records in the Southwell family, that he was publicly executed for robbery on Arbor-hill, Dublin."†

(LL)—" ſome of his deſcendants, of the name of *Nailor, &c.*"] See the preface to the *Hiſtory of George a Green*. As ſurnames were by no means in general uſe at the cloſe of the twelfth century, Little John may have obtained that of *Nailor* from his original profeſſion.

> (" Ye boaſted worthies of the knuckle,
> To Maggs and to the *Nailor* truckle.")

But however this, or the fact itſelf may be, a bow, ſaid to have belonged to Little John, with the name of *Naylor* upon it, is now, as the editor is informed, in the poſſeſſion of a gentleman in the weſt riding of Yorkſhire.

The quotation about *whetſtones* is from the Sloan MS. Thoſe, indeed, who recollect the equivocal meaning of the word may think that this production has not been altogether confined to the grave of Little John.

* *Deſcription of Ireland*, in Holinsheds chronicle, 1587.

† *Hiſtorical eſſay*, &c. p. 129. This allegation demands what the lawyers call a *profert in curiam*. It is, however, certain that there have been perſons who uſurped the name of *Little John*. In the year 1502, " about mydſomer, was taken a felow whyche had renned many of Robyn Hodes pagentes, which named hymſelfe *Greneleſ*." (*Fabyans chronicle*, 1559.) Therefor, beware of counterfeits!

THE END OF THE LIFE, &c.

CONTENTS

OF

VOLUME THE FIRST.

PART THE FIRST.

ROBIN HOOD.

PART I.

I.

A LYTELL GESTE OF ROBYN HODE.

This ancient legend is printed from the copy of an edition, in 4to. and black letter, by Wynken de Worde, preserved in the public library at Cambridge; compared with, and, in some places, corrected by, another impression (apparently from the former), likewise in 4to. and black letter, by William Copland; a copy of which is among the late mr. Garricks old plays, now in the British Museum. The full title of the first edition is as follows: " Here beginneth a mery geste of Robyn Hode and his meyne, and of the proude sheryfe of

Notyngham;" and the printers colophon runs thus: " Explycit. Kynge Edwarde and Robyn hode & Lytell Johan Entrented at London in Flete ſtrete at the ſygne of the ſone By Wynken de Worde." To Coplands edition is added " a newe playe for to be played in Maye games very pleſaunte and full of paſtyme;" which will be found at large in another place. No other copy of either edition is known to be extant; but, by the favour of the reverend dr. Farmer, the editor hath in his hands a few leaves of an old 4to. black letter impreſſion, judged by its late worthy poſſeſſor, than whom no one can decide in theſe matters with more certainty, to be of Raſtalls printing, and older, by ſome years, than the above edition of Wynken de Worde, which yet, though without date, we may ſafely place as high as the year 1520. Among the ſame gentlemans numerous literary curioſities is likewiſe another edition, "printed," after Coplands, " for Edward White," (4to, black letter, no date, but entered in the Stationers books 13 May, 1594) which, as well as the above fragment, hath been collated, and every variation worthy of notice either adopted or remarked in the margin. The only deſertion from all the copies (except in neceſſary corrections) is the diviſion of ſtanzas, the indenting of the lines, the addition of points, the diſuſe of abbreviations, and the occaſional introduction or rejection of a capital letter; liberties, if they may be ſo called, which have been taken with moſt of the other poems in this collection.

LITHE and lyſten, gentylmen,
That be of frebore blode;
I ſhall you tell of a good yemàn,
His name was Robyn Hode.

Robyn was a proude outlawe,
Whyles he walked on grounde,
So curteyſe an outlawe as he was one
Was never none y founde.

Robyn ſtode in Bernyſdale,
And lened hym to a tree,
And by hym ſtode Lytell Johan,
A good yeman was he;

And alſo dyde good Scathelock,
And Much the millers ſone;
There was no ynche of his body,
But it was worthe a grome.

Than be ſpake hym Lytell Johan
All unto Robyn Hode,
Mayſter, yf ye wolde dyne betyme,
It wolde do you moch good.

Then beſpake good Robyn,
To dyne I have no luſt,
Tyll I have ſome bolde baron,
Or ſome unketh geſt,
That may paye for the beſt;
Or ſome knyght or ſome ſquyere
That dwelleth here by weſt.

V. 25. The irregularity or defect of the verſification, in this and ſimilar paſſages, is probably owing to the loſs of a line.

A good maner than had Robyn,
In londe where that he were,
Every daye or he woulde dyne
Thre meſſes wolde he here:

The one in the worſhyp of the fader,
The other of the holy gooſt,
The thyrde was of our dere lady,
That he loved of all other moſte.

Robyn loved our dere lady,
For doute of dedely ſynne;
Wolde he never do company harme
That ony woman was ynne.

Mayſter, than ſayd Lytell Johan,
And we our borde ſhall ſprede,
Tell us whether we ſhall gone,
And what lyfe we ſhall lede;

Where we ſhall take, where we ſhall leve,
Where we ſhall abide behynde,
Where we ſhall robbe, where we ſhall reve,
Where we ſhall bete and bynde.

Ther of no fors, ſayd Robyn,
We ſhall do well ynough;
But loke ye do no houſbonde harme
That tylleth with his plough;

No more ye ſhall no good yemàn,
  That walketh by grene wode ſhawe,
Ne no knyght ne no ſquyer,
  That wolde be a good felawe.

Theſe bysſhoppes, and thyſe archebysſhoppes,
  Ye ſhall them bete and bynde;
The hye ſheryfe of Notynghame,
  Hym holde in your mynde.

This worde ſhall be holde, ſayd Lytyll Johan,
  And this leſſon ſhall we lere;
It is ferre dayes, god ſende us a geſt,
  That we were at our dynere.

Take thy good bowe in thy hande, ſaid Robyn,
  Let Moche wende with the,
And ſo ſhall Wyllyam Scathelocke,
  And no man abyde with me.

And walke up to the Sayles,
  And ſo to Watlynge ſtrete,*
And wayte after ſome unketh geſt,
  Up chaunce ye mowe them mete.

* *This ſeems to have been, and, in many parts, is ſtill the name generally uſed by the vulgar for* ERMING-STREET. *The courſe of the real Watling-ſtreet was from Dover to Cheſter.*

The SAYLES *appears to be ſome place in the neighbourhood of Barnſdale, but no mention of it has elſewhere occurred; though, it is believed, there is a field ſo called not far from Doncaſter.*

Be he erle or ony barȯn,
Abbot or ony knyght,
Brynge hym to lodge to me,
Hys dyner ſhall be dyght.

They wente unto the Sayles,
Theſe yemen all thre,
They loked eſt, they loked weſt,
They myght no man ſee.

But as they loked in Barnyſdale,
By a derne ſtrete,
Then came there a knyght rydynge,
Full ſone they gan hym mete.

All dreri then was his ſemblaunte,
And lytell was hys pryde,
Hys one fote in the ſterope ſtode,
That other waved beſyde.

Hys hode hangynge over hys eyen two,
He rode in ſymple a ray ;
A ſoryer man than he was one
Rode never in ſomers day.

Lytell Johan was curteyſe,
And ſet hym on his kne :
Welcome be ye, gentyll knyght,
Welcome are you to me,

V. 84. all his. *PCC.*

Welcome be thou to grene wood,
Hende knyght and fre;
My mayſter hath a byden you faſtynge,
Syr, all theſe oures thre.

Who is your mayſter? ſayd the knyght.
Johan ſayde, Robyn Hode.
He is a good yeman, ſayd the knyght,
Of hym I have herde moch good.

I graunte, he ſayd, with you to wende,
My brethren all in fere;
My purpoſe was to have deyned to day
At Blythe or Dankaſtere.

Forthe than went this gentyll knyght,
With a carefull chere,
The teres out of his eyen ran,
And fell downe by his lere.

They brought hym unto the lodge dore,
When Robyn gan hym ſe,
Full curteysly dyde of his hode,
And ſet hym on his kne.

Welcome, ſyr knyght, then ſaid Robyn,
Welcome thou arte to me,
I haue abyde you faſtynge, ſyr,
All theſe houres thre.

V. 105. *So R.* [Raſtall.] all thre. *W. C.* [de Worde *and* Copland.] *V.* 108. this. *R.* that. *W. C.* *V.* 111. ere. *R.*

Then anſwered the gentyll knyght,
With wordes fayre and fre,
God the ſave, good Robyn,
And all thy fayre meynè.

They waſhed togyder and wyped bothe,
And ſet tyll theyr dynere;
Brede and wyne they had ynough,
And nombles of the dere;

Swannes and feſauntes they had full good,
And foules of the revere;
There fayled never ſo lytell a byrde,
That ever was bred on brere.

Do gladly, ſyr knyght, ſayd Robyn.
Gramercy, ſyr, ſayd he,
Suche a dyner had I not
Of all theſe wekes thre:

If I come agayne, Robyn,
Here by this countrè,
As good a dyner I ſhall the make,
As thou haſt made to me.

Gramercy, knyght, ſayd Robyn,
My dyner whan I have,
I was never ſo gredy, by dere worthy god,
My dyner for to crave.

But pay or ye wende, ſayd Robyn,
  Me thynketh it is good ryght;
It was never the maner, by dere worthy god,
  A yeman to pay for a knyght.

I have nought in my coſers, ſayd the knyght,
  That I may profer for ſhame.
Lytell Johan, go loke, ſayd Robyn,
  Ne let not for no blame.

Tell me trouth, ſayd Robyn,
  So god have parte of the.
I have no more but ten ſhillings, ſayd the knyght,
  So god have parte of me.

Yf thou have no more, ſayd Robyn,
  I wyll not one peny;
And yf thou have nede of ony more,
  More ſhall I len the.

Go now forth, Lytell Johan,
  The trouthe tell thou me,
Yf there be no more but ten ſhillings,
  Not one peny that I ſe.

Lytell Johan ſpred downe his mantèll
  Full fayre upon the grounde,
And there he founde in the knyghtes coſer
  But even halfe a pounde.

V. 147. to pay. *R.* pay. *W. C.* *V.* 150. Robyn. *R.* Robyn Hoode. *W. C.*

Lytyll Johan let it lye full ſtyll,
And went to his mayſter full lowe.
What tydynge Johan? ſayd Robyn.
"Syr, the knyght is trewe inough."

Fyll of the beſt wyne, ſayd Robyn,
The knyght ſhall begynne;
Moch wonder thynketh me
Thy clothynge is ſo thynne.

Tell me one worde, ſayd Robyn,
And counſell ſhall it be;
I trowe thou were made a knyght of forſe,
Or elles of yemanry;

Or elles thou haſt ben a ſory houſband,
And leved in ſtroke and ſtryfe;
An okerer, or elles a lechoure, ſayd Robyn,
With wronge haſt thou lede thy lyfe.

I am none of them, ſayd the knyght,
By god that made me;
An hondreth wynter here before,
Myne aunſetters knyghtes have be.

But ofte it hath befal, Robyn,
A man hath be dyſgrate;
But god that ſyteth in heven above
May amend his ſtate.

Within two or thre yere, Robyn, he ſayd,
  My neyghbores well it ‘ kende,’
Foure hondreth pounde of good money
  Full wel than myght I ſpende.

Now have I no good, ſayd the knyght,
  But my chyldren and my wyfe;
God hath ſhapen ſuch an ende,
  Tyll god ‘ may amende my lyfe.’

In what maner, ſayd Robyn,
  Haſt thou lore thy rychès?
For my grete foly, he ſayd,
  And for my kindeneſſe.

I had a ſone, for ſoth, Robyn,
  That ſholde have ben my eyre,
When he was twenty wynter olde,
  In felde wolde juſte full feyre;

He ſlewe a knyght of Lancaſtſhyre,
  And a ſquyre bolde;
For to ſave hym in his ryght
  My goodes beth ſette and ſolde;

My londes beth ſet to wedde, Robyn,
  Untyll a certayne daye,
To a ryche abbot here beſyde,
  Of Saynt Mary abbay.

V. 192. two yere. *R.* *V.* 193. knowe. *PCC.* *V.* 199. it may amende. *PCC.* *V.* 208. lancaſcsſhyre. *R.*

What is the ſomme? ſayd Robyn,
Trouthe than tell thou me.
Syr, he ſayd, foure hondred pounde,
The abbot tolde it to me.

Now, and thou leſe thy londe, ſayd Robyn,
What ſhall fall of the?
Haſtely I wyll me buſke, ſayd the knyght,
Over the ſalte ſee,

And ſe where Cryſt was quycke and deed,
On the mounte of Caluarè.
Fare well, frende, and have good daye,
It may noo better be——

Teeres fell out of his eyen two,
He wolde haue gone his waye—
Farewell, frendes, and have good day,
I ne have more to pay.

Where be thy friendes? ſayd Robyn.
"Syr, never one wyll me know;
Whyle I was ryche inow at home
Grete boſt then wolde they blowe,

And now they renne awaye fro me,
As beſtes on a rowe;
They take no more heed of me
Then they me never ſawe."

V. 227. not. *W. C.* *V.* 232. by *W. C.* *V.* 233. *So R.* knowe me. *W. C.* *The fragment of Raſtalls edition ends with v.* 238.

For ruthe then wepte Lytell Johan,
Scathelocke and Much 'in fere.'
Fyll of the beſt wyne, ſayd Robyn,
For here is a ſymple chere.

Haſt thou ony frendes, ſayd Robyn,
Thy borowes that wyll be?
I have none, then ſayd the knyght,
But god that dyed on a tree.

Do waye thy japes, ſayd Robyn,
Therof wyll I right none;
Weneſt thou I wyll have god to borowe?
Peter, Poule or Johan?

Nay, by hym that me made,
And ſhope both ſonne and mone,
Fynde a better borowe, ſayd Robyn,
Or mony geteſt thou none.

I have none other, ſayd the knyght,
The ſothe for to ſay,
But yf it be our dere lady,
She ſayled me never or this day.

By dere worthy god, ſayd Robyn,
To ſeche all Englond thorowe,
Yet founde I never to my pay,
A moch better borowe.

V. 241. alſo. *PCC.* *V.* 242. Wyme. *PCC.*

Come now forthe, Lytell Johan,
And goo to my treſourè,
And brynge me foure hondred pounde.
And loke that it well tolde be.

Forthe then wente Lytell Johan,
And Scathelocke went before,
He tolde out foure houndred pounde,
By eyghtene ſcore.

Is this well tolde? ſayd lytell Much.
Johan ſayd, What greveth the?
It is almes to helpe a gentyll knyght
That is fall in povertè.

Mayſter, than ſayd Lytell Johan,
His clothynge is full thynne,
Ye muſt gyve the knyght a lyveray,
To 'lappe' his body ther in.

For ye have ſcarlet and grene, mayſter,
And many a ryche aray,
There is no marchaunt in mery Englonde
So ryche I dare well ſaye.

Take hym thre yerdes of every coloure,
And loke that well mete it be.
Lytell Johan toke none other meſure
But his bowe tre,

V. 279. helpe. *W.* wrappe. *C.*

And of every handfull that he met
  He lept ouer fotes thre.
What devilkyns draper, ſayd litell Much,
  Thynkyſt thou to be ?

Scathelocke ſtoode full ſtyll and lough,
  And ſayd, By god allmyght,
Johan may gyve hym the better meſure,
  By god, it coſt him but lyght.

Mayſter, ſayd Lytell Johan,
  All unto Robyn Hode,
Ye muſt gyve that knight an hors,
  To lede home al this good.

Take hym a gray courſer, ſayd Robyn,
  And a ſadell newe;
He is our ladyes meſſengere,
  God lene that he be true.

And a good palfraye, ſayd lytell Moch,
  To mayntayne hym in his ryght.
And a payre of botes, ſayd Scathelocke,
  For he is a gentyll knyght.

What ſhalt thou gyve hym, Lytel Johan? ſayd Robyn.
  Syr, a payre of gylte ſpores clene,
To pray for all this company:
  God brynge hym out of tene!

V. 303. leue. *W.* lende. *C.*

Whan ſhall my daye be, ſayd the knyght,
  Syr, and your wyll be ?
This daye twelve moneth, ſayd Robyn,
  Under this grene wode tre.

It were grete ſhame, ſayd Robyn,
  A knyght alone to ryde,
Without ſquyer, yeman or page,
  To walke by hys ſyde.

I ſhall the lene Lytyll Johan my man,
  For he ſhall be thy knave ;
In a yemans ſteed he may the ſtonde,
  Yf thou grete nede have.

THE SECONDE FYTTE.

NOWE is the knyght went on this way,
  This game he thought full good,
When he loked on Bernyſdale,
  He blyſſed Robyn Hode ;

And whan he thought on Bernyſdale,
  On Scathelock, Much, and Johan,
He blyſſed them for the beſt company
  That ever he in come.

Then ſpake that gentyll knyght,
To Lytel Johan gan he ſaye,
To morowe I muſt to Yorke toune,
To Saynt Mary abbay;

And to the abbot of that place
Foure hondred pounde I muſt pay:
And but I be there upon this nyght
My londe is loſt for ay.

The abbot ſayd to his covent,
There he ſtode on grounde,
This day twelfe moneth came there a knyght
And borowed foure hondred pounde.

[He borowed foure hondred pounde,]
Upon all his londe fre,
But he come this ylke day
Dysherytye ſhall he be.

It is full erely, ſayd the pryoure *,
The day is not yet ferre gone,
I had lever to pay an hondred pounde,
And lay it downe a none.

The knyght is ferre be yonde the ſee,
In Englonde is his ryght,
And ſuffreth honger and colde
And many a ſory nyght:

* *The prior, in an abbey, was the officer immediately under th abbot; in priories and conventral cathedrals he was the ſuperior.*

It were grete pytè, ſayd the pryoure,
  So to have his londe,
And ye be ſo lyght of your conſeyence
  Ye do to him moch wronge.

Thou arte euer in my berde, ſayd the abbot,
  By god and ſaynt Rycharde *.
With that cam in a fat heded monke,
  The heygh ſelerer;

He is dede or hanged, ſayd the monke,
  By god that bought me dere,
And we ſhall have to ſpende in this place
  Foure hondred pounde by yere.

The abbot and the hy ſelerer,
  Sterte forthe full bolde,
The high juſtyce of Englonde
  The abbot there dyde holde.

* *This was a " S. Richard king and confeſſour, ſonne to Lotharius king of Kent, who, for the love of Chriſt, taking upon him a long perregrination, went to Rome for devotion to that ſea, and in his way homward, died at Luca, about the year of Chriſt, ſeaven hundred and fifty, where his body is kept untill this day with great veneration, in the oratory and chappell of S. Frigidian, and adorned with an epitaph both in verſe and proſe."* Engliſh Martyrologe, 1608.

There were other ſaints of the ſame name, as Richard de la Wich, biſhop of Chicheſter, canonized in 1262; *and Richard biſhop of St. Andrews in Calabria. See Draytons* Poly Olbion, *Song* 24.

The hye juſtyce and many mo
  Had take into their honde
Holy all the knyghtes det,
  To put that knyght to wronge.

They demed the knyght wonder ſore,
  The abbot and hys meynè:
" But he come this ylke day
  Dysheryte ſhall he be."

He wyll not come yet, ſayd the juſtyce,
  I dare well under take.
But in ſorowe tyme for them all
  The knyght came to the gate.

Than be ſpake that gentyll knyght
  Untyll hys meynè,
Now put on your ſymple wedes
  That ye brought fro the ſee.

[They put on their ſymple wedes,]
  And came to the gates anone,
The porter was redy hymſelfe,
  And welcomed them everychone,

Welcome, ſyr knyght, ſayd the porter,
  My lorde to mete is he,
And ſo is many a gentyll man,
  For the love of the.

The porter ſwore a full grete othe,
By god that made me,
Here be the beſt coreſed hors
That ever yet ſawe I me.

Lede them into the ſtable, he ſayd,
That eaſed myght they be.
They ſhall not come therin, ſayd the knyght,
By god that dyed on a tre.

Lordes were to mete iſette
In that abbotes hall,
The knyght went forth and kneled downe
And ſalved them grete and ſmall.

Do gladly, ſyr abbot, ſayd the knyght,
I am come to holde my day.
The fyrſt word the abbot ſpake,
Haſt thou brought my pay?

Not one peny, ſayd the knyght,
By god that maked me.
Thou art a ſhrewed dettour, ſayd the abbot;
Syr juſtyce, drynke to me.

What dooſt thou here, ſayd the abbot,
But thou haddeſt brought thy pay?
For god, than ſayd the knyght,
To pray of a lenger daye.

Thy daye is broke, ſayd the juſtyce,
Londe geteſt thou none.
" Now, good ſyr juſtyce, be my frende,
And fende me of my fone.

I am holde with the abbot, ſayd the juſtyce,
Bothe with cloth and fee.
" Now, good ſyr ſheryf, be my frende."
Nay for god, ſayd he.

" Now, good ſyr abbot, be my frende,
For thy curteyſê,
And holde my londes in thy honde
Tyll I have made the gree;

And I wyll be thy true ſervaunte,
And trewely ſerve the,
Tyl ye have foure hondred pounde
Of money good and free."

The abbot ſware a full grete othe,
By god that dyed on a tree,
Get the londe where thou may,
For thou geteſt none of me.

By dere worthy god, then ſayd the knyght,
That all this worlde wrought,
But I have my londe agayne
Full dere it ſhall be bought;

God that was of a mayden borne
  Lene us well to ſpede,
For it is good to aſſay a frende
  Or that a man have nede.

The abbot lothely on hym gan loke
  And vylaynesly hym gan 'call,'
Out, he ſayd, thou falſe knyght,
  Spede the out of my hall.

Thou lyeſt, then ſayd the gentyll knyght,
  Abbot in thy hal;
Falſe knyght was I never,
  By god that made us all.

Up then ſtode that gentyll knyght,
  To the abbot ſayd he,
To ſuffre a knyght to knele ſo longe.
  Thou canſt no curteyſye;

In jouſtes and in tournement
  Full ferre than have I be,
And put myſelfe as ferre in prees
  As ony that ever I ſe.

What wyll ye gyve more? ſayd the juſtyce,
  And the knyght ſhall make a releyſe;
And elles dare I ſafly ſwere
  Ye holde never your londe in pees.

V. 122. leue. *W.* Sende us. *C.* *V.* 126. loke. *W. C.*

An hondred pounde, ſayd the abbot.
  The juſtyce ſaid, Gyve him two.
Nay, be god, ſayd the knyght,
  Yet gete ye it not ſoo:

Though ye wolde gyve a thouſande more,
  Yet were 'ye' never the nere;
Shall there never be myn eyre,
  Abbot, juſtyſe, ne frere.

He ſterte hym to a borde anone,
  Tyll a table rounde,
And there he ſhoke out of a bagge
  Even foure hondred pounde.

Have here thy golde, ſyr abbot, ſayd the knyght,
  Which that thou lenteſt me;
Haddeſt thou ben curteys at my comynge,
  Rewarde ſholdeſt thou have be.

The abbot ſat ſtyll, and ete no more,
  For all his ryall chere,
He caſte his hede on his ſholder,
  And faſt began to ſtare.

Take me my golde agayne, ſayd the abbot,
  Syr juſtyce, that I toke the.
Not a peny, ſayd the juſtyce,
  By god that dyed on a tree.

V. 148. grete. *W.* get. *C.* *V.* 150. thou. *PCC.*

"Syr abbot, and ye men of lawe,
Now have I holde my daye,
Now ſhall I have my londe agayne,
For ought that you can ſaye."

The knyght ſtert out of the dore,
Awaye was all his care,
And on he put his good clothynge,
The other he lefte there.

He wente hym forthe full mery ſyngynge,
As men have tolde in tale,
His lady met hym at the gate,
At home in Uteryſdale.

Welcome, my lorde, ſayd his lady;
Syr, loſt is all your good?
Be mery, dame, ſayd the knyght,
And praye for Robyn Hode,

That ever his ſoule be in blyſſe,
He holpe me out of my tene;
Ne had not be his kyndeneſſe,
Beggers had we ben.

The abbot and I acordyd ben,
He is ſerved of his pay,
The good yeman lent it me,
As I came by the way.

This knyght than dwelled fayre at home,
The foth for to fay,
Tyll he had got foure hondreth pounde,
All redy for too paye.

He purveyed hym an hondred bowes,
The ftrenges [were] welle dyght,
An hondred fhefe of arowes good,
The hedes burnyfhed full bryght,

And every arowe an elle longe,
With pecocke well y dyght,
Inocked all with whyte fylver,
It was a femly fyght.

He purveyed hym an hondreth men,
Well harneyfed in that ftede,
And hymfelfe in that fame fete,
And clothed in whyte and rede.

He bare a launsgay in his honde,
And a man ledde his male,
And reden with a lyght fonge,
Unto Bernyfdale.

As he went at a brydge ther was a wraftelyng,
And there taryed was he,
And there was all the beft yemen,
Of all the weft countree.

V. 207. fute. *C.*

A full fayre game there was upſet,
  A whyte bull up ipyght;
A grete courſer with ſadle and brydil,
  With golde burneyſhed full bryght;

A payre of gloves, a rede golde rynge,
  A pype of wyne, in good fay:
What man bereth him beſt I wys,
  The pryce ſhall bere away.

There was a yeman in that place,
  And beſt worthy was he,
And for he was ferre and frend beſtad,
  Iſlayne he ſholde have be.

The knyght had reuth of this yeman,
  In place where that he ſtode,
He ſaid that yoman ſholde have no harme,
  For love of Robyn Hode.

The knyght preſed into the place,
  An hondred folowed hym ' fre,'
With bowes bent, and arowes ſharpe,
  For to ſhende that company.

They ſholdred all, and made hym rome,
  To wete what he wolde ſay,
He toke the yeman by the honde,
  And gave hym all the playe;

V. 218. I up pyght. *W.* up ypyght. *C.* *V.* 234. fere. *W.* in fere. *C.*

He gave hym fyve marke for his wyne,
There it laye on the molde,
And bad it ſholde be ſette a broche,
Drynke who ſo wolde.

Thus longe taryed this gentyll knyght,
Tyll that playe was done,
So longe abode Robyn faſtynge,
Thre houres after the none.

THE THYRDE FYTTE.

LYTH and lyſten, gentyll men,
All that now be here,
Of Lytell Johan, that was the knyghtes man,
Good myrthe ye ſhall here.

It was upon a mery day,
That yonge men wolde go ſhete,
Lytell Johan fet his bowe anone,
And ſayd he wolde them mete.

Thre tymes Lytell Johan ſhot about,
And alway cleſt the wande,
The proude ſheryf of Notyngham
By the markes gan ſtande.

V. 6. ſhote. *W.* *V.* 10. he ſleſte (*ſliced?*) *W.*

The ſheryf ſwore a full grete othe,
By hym that dyed on a tree,
This man is the beſt archere
That yet ſawe I me.

Say me now, wyght yonge man,
What is now thy name?
In what countre were thou born,
And where is thy wonnynge wan?

" In Holderneſſe I was bore,
I wys all of my dame,
Men call me Reynolde Grenelefe,
Whan I am at hame."

" Say me, Reynaud Grenelefe,
Wolte thou dwell with me?
And every yere I wyll the gyve
Twenty marke to thy fee."

I have a mayſter, ſayd Lytell Johan,
A curteys knyght is he,
May ye gete leve of hym,
The better may it bee.

The ſheryfe gate Lytell Johan
Twelve monethes of the knyght,
Therfore he gave him ryght anone
A good hors and a wyght.

V. 19. thou waſt. *C.* waſt thou. *Wb.*

Now is Lytel Johan the ſheryffes man,
He gyve us well to ſpede,
But alway thought Lytell Johan
To quyte hym well his mede.

Now ſo god me helpe, ſayd Lytel Johan,
And be my trewe lewtè,
I ſhall be the worſte ſervaunte to hym
That ever yet had he.

It befell upon a wedneſday,
The ſheryfe on hontynge was gone,
And Lytel Johan lay in his bed,
And was foryete at home.

Therfore he was faſtynge
Tyl it was paſt the none.
Good ſyr ſtuard, I pray the,
Geve me to dyne, ſayd Lytel Johan,

It is to long for Grenelefe,
Faſtynge ſo long to be;
Therfore I pray the, ſtuarde,
My dyner gyve thou me.

Shalt thou never ete ne drynke, ſayd the ſtuarde,
Tyll my lord be come to towne.
I make myn avowe to god, ſayd Lytell Johan,
I had lever to cracke thy crowne.

V. 41. Ge. *W. f.* God.

The butler was ful uncurteys,
  There he ſtode on flore,
He ſterte to the buttery,
  And ſhet faſt the dore.

Lytell Johan gave the buteler ſuch a rap,
  His backe yede nygh on two,
Tho he lyved an hundreth wynter,
  The wors he ſholde go.

He ſporned the dore with his fote,
  It went up wel and fyne,
And there he made a large lyveray
  Both of ale and wyne.

Syth ye wyl not dyne, ſayd Lytel Johan,
  I ſhall gyve you to drynke,
And though ye lyve an hondred wynter,
  On Lytell Johan ye ſhall thynk.

Lytell Johan ete, and Lytell [Johan] dronke,
  The whyle that he wolde.
The ſheryfe had in his kechyn a coke,
  A ſtoute man and a bolde.

I make myn avowe to god, ſayd the coke,
  Thou arte a ſhrewde hynde,
In an houſholde to dwel,
  For to aſk thus to dyne.

And there he lent Lytel Johan
  Good ſtrokes thre.
I make myn avowe, ſayd Lytell Johan,
  Theſe ſtrokes lyketh well me.

Thou arte a bolde man and an hardy,
  And ſo thynketh me ;
And or I paſſe fro this place,
  Aſayed better ſhalt thou be.

Lytell Johan drewe a good ſwerde,
  The coke toke another in honde ;
They thought nothynge for to fle,
  But ſtyfly for to ſtonde.

There they fought ſore to gyder,
  Two myle way and more,
Myght neyther other harme done,
  The mountenaunce of an houre.

I make myn avowe to god, ſayd Lytell Johan,
  And be my trewe lewtè,
Thou art one of the beſt ſwerdemen,
  That ever yet ſawe I me.

Coowdeſt thou ſhote as well in a bowe,
  To grene wood thou ſholdeſt with me,
And two tymes in the yere thy clothynge
  Ichaunged ſholde be ;

And every yere of Robyn Hode
  Twenty marke to thy fee.
Put up thy ſwerde, ſayd the coke,
  And felowes wyll we be.

Then he fette to Lytell Johan
  The numbles of a doo,
Good brede and full good wyne,
  They ete and dranke therto.

And whan they had dronken well,
  Ther trouthes togyder they plyght,
That they wolde be with Robyn
  That ylke ſame day at nyght.

The dyde them to the treſure hous,
  As faſt as they myght gone,
The lockes that were of good ſtele
  They brake them everychone;

They toke away the ſylver veſſell,
  And all that they myght get,
Peces, maſars, and ſpones,
  Wolde they non forgete;

Alſo they toke the good pence,
  Thre hondred pounde and three;
And dyde them ſtrayt to Robyn Hode,
  Under the grene wode tre.

V. 121. hyed. *C.*

" God the ſave, my dere mayſtèr,
And Cryſt the ſave and ſe."
And than ſayd Robyn to Lytell Johan,
Welcome myght thou be;

And alſo be that fayre yeman
Thou bryngeſt there with the.
What tydynges fro Notyngham?
Lytell Johan tell thou me.

" Well the greteth the proude ſheryfe,
And ſende the here by me
His coke and his ſylver veſſell,
And thre hondred pounde and thre."

I make myn avow to god, ſayd Robyn,
And to the trenytè,
It was never by his good wyll,
This good is come to me.

Lytell Johan hym there bethought,
On a ſhrewed wyle,
Fyve myle in the foreſt he ran,
Hym happed at his wyll;

Than he met the proud ſheryf,
Huntynge with hounde and horne,
Lytell Johan coud his curteyſye,
And kneled hym beforne:

V. 150. whyle. *W.*

"God the ſave, my dere mayſtèr,
And Cryſt the ſave and ſee."
Raynolde Grenelefe, ſayd the ſheryfe,
Where haſt thou nowe be?

"I have be in this foreſt,
A fayre ſyght can I ſe,
It was one of the fayreſt ſyghtes
That ever yet ſawe I me;

Yonder I ſe a ryght fayre hart,
His coloure is of grene,
Seven ſcore of dere upon an herde
Be with hym all bedene;

His tynde are ſo ſharp, mayſtèr,
Of ſexty and well mo,
That I durſt not ſhote for drede
Leſt they wolde me ſloo."

I make myn avowe to god, ſayd the ſheryf,
That ſyght wolde I fayn ſe.
"Buſke you thyderwarde, my dere mayſtèr,
Anone and wende with me."

The ſheryfe rode, and Lytell Johan
Of fote he was full ſmarte,
And whan they came afore Robyn:
"Lo, here is the mayſter harte!"

V. 163. ſyght. *W.* ſightes. *C.*

Styll ſtode the proude ſheryf,
A ſory man was he:
"Wo worthe the, Raynolde Grenelefe
Thou haſt now betrayed me."

I make myn avowe to god, ſayd Lytell Johan,
Mayſter, ye be to blame,
I was myſſerved of my dynere,
When I was with you at hame.

Soone he was to ſuper ſette,
And ſerved with ſylver whyte;
And whan the ſheryf ſe his veſſell,
For ſorowe he myght not ete.

Make good chere, ſayd Robyn Hode,
Sheryfe, for charytè,
And for the love of Lytell Johan,
Thy lyfe is graunted to the.

When they had ſupped well,
The day was all agone,
Robyn commaunded Lytell Johan
To drawe of his hoſen and his ſhone,

His kyrtell and his cote a pye,
That was furred well fyne,
And take him a grene mantèll,
To lappe his body therin.

V. 183. wo the worth. *W.*

Robyn commaunded his wyght yong men,
  Under the grene wood tre,
They ſhall lay in that ſame ſorte;
  That the ſheryf myght them ſe.

All nyght laye that proud ſheryf,
  In his breche and in his ſherte,
No wonder it was in grene wode,
  Tho his ſydes do ſmerte.

Make glad chere, ſayd Robyn Hode,
  Sheryfe, for charytè,
For this is our order I wys,
  Under the grene wood tre.

This is harder order, ſayd the ſheryfe,
  Than ony anker or frere;
For al the golde in mery Englonde
  I wolde not longe dwell here.

All theſe twelve monethes, ſayd Robyn,
  Thou ſhalte dwell with me;
I ſhall the teche, proud ſheryfe,
  An outlawe for to be.

Or I here another nyght lye, ſayd the ſheryfe,
  Robyn, nowe I praye the,
Smyte of my hede rather to morne,
  And I forgyve it the.

Lete me go, then ſayd the ſheryf,
For ſaynt Charytè,
And I wyll be thy beſt frende
That ever yet had the.

Thou ſhalte ſwere me an othe, ſayd Robyn,
On my bryght bronde,
Thou ſhalt never awayte me ſcathe,
By water ne by londe;

And if thou fynde ony of my men,
By nyght or by day,
Upon thyne othe thou ſhalt ſwere,
To helpe them that thou may.

Now have the ſheryf iſwore his othe,
And home he began to gone,
He was as full of grene wode
As ever was hepe of ſtone.

THE FOURTH FYTTE.

THE ſheryf dwelled in Notynghame,
He was fayne that he was gone,
And Robyn and his mery men
Went to wode anone.

Go we to dyner, ſayd Lytell Johan.
  Robyn Hode ſayd, Nay;
For I drede our lady be wroth with me,
  For ſhe ſent me not my pay.

Have no dout, mayſter, ſayd Lytell Johan,
  Yet is not the ſonne at reſt,
For I dare ſaye, and ſaufly ſwere,
  The knyght is trewe and truſt.

Take thy bowe in thy hande, ſayd Robyn,
  Let Moch wende with the,
And ſo ſhall Wyllyam Scathelock,
  And no man abyde with me,

And walke up into the Sayles,
  And to Watlynge ſtrete,
And wayte after 'ſome' unketh geſt,
  Up chaunce ye may them mete.

Whether he be meſſengere,
  Or a man that myrthes can,
Or yf he be a pore man,
  Of my good he ſhall have ſome.

Forth then ſtert Lytel Johan,
  Half in tray and tene,
And gyrde hym with a full good ſwerde,
  Under a mantel of grene.

V. 19. ſuch. *W.*

They went up to the Sayles,
  Thefe yemen all thre ;
They loked eft, they loked weft,
  They myght no man fe.

But as ' they' loked in Bernyfdale,
  By the hye waye,
Than were they ware of two blacke monkes,
  Eche on a good palferay.

Then befpake Lytell Johan,
  To Much he gan fay,
I dare lay my lyfe to wedde,
  That thefe monkes have brought our pay.

Make glad chere, fayd Lytell Johan,
  And frefe our bowes of ewe,
And loke your hertes be feker and fad,
  Your ftrynges trufty and trewe.

The monke hath fifty two men,
  And feven fomers full ftronge,
There rydeth no byfhop in this londe
  So ryally, I underftond.

Brethern, fayd Lytell Johan,
  Here are no more but we thre ;
But we brynge them to dyner,
  Our mayfter dare we not fe.

V. 33. he. *Old copies.*

Bende your bowes, ſayd Lytell Johan,
  Make all yon preſe to ſtonde,
The formoſt monke, his lyfe and his deth
  Is cloſed in my honde.

Abyde, chorle monke, ſayd Lytell Johan,
  No ferther that thou gone ;
Yf thou dooſt, by dere worthy god,
  Thy deth is in my honde.

And evyll thryfte on thy hede, ſayd Lytell Johan,
  Ryght under thy hattes bonde,
For thou haſt made our mayſter wroth,
  He is faſtynge ſo longe.

Who is your mayſter? ſayd the monke.
  Lytell Johan ſayd, Robyn Hode.
He is a ſtronge thefe, ſayd the monke,
  Of hym herd I never good.

Thou lyeſt, than ſayd Lytell Johan,
  And that ſhall rewe the ;
He is a yeman of the forèſt,
  To dyne he hath bode the.

Much was redy with a bolte,
  Redly and a none,
He ſet the monke to fore the breſt,
  To the grounde that he can gone.

V. 59. you. *W.* Make you yonder preſte. *C.*

Of fyfty two wyght yonge men,
There abode not one,
Saf a lytell page, and a grome
To lede the somers with Johan.

They brought the monke to the lodge dore,
Whether he were loth or lefe,
For to speke with Robyn Hode,
Maugre in theyr tethe.

Robyn dyde adowne his hode,
The monke whan that he se;
The monke was not so curteyse,
His hode then let he be.

He is a chorle, mayster, by dere worthy god,
Than said Lytell Johan.
Thereof no force, sayd Robyn,
For curteysy can he none.

How many men, sayd Robyn,
Had this monke, Johan?
"Fyfty and two whan that we met,
But many of them be gone."

Let blowe a horne, sayd Robin,
That felaushyp may us knowe;
Seven score of wyght yemen,
Came pryckynge on a rowe,

V. 82. yemen. *C.* *V.* 85. Lytell Johan. *O. CC.*

And everych of them a good mantèll,
Of ſcarlet and of raye,
All they came to good Robyn,
To wyte what he wolde ſay.

They made the monke to waſhe and wype,
And ſyt at his denere,
Robyn Hode and Lytel Johan
They ſerved ' him' bothe in fere.

Do gladly, monke, ſayd Robyn,
Gramercy, ſyr, ſaid he.
" Where is your abbay, whan ye are at home,
And who is your avowè ?"

Saynt Mary abbay, ſayd the monke,
Though I be ſymple here.
In what offyce ? ſayd Robyn.
" Syr, the hye ſelerer."

Ye be the more welcome, ſayd Robyn,
So ever mote I the.
Fyll of the beſt wyne, ſayd Robyn,
This monke ſhall drynke to me.

But I have grete mervayle, ſayd Robyn,
Of all this longe day,
I drede our lady be wroth with me,
She ſent me not my pay.

V. 113. them. *O. CC.*

Have no doute, mayſter, ſayd Lytell Johan,
Ye have no nede J ſaye,
This monke it hath brought, I dare well ſwere,
For he is of her abbay.

And ſhe was a borowe, ſayd Robyn,
Betwene a knyght and me,
Of a lytell money that I hym lent,
Under the grene wode tree;

And yf thou haſt that ſylver ibroughte,
I praye the let me ſe,
And I ſhall helpe the eft ſones,
Yf thou have nede of me.

The monke ſwore a full grete othe,
With a ſory chere,
Of the borowehode thou ſpekeſt to me,
Herde I never ere.

I make myn avowe to god, ſayd Robyn,
Monke, thou arte to blame,
For god is holde a ryghtwys man,
And ſo is his dame.

Thou toldeſt with thyn owne tonge,
Thou may not ſay nay,
How thou arte her ſervaunt,
And ſerveſt her every day.

V. 141. to. *W.*

And thou art made her meſſengere,
  My money for to pay,
Therfore I cun the more thanke,
  Thou arte come at thy day.

What is in your cofers? ſayd Robyn,
  Trewe than tell thou me.
Syr, he ſayd, twenty marke,
  Al ſo mote I the.

Yf there be no more, ſayd Robyn,
  I wyll not one peny;
Yf thou haſt myſter of ony more,
  Syr, more I ſhall lende to the;

And yf I fynde more, ſayd Robyn,
  I wys thou ſhalte it forgone;
For of thy ſpendynge ſylver, monk,
  Therof wyll I ryght none.

Go nowe forthe, Lytell Johan,
  And the trouth tell thou me;
If there be no more but twenty marke,
  No peny that I ſe.

Lytell Johan ſpred his mantell downe,
  As he had done before,
And he tolde out of the monkes male,
  Eyght hundreth pounde and more.

V. 154. nade. *W. not in C.* *V.* 177. Eyght pounde. *W.*

Lytell Johan let it lye full ſtyll,
  And went to his mayſter in haſt;
Syr, he ſayd, the monke is trewe ynowe,
  Our lady hath doubled your coſt.

I make myn avowe to god, ſayd Robyn,
  Monke, what tolde I the?
Our lady is the treweſt womàn,
  That ever yet founde I me.

By dere worthy god, ſayd Robyn,
  To ſeche all Englond thorowe,
Yet founde I never to my pay
  A moche better borowe.

Fyll of ye beſt wyne, do hym drynke, ſayd Robyn,
  And grete well thy lady hende,
And yf ſhe have nede of Robyn Hode,
  A frende ſhe ſhall hym fynde;

And yf ſhe nedeth ony more ſylver,
  Come thou agayne to me,
And by this token ſhe hath me ſent,
  She ſhall have ſuch thre.

The monke was going to London ward,
  There to holde grete mote,
The knyght that rode ſo hye on hors,
  To brynge hym under fote.

V. 192. to. *W*.

Whether be ye away? ſayd Robyn.
"Syr, to maners in this londe,
Too reken with our reves,
That have done moch wronge."

"Come now forth, Lytell Johan,
And harken to my tale,
A better yeman I knowe none,
To ſeke a monkes male."

How moch is in yonder other 'cofer?' ſayd Robyn,
The ſoth muſt we ſee.
By our lady, than ſayd the monke,
That were no curteyſye,

To bydde a man to dyner,
And ſyth hym bete and bynde.
It is our olde maner, ſayd Robyn,
To leve but lytell behynde.

The monke toke the hors with ſpore,
No lenger wolde he abyde.
Aſke to drynke, than ſayd Robyn,
Or that ye forther ryde.

Nay, for god, than ſayd the monke,
Me reweth I cam ſo nere,
For better chepe I myght have dyned,
In Blythe or in Dankeſtere.

V. 210. corſer. *W*. courſer. *C*.

Grete well your abbot, ſayd Robyn,
And your pryour, I you pray,
And byd hym ſend me ſuch a monke,
To dyner every day.

Now lete we that monke be ſtyll,
And ſpeke we of that knyght,
Yet he came to holde his day
Whyle that it was lyght.

He dyde hym ſtreyt to Bernyſdale,
Under the grene wode tre,
And he founde there Robyn Hode,
And all his mery meynè.

The knyght lyght downe of his good palfrày,
Robyn whan he gan ſee,
So curteysly he dyde adoune his hode,
And ſet hym on his knee.

"God the ſave, good Robyn Hode,
And al this company."
"Welcome be thou, gentyll knyght,
And ryght welcome to me."

Than beſpake hym Robyn Hode,
To that knyght ſo fre,
What nede dryveth the to grene wode?
I pray the, ſyr knyght, tell me.

And welcome be thou, gentyl knyght,
  Why haſt thou be ſo longe?
"For the abbot and the hye juſtyce
  Wolde have had my londe."

Haſt thou thy lond agayne? ſayd Robyn,
  Treuth than tell thou me.
Ye, for god, ſayd the knyght,
  And that thanke I god and the.

But take not a grefe, I have be ſo longe;
  I came by a wraſtelynge,
And there I dyd holpe a pore yemàn,
  With wronge was put behynde.

Nay, for god, ſayd Robyn,
  Syr knyght, that thanke I the;
What man that helpeth a good yemàn,
  His frende than wyll I be.

Have here foure hondred pounde, than ſayd the [knyght,
  The whiche ye lent to me;
And here is alſo twenty marke
  For your curteyſy.

Nay, for god, than ſayd Robyn,
  Thou broke it well for ay,
For our lady, by her ſelerer,
  Hath ſent to me my pay;

V. 254. gayne. *W.*

V. 258. But take not a grefe, ſayd the knyght,
That I have be ſo longe. *O. CC.*

And yf I toke it twyſe,
A ſhame it were to me:
But trewely, gentyll knyght,
Welcom arte thou to me.

Whan Robyn had tolde his tale,
He leugh and had good chere.
By my trouthe, then ſayd the knyght,
Your money is redy here.

Broke it well, ſayd Robyn,
Thou gentyll knyght ſo fre;
And welcome be thou, gentill knyght,
Under my tryſtell tree.

But what ſhall theſe bowes do? ſayd Robyn,
And theſe arowes ifedered fre?
By god, than ſayd the knyght,
A pore preſent to the.

"Come now forth, Lytell Johan,
And go to my treaſurè,
And brynge me there foure hondred pounde,
The monke over tolde it me.

Have here foure hondred pounde,
Thou gentyll knyght and trewe,
And bye hors and harnes good,
And gylte thy ſpores all newe:

V. 49. I twyſe. *W.* *V.* 285. thi truſty. *C.*

And yf thou fayle ony ſpendynge,
Com to Robyn Hode,
And by my trouth thou ſhalt none fayle
The whyles I have any good.

And broke well thy four hundred pound,
Whiche I lent to the,
And make thy ſelfe no more ſo bare,
By the counſell of me.

Thus than holpe hym good Robyn,
The knyght all of his care.
God, that ſytteth in heven hye,
Graunte us well to fare.

THE FYFTH FYTTE.

NOW hath the knyght his leve itake,
And wente hym on his way;
Robyn Hode and his mery men
Dwelled ſtyll full many a day.

Lyth and lyſten, gentil men,
And herken what I ſhall ſay,
How the proud ſheryfe of Notyngham
Dyde crye a full fayre play;

V. 307. this care. *W.* *V* 308. ſyt. *W.*

That all the beſt archers of the north
Sholde come upon a day,
And they that ſhoteth 'alder' beſt
The game ſhall bere away.

"He that ſhoteth 'alder' beſt
Furtheſt fayre and lowe,
At a payre of fynly buttes,
Under the grene wode ſhawe,

A ryght good arowe he ſhall have,
The ſhaft of ſylver whyte,
The heade and the feders of ryche rede golde,
In Englond is none lyke."

This then herde good Robyn,
Under his tryſtell tre:
"Make you redy, ye wyght yonge men,
That ſhotynge wyll I ſe.

Buſke you, my mery yonge men,
Ye ſhall go with me;
And I wyll wete the ſhryves fayth,
Trewe and yf he be."

Whan they had theyr bowes ibent,
Theyr takles fedred fre,
Seven ſcore of wyght yonge men
Stode by Robyns kne.

V. 11. And that ſhoteth al ther beſt. *W.*
And they that ſhote al of the beſt. *C.*
V. 13. al theyre. *W.* al of the. *C.*

Whan they cam to Notyngham,
The buttes were fayre and longe,
Many was the bolde archere
That ſhoted with bowes ſtronge.

" There ſhall but ſyx ſhote with me,
The other ſhal kepe my hede,
And ſtande with good bowes bent
That I be not deſceyved. "

The fourth outlawe his bowe gan bende,
And that was Robyn Hode,
And that behelde the proude ſheryfe,
All by the but he ſtode.

Thryes Robyn ſhot about,
And alway he ſliſt the wand,
And ſo dyde good Gylberte ,
With the whyte hande.

Lytell Johan and good Scatheloke
Were archers good and fre ;
Lytell Much and good Reynolde,
The worſte wolde they not be.

Whan they had ſhot aboute,
Theſe archours fayre and good,
Evermore was the beſt,
Forſoth, Robyn Hode.

V. 46. they ſliſt. *W.* he clefte. *C.*

Hym was delyvered the goode arow,
For beſt worthy was he;
He toke the yeſt ſo curteysly,
To grene wode wolde he,

They cryed out on Robyn Hode,
And great hornes gan they blowe,
Wo worth the, treaſon! ſayd Robyn,
Full evyl thou art to knowe.

And wo be thou, thou proud ſheryf,
Thus gladdynge thy geſt,
Other wyſe thou behote me
In yonder wylde foreſt;

But had I the in grene wode,
Under my tryſtell tre,
Thou ſholdeſt leve me a better wedde
Than thy trewe lewtè.

Full many a bowe there was bent,
And arowes let they glyde,
Many a kyrtell there was rent,
And hurt many a ſyde.

The outlawes ſhot was ſo ſtronge,
That no man myght them dryve,
And the proud ſheryfes men
They fled away full blyve.

V. 80. belyve. *C.*

Robyn ſawe the busſhement to broke,
In grene wode he wolde have be,
Many an arowe there was ſhot
Amonge that company.

Lytell Johan was hurte full ſore,
With an arowe in his kne,
That he myght neyther go nor ryde;
It was full grete pytè.

Mayſter, then ſayd Lytell Johan,
If ever thou loveſt me,
And for that ylke lordes love,
That dyed upon a tre,

And for the medes of my ſervyce,
That I have ſerved the,
Lete never the proude ſheryf
Alyve now fynde me;

But take out thy browne ſwerde,
And ſmyte all of my hede,
And gyve me woundes dede and wyde,
No lyfe on me be lefte.

I wolde not that, ſayd Robyn,
Johan, that thou were ſlawe,
For all the golde in mery Englond,
Though it lay now on a rawe.

V. 100. That I after eate no bread. *C.*

God forbede, ſayd lytell Much,
  That dyed on a tre,
That thou ſholdeſt, Lytell Johan,
  Parte our company.

Up he toke him on his backe,
  And bare hym well a myle,
Many a tyme he layd hym downe,
  And ſhot another whyle.

Then was there a fayre caſtèll,
  A lytell within the wode,
Double dyched it was about,
  And walled, by the rode;

And there dwelled that gentyll knyght,
  Syr Rychard at the Lee,
That Robyn had lent his good,
  Under the grene wode tree.

In he toke good Robyn,
  And all his company:
"Welcome be thou, Robyn Hode,
  Welcome arte thou [to] me;

And moche [I] thanke the of thy confort,
  And of thy curteyſye,
And of thy grete kyndeneſſe,
  Under the grene wode tre;

I love no man in all this worlde
  So moch as I do the;
For all the proud ſheryf of Notyngham,
  Ryght here ſhalt thou be.

Shyt the gates, and drawe the bridge,
  And let no man com in;
And arme you well and make you redy,
  And to the walle ye wynne.

For one thyng, Robyn, I the behote,
  I ſwere by ſaynt Quyntyn,
Theſe twelve dayes thou woneſt with me,
  To ſuppe, ete, and dyne.

Bordes were layed, and clothes ſpred,
  Reddely and anone;
Robyn Hode and his mery men
  To mete gan they gone.

THE SYXTE FYTTE.

LYTHE and lyſten, gentylmen,
  And herken unto your ſonge,
How the proude ſheryfe of Notyngham,
  And men of armes ſtronge,

Full faste came to the hye sheryfe,
The countre up to rout,
And they beset the knyghts castèll,
The walles all about.

The proude sheryf loude gan crye,
And sayd, Thou traytour knyght,
Thou kepeste here the kynges enemye,
Agayne the lawes and ryght.

"Syr, I wyll avowe that I have done,
The dedes that here be dyght,
Upon all the londes that I have,
As a am a trewe knyght.

Wende forthe, syrs, on your waye,
And doth no more to me,
Tyll ye wytte our kynges wyll
What he woll say to the."

The sheref thus had his answere,
With out ony leasynge,
Forthe he yode to London toune,
All for to tel our kynge.

There he tolde him of that knyght,
And eke of Robyn Hode,
And also of the bolde archeres,
That noble were and good.

V. 14. thou. *W.*

"He wolde avowe that he had done,
To mayntayne the outlawes ſtronge,
He wolde be lorde, and ſet you at nought,
In all the north londe."

I woll be at Notyngham, ſayd the kynge,
Within this fourtynyght,
And take I wyll Robyn Hode,
And ſo I wyll that knyght.

Go home, thou proud ſheryf,
And do as I bydde the,
And ordayne good archeres inowe,
Of all the wyde countree.

The ſheryf had his leve itake,
And went hym on his way;
And Robyn Hode to grene wode,
Upon a certayn day;

And Lytell Johan was hole of the arowe,
That ſhote was in his kne,
And dyde hym ſtrayte to Robyn Hode,
Under the grene wode tre.

Robyn Hode walked in the foreſte,
Under the leves grene,
The proud ſheryfe of Notyngham
Therfore he had grete tene.

V. 38. the bydde. *OCC.*

The ſheryf there fayled of Robyn Hode,
He myght not have his pray,
Then he awayted that gentyll knyght,
Bothe by nyght and by daye.

Ever he awayted that gentyll knyght,
Syr Rychard at the Lee;
As he went on haukynge by the ryver ſyde,
And let his haukes flee,

Toke he there this gentyll knyght,
With men of armes ſtronge,
And lad hym home to Notyngham warde,
Ibonde both fote and honde.

The ſheryf ſwore a full grete othe,
By hym that dyed on a tre,
He had lever than an hondrede pounde,
That Robyn Hode had he!

Then the lady, the knyghtes wyfe,
A fayre lady and fre,
She ſet her on a gode palfray,
To grene wode anon rode ſhe.

When ſhe came to the forèſt,
Under the grene wode tre,
Founde ſhe there Robyn Hode,
And all his fayre meynè.

V. 64. honde and fote. *W.* foote and hande. *C.* *V.* 68. That he had Robyn Hode. *W.*

"God the ſave, good Robyn Hode,
And all thy company;
For our dere ladyes love,
A bone graunte thou me.

Let thou never my wedded lorde
Shamfully ſlayne to be;
He is faſt ibounde to Notyngham warde,
For the love of the."

Anone then ſayd good Robyn,
To that lady fre,
What man hath your lorde itake?
The proude ſhirife, than ſayd ſhe.

[The proude ſheryfe hath hym itake]
Forſoth as I the ſay;
He is not yet thre myles,
Paſſed on 'his' waye.

Up then ſterte good Robyn,
As a man that had be wode:
"Buſke you, my mery younge men,
For hym that dyed on a rode;

V. 77. God the good Robyn. *W.* *V.* 79. lady. *W.* *V.* 81. Late. *V.* 82. Shamly I ſlayne be. *W.* *V.* 88. For ſoth as I the ſay. *W.* *V.* 92. your. *W.* You may them overtake. *C.*

And he that this ſorowe forſaketh,
  By hym that dyed on a tre,
And by him that al thinges maketh,
  No lenger ſhall dwell with me."

Sone there were good bowes ibent,
  Mo than ſeven ſcore,
Hedge ne dyche ſpared they none,
  That was them before.

I make myn avowe to god, ſayd Robyn,
  The knyght wolde I fayn ſe,
And yf I may hym take,
  Iquyt than ſhall he bee.

And whan they came to Notyngham,
  They walked in the ſtrete,
And with the proud ſheryf, I wys,
  Sone gan they mete.

Abyde, thou proud ſheryf, he ſayd,
  Abyde and ſpeake with me,
Of ſome tydynges of our kynge,
  I wolde fayne here of the.

This ſeven yere, by dere worthy god,
  Ne yede I ſo faſt on fote,
I make myn avowe to god, thou proud ſheryfe,
  ‘ It’ is not for thy good.

V. 99, 100. Shall he never in grene wode be Nor longer dwell with me. *W.* *V.* 108. it. *W.* *V.* 120. At. *W.* That. *C.* — good] boote. *Wb.*

Robyn bent a good bowe,
An arrowe he drewe at his wyll,
He hyt ſo the proud ſheryf,
Upon the grounde he lay full ſtyll;

And or he myght up aryſe,
On his fete to ſtonde,
He ſmote of the ſheryves hede,
With his bryght bronde.

"Lye thou there, thou proud ſheryf,
Evyll mote thou thryve;
There myght no man to the truſt,
The whyles thou were alyve."

His men drewe out theyr bryght ſwerdes,
That were ſo ſharpe and kene,
And layde on the ſheryves men,
And dryved them downe by dene.

Robyn ſtert to that knyght,
And cut a two his bonde,
And toke him in his hand a bowe,
And bade hym by hym ſtonde.

"Leve thy hors the behynde,
And lerne for to renne;
Thou ſhalt with me to grene wode,
Through myre, moſſe and fenne,

V. 138. hoode. *W.* bande. *C.*

Thou ſhalt with me to grene wode,
Without ony leaſynge,
Tyll that I have gete us grace,
Of Edwarde our comly kynge."

THE SEVENTH FYTTE.

THE kynge came to Notynghame,
With knyghtes in grete araye,
For to take that gentyll knyght,
And Robyn Hode, yf he may.

He aſked men of that countrè,
After Robyn Hode,
And after that gentyll knyght,
That was ſo bolde and ſtout.

Whan they had tolde hym the caſe,
Our kynge underſtonde ther tale,
And ſeaſed in his honde
The knyghtes londes all,

All the paſſe of Lancaſhyre,
He went both ferre and nere,
Tyll he came to Plomton parke,
He faylyd many of his dere.

V. 4. and yf. *P.*

There our kynge was wont to ſe
  Herdes many one,
He coud unneth fynde one dere,
  That bare ony good horne.

The kynge was wonder wroth with all,
  And ſwore by the trynytè,
" I wolde I had Robyn Hode,
  With eyen I myght hym ſe ;

And he that wolde ſmyte of the knyghtes hede,
  And brynge it to me,
He ſhall have the knyghtes londes,
  Syr Rycharde at the Le ;

I gyve it hym with my chartèr,
  And ſele it with my honde,
To have and holde for ever more,
  In all mery Englonde."

Than beſpake a fayre olde knyght,
  That was treue in his fay,
A, my lege lorde the kynge,
  One worde I ſhall you ſay ;

There is no man in this countrè
  May have the knyghtes londes,
Whyle Robyn Hode may ryde or gone,
  And bere a bowe in his hondes ;

That he ne ſhall leſe his hede,
  That is the beſt ball in his hode:
Give it no man, my lorde the kynge,
  That ye wyll any good.

Half a yere dwelled our comly kynge,
  In Notyngham, and well more,
Coude he not here of Robyn Hode,
  In what countre that he were;

But alway went good Robyn
  By halke and eke by hyll,
And alway ſlewe the kynges dere,
  And welt them at his wyll.

Than beſpake a proude foſtere,
  That ſtode by our kynges kne,
If ye wyll ſe good Robyn,
  Ye muſt do after me;

Take fyve of the beſt knyghtes
  That be in your lede,
And walke downe by 'yon' abbay,
  And gete you monkes wede.

And I wyll be your ledes man,
  And lede you the way,
And or ye come to Notyngham,
  Myn hede then dare I lay,

V. 59. your. *OCC.*

That ye ſhall mete with good Robyn,
On lyve yf that he be,
Or ye come to Notyngham,
With eyen ye ſhall hym ſe.

Full haſtly our kynge was dyght,
So were his knyghtes fyve,
Everych of them in monkes wede,
And haſted them thyder blyth.

Our kynge was grete above his cole,
A brode hat on his crowne,
Ryght as he were abbot lyke,
They rode up in to the towne.

Styf botes our kynge had on,
Forſoth as I you ſay,
He rode ſyngynge to grene wode,
The covent was clothed in graye,

His male hors, and his grete ſomers,
Folowed our kynge be hynde,
Tyll they came to grene wode,
A myle under the lynde,

There they met with good Robyn,
Stondynge on the waye,
And ſo dyde many a bolde archere,
For ſoth as I you ſay.

Robyn toke the kynges hors,
Haſtely in that ſtede,
And ſayd, Syr abbot, by your leve,
A whyle ye muſt abyde;

We be yemen of this foreſte,
Under the grene wode tre,
We lyve by our kynges dere,
Other ſhyft have not we;

And ye have chyrches and rentes both,
And gold full grete plentè;
Gyve us ſome of your ſpendynge,
For ſaynt Charyte.

Than beſpake our cumly kynge,
Anone than ſayd he,
I brought no more to grene wode,
But forty pounde with me;

I have layne at Notyngham,
This fourtynyght with our kynge,
And ſpent I have full moche good,
On many a grete lordynge;

And I have but forty pounde,
No more than have I me,
But yf I had an hondred pounde,
I would geve it to the.

V 96. Under the grene wode tre. *W.* *V.* 112. I vouche it halfe on the. *W.*

Robyn toke the forty pounde,
And departed it in two partye,
Halfendell he gave his mery men,
And bad them mery to be.

Full curteysly Robyn gan ſay,
Syr, have this for your ſpendyng,
We ſhall mete a nother day.
Gramercy, than ſayd our kynge;

But well the greteth Edwarde our kynge,
And ſent to the his ſeale,
And byddeth the com to Notyngham,
Both to mete and mele.

He toke out the brode tarpe,
And ſone he lete hym ſe;
Robyn coud his courteyſy,
And ſet hym on his kne:

"I love no man in all the worlde
So well as I do my kynge,
Welcome is my lordes ſeale;
And, monke, for thy tydynge,

Syr abbot, for thy tydynges,
To day thou ſhalt dyne with me
For the love of my kynge
Under my tryſtell tre."

V. 125. ſeale. *C.*

Forth he lad our comly kynge,
Full fayre by the honde,
Many a dere there was ſlayne,
And full faſt dyghtande.

Robyn toke a full grete horne,
And loude he gan blowe,
Seven ſcore of wyght yonge men,
Came redy on a rowe,

All they kneeled on theyr kne,
Full fayre before Robyn.
The kynge ſayd hymſelfe untyll,
And ſwore by ſaynt Auſtyn,

Here is a wonder ſemely ſyght,
Me thynketh, by goddes pyne;
His men are more at his byddynge,
Then my men be at myn.

Full haſtly was theyr dyner idyght,
And therto gan they gone,
They ſerved our kynge with al theyr myght,
Both Robyn and Lytell Johan.

Anone before our kynge was ſet
The fatte venyſon,
The good whyte brede, the good red wyne,
And therto the fyne ale browne.

V. 160. and browne. *W.*

Make good chere, ſayd Robyn,
Abbot, for charyte;
And for this ylke tydynge,
Blyſſed mote thou be.

Now ſhalte thou ſe what lyfe we lede,
Or thou hens wende,
Than thou may enfourme our kynge,
Whan ye togyder lende.

Up they ſterte all in haſt,
Theyr bowes were ſmartly bent,
Our kynge was never ſo ſore agaſt,
He wende to have be ſhente.

Two yerdes there were up ſet,
There to gan they gange;
By fifty paſe, our kynge ſayd,
The merkes were to longe,

On every ſyde a roſe garlonde,
They ſhot under the lyne.
Who ſo fayleth of the roſe garlonde, ſayd Robyn,
His takyll he ſhall tyne,

And yelde it to his mayſter,
Be it never ſo fyne,
For no man wyll I ſpare,
So drynke I ale or wyne.

And bere a buffet on his hede,
  I wys ryght all bare.
And all that fell in Robyns lote,
  He ſmote them wonder ſare.

Twyſe Robyn ſhot aboute,
  And ever he cleved the wande,
And ſo dyde good Gylberte,
  With the whyte hand;

Lytell Johan and good Scathelocke,
  For nothyng wolde they ſpare,
When they fayled of the garlonde,
  Robyn ſmote them full ſare:

At the laſt ſhot that Robyn ſhot,
  For all his frendes fare,
Yet he fayled of the garlonde,
  Thre fyngers and mare.

Than beſpake good Gylberte,
  And thus he gan ſay,
Mayſter, he ſayd, your takyll is loſt,
  Stand forth and take your pay.

If it be ſo, ſayd Robyn,
  That may no better be;
Syr abbot, I delyver the myn arowe,
  I pray the, ſyr, ſerve thou me.

V. 186. A wys. *W.* For that ſhall be his fyne. *C.* *V.* 193. good whyte. *W.* lilly white. *C.*

It falleth not for myn order, ſayd our kynge,
Robyn, by thy leve,
For to ſmyte no good yemàn,
For doute I ſholde hym greve.

Smyte on boldely, ſayd Robyn,
I give the large leve.
Anone our kynge, with that worde,
He folde up his ſleve,

And ſych a buffet he gave Robyn,
To grounde he yede full nere.
I make myn avowe to god, ſayd Robyn,
Thou arte a ſtalworthe frere ;

There is pith in thyn arme, ſayd Robyn,
I trowe thou canſt well ſhote.
Thus our kynge and Robyn Hode
Togeder than they met.

Robyn behelde our comly kynge
Wyſtly in the face,
So dyde ſyr Richarde at the Le,
And kneled downe in that place ;

And ſo dyde all the wylde outlawes,
Whan they ſe them knele.
" My lorde the kynge of Englonde,
Now I knowe you well."

Mercy, then Robyn ſayd to our kynge,
  Under your tryſtyll tre,
Of thy goodneſſe and thy grace
  For my men and me!

Yes, for god, ſayd Robyn,
  And alſo god me ſave;
I aſke mercy, my lorde the kynge,
  And for my men I crave.

Yes, for god, than ſayd our kynge
  Thy peticion I graunt the,
With that thou leve the grene wode,
  And all thy company;

And come home, ſyr, to my courte,
  And there dwell with me.
I make myn avowe to god, ſayd Robyn,
  And ryght ſo ſhall it be;

I wyll come to your courte,
  Your ſervyſe for to ſe,
And brynge with me of my men
  Seven ſcore and thre.

But me lyke well your ſervyſe,
  I come agayne full ſoone,
And ſhote at the donne dere,
  As I am wonte to done.

V. 248. And therto ſent I me. *W.*

THE EIGHTH FYTTE.

HASTE thou ony grene cloth? ſayd our kynge,
That thou wylte ſell nowe to me.
Ye, for god, ſayd Robyn,
Thyrty yerdes and thre.

Robyn, ſayd our kynge,
Now pray I the,
To ſell me ſome of that cloth,
To me and meynè.

Yes, for god, then ſayd Robyn,
Or elles I were a fole;
A nother day ye wyll me clothe,
I trowe, ayenſt the Yole.

The kynge keſt of his cote then,
A grene garment he dyde on,
And every knyght had ſo, I wys,
They clothed them full ſoone.

Whan they were clothed in Lyncolne grene,
They keſt away theyr graye.
Now we ſhall to Notyngham,
All thus our kynge gan ſay.

V. 9. good. *OCC.* *V.* 16. Another had full ſone. *W.*

Theyr bowes bente and forth they went,
Shotynge all in fere,
Towarde the towne of Notyngham,
Outlawes as they were.

Our kynge and Robyn rode togyder,
For ſoth as I you ſay,
And they ſhote plucke buffet,
As they went by the way;

And many a buffet our kynge wan,
Of Robyn Hode that day;
And nothynge ſpared good Robyn
Our kynge in his pay.

So god me helpe, ſayd our kynge,
Thy game is nought to lere,
I ſholde not get a ſhote of the,
Though I ſhote all this yere.

All the people of Notyngham
They ſtode and behelde,
They ſawe nothynge but mantels of grene,
That covered all the felde;

Than every man to other gan ſay,
I drede our kynge be ſlone;
Come Robyn Hode to the towne, I wys,
On lyve he leveth not one.

V. 44. Lefte never one. *W.*

Full haſtly they began to fle,
  Both yemen and knaves,
And olde wyves that myght evyll goo,
  They hypped on theyr ſtaves,

The kynge loughe full faſt,
  And commanded theym agayne;
When they ſe our comly kynge,
  I wys they were full fayne.

They ete and dranke, and made them glad,
  And ſange with notes hye.
Than beſpake our comly kynge
  To ſyr Rycharde at the Lee:

He gave hym there his londe agayne,
  A good man he bad hym be.
Robyn thanked our comly kynge,
  And ſet hym on his kne.

Had Robyn dwelled in the kynges courte,
  But twelve monethes and thre,
That he had ſpent an hondred pounde,
  And all his mennes fe.

In every place where Robyn came,
  Ever more he layde downe,
Both for knyghtes and for ſquyres,
  To gete hym grete renowne,

V. 49. lughe. *W.*

By than the yere was all agone,
He had no man but twayne
Lytell Johan and good Scathelocke,
Wyth hym all for to gone.

Robyn ſawe yonge men ſhote,
Full fayre upon a day,
Alas! than ſayd good Robyn,
My welthe is went away.

Somtyme I was an archere good,
A ſtyffe and eke a ſtronge,
I was commytted the beſt archere,
That was in mery Englonde.

Alas! then ſayd good Robyn,
Alas and well a woo!
Yf I dwele lenger with the kynge,
Sorowe wyll me ſloo.

Forth than went Robyn Hode,
Tyll he came to our kynge:
" My lorde the kynge of Englonde,
Graunte me myn aſkynge.

I made a chapell in Bernyſdale,
That ſemely is to ſe,
It is of Mary Magdalene,
And thereto wolde I be;

V. 74. ferre. *W.* *V.* 75. commended for. *C.*

I myght never in this ſeven nyght,
No tyme to ſlepe ne wynke,
Nother all theſe ſeven dayes,
Nother ete ne drynke.

Me longeth ſore to Bernyſdale,
I may not be therfro,
Barefote and wolwarde I have hyght
Thyder for to go."

Yf it be ſo, than ſayd our kynge,
It may no better be;
Seven nyght I gyve the leve,
No lengre, to dwell fro me.

Gramercy, lorde, then ſayd Robyn,
And ſet hym on his kne;
He toke his leve full courteysly,
To grene wode then went he.

Whan he came to grene wode,
In a mery mornynge,
There he herde the notes ſmall,
Of byrdes mery ſyngynge.

It is ferre gone, ſayd Robyn,
That I was laſt here,
Me lyſte a lytell for to ſhote,
At the donne dere.

Robyn ſlewe a full grete harte,
His horne than gan he blow,
That all the outlawes of that forèſt,
That horne coud they knowe,

And gadred them togyder,
In a lytell throwe,
Seven ſcore of wight yonge men,
Came redy on a rowe;

And fayre dyde of theyr hodes,
And ſet them on theyr kne:
Welcome, they ſayd, our mayſtèr,
Under this grene wode tre.

Robyn dwelled in grene wode,
Twenty yere and two,
For all drede of Edwarde our kynge,
Agayne wolde he not goo.

Yet he was begyled, I wys,
Through a wycked womàn,
The pryoreſſe of Kyrkesly,
That nye was of his kynne,

For the love of a knyght,
Syr Roger of Donkeſtèr,
That was her owne ſpeciall,
Full evyll mote they 'fare,'

V. 134. donkeſley. *W.* *V.* 136. the. *OCC.*

They toke togyder theyr counſell
  Robyn Hode for to ſle,
And how they myght beſt do that dede,
  His banis for to be.

Than beſpake good Robyn,
  In place where as he ſtode,
To morow I muſte to Kyrkesley,
  Craftely to be leten blode.

Syr Roger of Donkeſtere,
  By the pryoreſſe he lay,
And there they betrayed good Robyn Hode,
  Through theyr falſe playe.

Cryſt have mercy on his ſoule,
  That dyed on the rode!
For he was a good out lawe,
  And dyde pore men moch god.

II.

ROBYN HODE [AND THE POTTER].

This curious, and hitherto unpublished, and even unheard of old piece is given from a manuscript, among bishop Mores collections, in the public library of the university of Cambridge (Ee. 4. 35). The writing, which is evidently that of a vulgar and illiterate person, appears to be of the age of Henry the seventh, that is about the year 1500; *but the composition (which he has irremediably corrupted) is probably of an earlyer period, and much older, no doubt, than "The play of Robyn Hode," which ſeems alluſive to the ſame ſtory. At the end of the original is "Expleycyt Robyn Hode."*

IN ſchomer, when the leves ſpryng,
The bloſchems on every bowe,
So merey doyt the berdys ſyng,
Yn wodys merey now.

Herkens, god yemen,
Comley, corteſſey, and god,
On of the beſt that yever bar bou,
Hes name was Roben Hode.

Roben Hood was the yemans name,
That was boyt corteys and fre;
For the loffe of owr ladey,
All wemen werſchep 'he.'

Bot as the god yeman ſtod on a day,
Among hes mery maney,
He was war of a prowd potter,
Cam dryfyng owyr the 'ley.'

Yonder comet a prod potter, ſeyde Roben,
That long hayt hantyd this wey,
He was never ſo corteys a man
On peney of pawage to pay.

V. 12. ye. *V.* 16. leſe. *V.* 17. ſyde.

Y met hem bot at Wentbreg, ſeyde Lytyll John,
And therfor yeffell mot he the,
Seche thre ſtrokes he me gafe,
Yet they cleffe by my ſeydys.

Y ley forty ſhillings, ſeyde Lytyll John,
To pay het thes ſame day,
Ther ys nat a man among hus all
A wed ſchall make hem ley.

Her ys forty ſhillings, ſeyde Roben,
Mor, and thow dar ſay,
That y ſchall make that prowde potter,
A wed to me ſchall he ley.

Ther thes money they leyde,
They toke het a yeman to kepe;
Roben befor the potter he breyde,
'And up to hem can lepe.'

Handys apon hes horſe he leyde,
And bad 'hem' ſtonde foll ſtell.
The potter ſchorteley to hem ſeyde,
Felow, what ys they well?

All thes thre yer, and mor, potter, he ſeyde,
Thow haſt hantyd thes wey,
Yet wer tow never ſo cortys a man
One peney of pauage to pay.

V. 21. ſyde. *V.* 27. hys. *V.* 28. leſſe. *V.* 36. A bad hem ſtond ſtell. *V.* 38. the potter.

What ys they name? ſeyde the potter;
For pauage thow aſke of me.
"Roben Hod ys mey name,
A wed ſchall thow leffe me."

Wed well y non leffe, ſeyde the potter,
Nor pavag well y non pay;
Awey they honde fro mey horſe,
Y well the tene eyls, be mey fay.

The potter to hes cart he went,
He was not to ſeke,
A god to-hande ſtaffe therowt he hent,
Befor Roben he 'lepe.'

Roben howt with a ſwerd bent,
A bokeler en hes honde [therto];
The potter to Roben he went,
And ſeyde, Felow, let mey horſe go.

Togeder then went thes two yemen,
Het was a god ſeyt to ſe;
Therof low Robyn hes men,
Ther they ſtod onder a tre.

Leytell John to hes felow he ſeyde,
Yend potter welle ſteffeley ſtonde.
The potter, with a caward ſtroke,
Smot the bokeler owt of hes honde;

V. 56. leppyd.

And ar Roben meyt get het agen,
Hes bokeler at hes fette,
The potter yn the neke hem toke,
To the gronde sone he yede.

That saw Roben hes men,
As thay stode ender a bow:
Let us helpe owr master, seyed Lytell John,
Yonder potter els well hem sclo.

Thes yemen went with a breyde,
To 'ther' master they cam.
Leytell John to hes master seyde,
Ho haet the wager won?

Schall y haff yowr forty shillings, seyde Lytel John,
Or ye, master, schall haffe myne?
Yeff they wer a hundred, seyde Roben,
Y feythe, they ben all theyne.

Het ys fol leytell cortesey, seyde the potter,
As y haffe harde weyse men saye,
Yeff a por yeman com drywyng ower the wey,
To let hem of hes gorney.

Be mey trowet, thow seys soyt, seyde Roben,
Thow seys god yemenrey;
And thow dreyffe forthe yevery day,
Thow schalt never be let for me.

V. 69. A. *V.* 76. seyde hels. *V.* 77. went yemen.
V. 78. thes. *V.* 82. lytl. *V.* 90. yemerey.

Y well prey the, god potter,
A feliſchepe well thow haffe?
Geffe me they clothyng, and thow ſchalt hafe myne,
Y well go to Notynggam.

Robyn went to Notynggam,
Thes pottes for to ſell;
The potter abode with Robens men,
Ther he fered not eylle.

Y grant therto, ſeyde the potter,
Thow ſchalt feynde me a felow gode;
Bot thow can ſell mey pottes well,
Com ayen as thow yode.

Nay, be mey trowt, ſeyde Roben,
And then y beſcro mey hede,
Yeffe y bryng eney pottes ayen,
And eney weyffe well hem chepe.

Than ſpake Leytell John,
And all hes felowhes heynd,
Maſter, be well war of the ſcreffe of Notynggam,
For he ys leytell howr frende.

Thorow the helpe of howr ladey,
Felowhes, let me alone;
Heyt war howte, ſeyde Roben,
To Notynggam well y gon.

V. 101. grat. *V.* 104. yede.

Tho Roben droffe on hes wey,
So merey ower the londe.
Heres mor and affter ys to ſaye,
The beſt ys beheynde.

[THE SECOND FIT.]

WHEN Roben cam to Notynggam,
The ſoyt yef y ſcholde ſaye,
He ſet op hes horſe anon,
And gaffe hem hotys and haye.

Yn the medys of the towne,
Ther he ſchowed hes war,
Pottys! pottys! he gan crey foll ſone,
Haffe hanſell for the mar.

Foll effen ageneſt the ſcreffeys gate,
Schowed he hes chaffar;
Weyffes and wedowes abowt hem drow,
And chepyd faſt of hes war.

Yet, Pottys, gret chepe! creyed Robyn,
Y loffe yeffell thes to ſtonde.
And all that ſaw hem ſell,
Seyde he had be no potter long.

V. 135. ſay.

The pottys that wer werthe pens feyffe,
He ſolde tham for pens thre:
Preveley ſeyde man and weyffe,
Ywnder potter ſchall never the.

Thos Roben ſolde foll faſt,
Tell he had pottys bot feyffe;
Op he hem toke of his car,
And ſende hem to the ſcreffeys weyffe.

Therof ſche was foll fayne,
Gereamarſey, ſir, than ſeyde ſche,
When ye com to thes contre ayen,
Y ſchall bey of ' they' pottys, ſo mot y the.

Ye ſchall haffe of the beſt, ſeyde Roben,
And ſwar be the treneytè.
Foll corteysley ' ſhe' gan hem call,
Com deyne with the ſcrefe and me.

Godamarſey, ſeyde Roben,
Yowr bedyng ſchall be doyn.
A mayden yn the pottys gan ber,
Roben and the ſcreffe weyffe folowed anon.

Whan Roben ynto the hall cam,
The ſcreffe ſone he met,
The potter cowed of corteyſey,
And ſone the ſcreffe he gret.

V. 146. ſeyde ſche ſ' than. *V.* 148. the. *V.* 151. he.

"Loketh what thes potter hayt geffe yow and me,
Feyffe pottys ſmalle and grete!"
He ys fol wellcom, ſeyd the ſcreffe,
Let os was, and 'go' to mete.

As they ſat at her methe,
With a nobell cher,
Two of the ſcreffes men gan ſpeke
Off a gret wagèr,

Was made the thother daye,
Off a ſchotyng was god and feyne,
Off forty ſhillings, the ſoyt to ſaye,
Who ſcholde thes wager wen.

Styll than ſat thes prowde potter,
Thos than thowt he,
As y am a trow Cerſtyn man,
Thes ſchotyng well y ſe.

Whan they had fared of the beſt,
With bred and ale and weyne,
To the 'bottys they' made them preſt,
With bowes and boltys foll feyne.

The ſcreffes men ſchot foll faſt,
As archares that weren godde,

V. 161, Loſeth. *V.* 164. to. *VV.* 169. 170. *Theſe two lines are tranſpoſed in the MS.* *V.* 179. pottys the. *V.* 180. bolt yt.

Ther cam non ner ney the marke
  Bey halfe a god archares bowe.

Stell then ſtod the prowde potter,
  Thos than ſeyde he,
And y had a bow, be the rode,
  On ſchot ſcholde yow ſe.

Thow ſchall haffe a bow, ſeyde the ſcreffe,
  The beſt that thow well cheys of thre ;
Thow ſemyſt a ſtalward and a ſtronge,
  Aſay ſchall thow be.

The ſcreffe comandyd a yeman that ſtod hem bey
  Affter bowhes to wende ;
The beſt bow that the yeman browthe
  Roben ſet on a ſtryng.

" Now ſchall y wet and thow be god,
  And polle het op to they ner."
So god me helpe, ſeyde the prowde potter,
  Thys ys bot rygzt weke ger.

To a quequer Roben went,
  A god bolt owthe he toke,
So ney on to the marke he went,
  He fayled not a fothe.

V 191. ſenyſt.

All they ſchot abowthe agen,
The ſcreffes men and he,
Off the marke he welde not fayle,
He cleffed the preke on thre.

The ſcreffes men thowt gret ſchame,
The potter the maſtry wan;
The ſcreffe lowe and made god game,
And ſeyde, Potter, thow art a man;
Thow art worthey to ber a bowe,
Yn what plas that thow 'gang.'

Yn mey cart y haffe a bowe,
Forſoyt, he ſeyde, and that a godde;
Yn mey cart ys the bow
That 'I had of Robyn Hode.'

Knoweſt thow Robyn Hode? ſeyde the ſcreffe,
Potter, y prey the tell thou me.
"A hundred torne y haffe ſchot with hem,
Under hes tortyll tre."

Y had lever nar a hundred ponde, ſeyde the ſcreffe,
And ſwar be the trenitè,
[Y had lever nar a hundred ponde, he ſeyde,]
That the fals owtelawe ſtod be me.

And ye well do afftyr mey red, ſeyde the potter,
And boldeley go with me,

V. 214. goe. *V.* 218. that Robyng gaffe me.

And to morow, or we het bred,
  Roben Hode wel we ſe.

Y well queyt the, kod the ſcreffe,
  And ſwer be god of meythe.
Schetyng thay left, and hom they went,
  Her ſcoper was redey deythe.

Upon the morow, when het was day,
  He boſkyd hem forthe to reyde;
The potter hes carte forthe gan ray,
  And wolde not [be] leffe beheynde.

He toke leffe of the ſcreffys wyffe,
  And thankyd her of all thyng;
"Dam, for mey loffe, and ye well thys wer,
  Y geffe yow her a golde ryng."

Gramarſey, ſeyde the weyffe,
  Sir, god eylde het the.
The ſcreffes hart was never ſo leythe,
  The feyr foreſt to ſe.

And when he cam ynto the foreyſt,
  Yonder the leffes grene,
Berdys ther ſange on bowhes preſt,
  Het was gret goy to ſene.

Her het ys merey to be, ſeyde Roben,
  For a man that had hawt to ſpende:

V. 232. mey they. *V.* 251. ſe.

Be mey horne ‘ we’ ſchall awet
Yeff Roben Hode be ‘ ner hande.’

Roben ſet hes horne to hes mowthe,
And blow a blaſt that was foll god,
That herde hes men that ther ſtode,
Fer downe yn the wodde.
I her mey maſter, ſeyde Leytyll John:
They ran as thay wer wode.

Whan thay to thar maſter cam,
Leytell John wold not ſpar:
“ Maſter, how haffe yow far yn Notynggam?
“ Haffe yow ſolde yowr war?”

“ Ye, be mey trowthe, Leytyll John,
Loke thow take no car;
Y haffe browt the ſcreffe of Notynggam,
For all howr chaffar.”

He ys foll wellcom, ſeyde Lytyll John,
Thes tydyng ys foll godde.
The ſcreffe had lever nar a hundred ponde
[He had never ſene Roben Hode].

“ Had I weſt that beforen,
At Notynggam when we wer,
Thow ſcholde not com yn feyr foreſt
Of all thes thowſande eyr.

V. 254. he. *V.* 255. her. *V.* 259. For. *V.* 265 How haffe. *V.* 266. I leyty. *V.* 274. He had weſt.

That wot y well, ſeyde Roben,
Y thanke god that y be her;
Therfor ſchall ye leffe yowr horſe with hos,
And all your hother ger.

That fend I godys forbode, kod the ſcreffe,
So to leſe mey godde.
" Hether ye cam on horſe foll hey,
And hom ſchall ye go on fote;
And gret well they weyffe at home,
The woman ys foll godde.

Y ſchall her ſende a wheyt palffrey,
Het hambellet as the weynde;
Ner for the loffe of yowr weyffe,
Off mor ſorow ſcholde yow ſeyng."

Thes parted Robyn Hode and the ſcreffe,
To Notynggam he toke the waye;
Hes weyffe feyr welcomed hem hom,
And to hem gan ſche ſaye:

Seyr, how haffe yow fared yn grene foreyſt?
Haffe ye browt Roben hom?
" Dam, the deyell ſpede hem, bothe bodey and bon,
Y haffe hade a foll grete ſkorne.

V. 279. that ye be. *V.* 284. y. *V.* 288. *The MS. repeats this line after the following.* Het ambellet be mey ſey.

Of all the god that y haffe lade to grene wod,
He hayt take het fro me,
All bot this feyr palffrey,
That he hayt fende to the."

With that fche toke op a lowde lawhyng,
And fwhar be hem that deyed on tre,
Now haffe yow payed for all the pottys
That Roben gaffe to me.

Now ye be com hom to Notynggam,
Ye fchall haffe god ynowe."
Now fpeke we of Roben Hode,
And of the pottyr onder the grene bowhe.

" Potter, what was they pottys worthe
To Notynggam that y ledde with me?"
They wer worth two nobellys, feyd he,
So mot y treyffe or the;
So cowde y had for tham,
And y had ther be.

Thow fchalt hafe ten ponde, feyde Roben,
Of money feyr and fre;
And yever whan thow comeft to grene wod,
Wellcom, potter, to me.

V. 311. bowhes. *V.* 317. be ther.

Thes partyd Robyn, the ſcreffe, and the potter,
  Ondernethe the grene wod tre.
God haffe merſey on Roben Hodys ſolle,
  And ſaffe all god yemanrey!

III.

ROBIN HOOD AND THE BEGGAR.

This poem, a north country (or, perhaps, Scotish) compofition of fome antiquity, is given from a modern copy printed at Newcaftle, where the editor accidentally picked it up: no other having, to his knowlege, been ever feen or heard of. The corruptions of the prefs being equally numerous and minute, fome of the moft trifling have been corrected without notice. But it may be proper to mention that each line of the printed copy is here thrown into two: a ftep which, though abfolutely neceffary from the narrownefs of the page, is fufficiently juftified by the frequent recurrence of the double rime. The divifion of ftanzas was conceived to be a ftill further improvement.—The original title is, "A pretty dialogue betwixt Robin Hood and a beggar."

LYTH and liften, gentlemen,
  That be of high born blood,
I'll tell you of a brave booting
  That befell Robin Hood.

Robin Hood upon a day,
He went forth him alone,
And as he came from Barnſdale
Into fair evening,

He met a beggar on the way,
Who ſturdily could gang;
He had a pike-ſtaff in his hand
That was both ſtark and ſtrang;

A clouted clock about him was,
That held him frae the cold,
The thinneſt bit of it, I gueſs,
Was more then twenty fold.

His meal-poke hang about his neck,
Into a leathern whang,
Well faſten'd to a broad bucle,
That was both ſtark and 'ſtrang.'

He had three hats upon his head,
Together ſticked faſt,
He car'd neither for wind nor wet,
In lands where'er he paſt.

Good Robin caſt him in the way,
To ſee what he might be,
If any beggar had monèy,
He thought ſome part had he.

V. 24. wher'e.

Tarry, tarry, good Robin ſays,
Tarry, and ſpeak with me.
He heard him as he heard him not,
And faſt on his way can hy.

'Tis be not ſo, ſays [good] Robìn,
Nay, thou muſt tarry ſtill.
By my troth, ſaid the bold beggàr,
Of that I have no will.

It is far to my lodging houſe,
And it is growing late,
If they have ſupt e'er I come in
I will look wondrous blate.

Now, by my truth, ſays good Robìn,
I ſee well by thy fare,
If thou ſhares well to thy ſuppèr,
Of mine thou doſt not care,

Who wants my dinner all this day,
And wots not where to ly,
And would I to the tavern go,
I want money to buy.

Sir, you muſt lend me ſome monèy
Till we meet again.
The beggar anſwer'd cankardly,
I have no money to lend.

Thou art a young man as I,
And ſeems to be as ſweer;
If thou faſt till thou get from me,
Thou ſhalt eat none this year.

Now, by my truth, ſays [good] Robìn,
Since we are aſembled ſo,
If thou has but a ſmall farthìng,
I'll have it e'er thou go.

Come, lay down thy clouted cloak,
And do no longer ſtand,
And looſe the ſtrings of all thy pokes,
I'll ripe them with my hand.

And now to thee I make a vow,
If 'thou' make any din,
I ſhall ſee a broad arròw,
Can pierce a beggar's ſkin.

The beggar ſmil'd, and anſwer made,
Far better let me be;
Think not that I will be afraid,
For thy nip crooked tree;

Or that I fear thee any whit,
For thy curn nips of ſticks,
I know no uſe for them ſo meet
As to be puding-pricks.

Here I defy thee to do me ill,
For all thy boiſterous fair,
Thou's get nothing from me but ill,
Would'ſt thou ſeek evermair.

Good Robin bent his noble bow,
He was an angery man,
And in it ſet a broad arròw;
Lo! e'er 'twas drawn a ſpan,

The beggar, with his noble tree,
Reach'd him ſo round a rout,
That his bow and his broad arròw
In flinders flew about.

Good Robin bound him to his brand,
But that prov'd likewiſe vain,
The beggar lighted on his hand
With his pike-ſtaff again:

[I] wot he might not draw a ſword
For forty days and mair.
Good Robin could not ſpeak a word,
His heart was ne'er ſo ſair.

He could not fight, he could not flee,
He wiſt not what to do;
The beggar with his noble tree
Laid luſty ſlaps him to.

He paid good Robin back and ſide,
  And baiſt him up and down,
And with his pyke-ſtaff laid on loud,
  Till he fell in a ſwooon.

Stand up, man, the beggar ſaid,
  'Tis ſhame to go to reſt;
Stay till thou get thy money told,
  I think it were the beſt:

And ſyne go to the tavern houſe,
  And buy both wine and ale;
Hereat thy friends will crack full crouſe,
  Thou haſt been at the dale.

Good Robin anſwer'd ne'er a word,
  But lay ſtill as a ſtane;
His cheeks were pale as any clay,
  And cloſed were his een.

The beggar thought him dead but fail,
  And boldly bound his way.—
I would ye had been at the dale,
  And gotten part of the play.

V. 116. cloſd. *We might read:*
And clos'd were [baith] his een.

THE SECOND PART.

NOW three of Robin's men, by chance,
  Came walking by the way,
And found their maſter in a trance,
  On ground where that he lay.

Up have they taken good Robìn,
  Making a pitious bear,
Yet ſaw they no man there at whom
  They might the matter ſpear.

They looked him all round about,
  But wound on him ſaw ' nane',
Yet at his mouth came bocking out
  The blood of a good vain.

Cold water they have gotten ſyne,
  And caſt unto his face;
Then he began to hitch his ear,
  And ſpeak within ſhort ſpace.

Tell us, dear maſter, ſaid his men,
  How with you ſtands the caſe.
Good Robin ſigh'd e'er he began
  To tell of his diſgrace.

"I have been watchman in this wood
Near hand this twenty year,
Yet I was never ſo hard beſtead
As ye have found me here;

A beggar with a clouted clock,
Of whom I fear'd no ill
Hath with his pyke-ſtaff cla'd my back,
I fear'twill never be well.

See, where he goes o'er yon hill,
With hat upon his head;
If e'er ye lov'd your maſter well,
Go now revenge this deed;

And bring him back again to me,
If it lie in your might,
That I may ſee, before I die,
Him puniſh'd in my ſight:

And if you may not bring him back,
Let him not go looſe on;
For to us all it were great ſhame
If he eſcape again."

"One of us ſhall with you remain,
Becauſe you're ill at eaſe,
The other two ſhall bring him back,
To uſe him as you pleaſe."

Now, by my truth, ſays good Robìn,
I true there's enough ſaid;
And he get ſcouth to wield his tree,
I fear you'll both be paid.

" Be not fear'd, our maſtèr,
That we two can be dung
With any bluter baſe beggàr,
That has nought but a rung.

His ſtaff ſhall ſtand him in no ſtead,
That you ſhall ſhortly ſee,
But back again he ſhall be led,
And faſt bound ſhall he be,
To ſee if ye will have him ſlain,
Or hanged on a tree."

" But caſt you ſliely in his way,
Before he be aware,
And on his pyke-ſtaff firſt hands lay,
Ye'll ſpeed the better far."

Now leave we Robin with his man,
Again to play the child,
And learn himſelf to ſtand and gang
By halds, for all his eild.

Now paſs we to the bold beggàr,
That raked o'er the hill,

Who never mended his pace more,
  Then he had done no ill.

. . . .
. . . .

And they have taken another way,
  Was nearer by miles three.

They ſtoutly ran with all their might,
  Spared neither dub ‘ nor’ mire,
They ſtarted at neither how nor height,
  No travel made them tire,

Till they before the beggar wan,
  And caſt them in his way;
A little wood lay in a glen,
  And there they both did ſtay;

They ſtood up cloſely by a tree,
  In each ſide of the gate,
Untill the beggar came them nigh,
  That thought of no ſuch late:

And as he was betwixt them paſt,
  They leapt upon him baith;
The one his pyke-ſtaff gripped faſt,
  They feared for its ſkaith.

The other he held in his ſight
  A drawen durk to his breaſt,

V. 72. The preceding lines of this ſtanza are wanting in the original.

And ſaid, Falſe 'carel,' quit thy ſtaff,
Or I ſhall be thy prieſt.

His pyke-ſtaff they have taken him frae,
And ſtuck it in the green,
He was full loath to let it gae,
An better might it been.

The beggar was the feardeſt man
Of any that e'er might be,
To win away no way he can,
Nor help him with his tree.

Nor wiſt he wherefore he was ta'en,
Nor how many was there;
He thought his life days had been gane,
He grew into diſpair.

Grant me my life, the beggar ſaid,
For him that dy'd on the tree,
And hold away that ugly knife,
Or elſe for fear I'll die.

I griev'd you never in all my life,
Neither by late or air,
You have great ſin if you would ſlay
A ſilly poor beggàr.

Thou lies, falſe lown, they ſaid again,
For all that may be ſworn;
Thou haſt 'near' ſlain the gentleſt man
Of one that e'er was born;

And back again thou ſhall be led,
And faſt bound ſhalt thou be,
To ſee if he will have thee ſlain,
Or hanged on a tree.

The beggar then thought all was wrong,
They were ſet for his wrack,
He ſaw nothing appearing then,
But ill upon warſe back.

Were he out of their hands, he thought,
And had again his tree,
He ſhould not be led back for nought,
With ſuch as he did ſee.

Then he bethought him on a wile,
If it could take effect,
How he might the young men beguile,
And give them a begeck.

Thus to do them ſhame for ill
His beaſtly breaſt was bent,
He found the wind blew ſomething ſhrill,
To further his intent.

He ſaid, Brave gentlemen, be good,
And let a poor man be;
When ye have taken a beggar's blood,
It helps you not a flee.

V. 132. gave. begack.

It was but in my own defence,
  If he has gotten ſkaith ;
But I will make a recompence
  Is better for you baith.

If ye will ſet me fair and free,
  And do me no more dear,
An hundred pounds I will you give,
  And much more odd ſilvèr,

That I have gather'd this many years,
  Under this clouted cloak,
And hid up wonder privately,
  In bottom of my poke.

The young men to the council yeed,
  And let the beggar gae ;
They wiſt full well he had no ſpeed
  From them to run away.

They thought they would the money take,
  Come after what ſo may ;
And yet they would not take him back,
  But in that place him ſlay.

By that good Robin would not know
  That they had gotten coin,
It would content him [well] to ſhow
  That there they had him ſlain.

V. 153. yeen.

They ſaid, Falſe carel, ſoon have done,
And tell forth thy monèy,
For the ill turn that thou haſt done
It's but a ſimple plee.

And yet we will not have thee back,
Come after what ſo may,
If thou will do that which thou ſpak,
And make us preſent pay.

O then he looſed his clouted clock,
And ſpread it on the ground,
And thereon lay he many a poke,
Betwixt them and the wind.

He took a great bag from his hals,
It was near full of meal,
Two pecks in it at leaſt there was,
And more, I wot full well.

Upon this cloak he ſet it down,
The mouth he opened wide,
To turn the ſame he made him bown,
The young men ready ſpy'd;

In every hand he took a nook
Of that great leathren 'mail,'
And with a fling the meal he ſhook
Into their face all hail:

V. 171. ſpok. *V.* 177. half. *V.* 183. bound. *V.* 186. bag.

Wherewith he blinded them ſo cloſe,
A ſtime they could not ſee;
And then in heart he did rejoice,
And clap'd his luſty tree.

He thought if he had done them wrong,
In mealing of their cloaths,
For to ſtrike off the meal again
With his pyke-ſtaff he goes.

E'er any of them could red their een,
Or a glimmring might ſee,
Ilke one of them a dozen had,
Well laid on with his tree.

The young men were right ſwift of foot,
And boldly bound away,
The beggar could them no more hit,
For all the haſte he may.

What's all this haſte? the beggar ſaid,
May not you tarry ſtill,
Untill your money be received?
I'll pay you with good will.

The ſhaking of my pokes, I fear,
Hath blown into your een;
But I have a good pyke-ſtaff here
Can ripe them out full clean.

V. 194. cloath. *V.* 206. thou.

The young men anſwered never a word,
  They were dum as a ſtane;
In the thick wood the beggar fled,
  E'er they riped their een :

And ſyne the night became ſo late,
  To ſeek him was in vain :
But judge ye if they looked blate
  When they cam home again.

Good Robin ſpeer'd how they had ſped.
  They anſwered him, Full ill.
That can not be, good Robin ſays,
  Ye have been at the mill.

The mill it is a meat rife part,
  They may lick what they pleaſe,
Moſt like ye have been at the art,
  Who would look at your ' claiths.'

They hang'd their heads, they drooped down,
  A word they could not ſpeak.
Robin ſaid, Becauſe I fell a ſound,
  I think ye'll do the like.

Tell on the matter, leſs or more,
  And tell me what and how
Ye have done with the bold beggàr
  I ſent you for right now.

V. 221. ſpeed. *V*. 228. cloaths.

And when they told him to an end,
  As i have ſaid before,
How that the beggar did them blind,
  What miſters preſſes more?

. . . .
  . . . .

And how in the thick woods he fled,
  E'er they a ſtime could ſee;

And how they ſcarcely could win home,
  Their bones were baſte ſo ſore;
Good Robin cry'd, Fy! out! for ſhame!
  We're ſham'd for evermore.

Altho good Robin would full fain
  Of his wrath revenged be,
He ſmil'd to ſee his merry young men
  Had gotten a taſte of the tree.

IV.

ROBIN HOOD AND GUY OF GISBORNE,

is reprinted from the " Reliques of ancient English poetry," published by Dr. Percy, (Vol. I. p. 81.) who there gives it from his " folio MS." as " never before printed, and ' carrying' marks of much greater antiquity than any of the common popular songs on this subject :" sentiments, to which, if the authority be genuine, and the publication faithful, (both which, by the way, they who are acquainted with Dr. Percys book, will have sufficient reason to doubt,) the present editor has nothing to object.

As for Guy of Gisborne, the only further memorial which has occured concerning him is in an old satyrical piece by William Dunbar, a celebrated Scotiſh poet, of the 15th century, on one "Schir Thomas Nory," (MS. Maitland, p. 3. MSS. More, Ll. 5. 10.) where he is named along with our hero, Adam Bell, and other worthies, it is conjectured, of a ſimilar ſtamp, but whoſe merits have not, leſs fortunately, come to the knowlege of poſterity.

"*Was neuir* WEILD ROBEINE *vnder bewch,*
"*Nor zitt Roger of Clekkinſlewch,*
"*So bauld a bairne as he;*
"GY OF GYSBURNE, *na Allane Bell,*
"*Na Simones ſones of Quhynſell,*
"*Off thocht war neuir ſo ſlie.*"

Gisborne is a market town in the weſt riding of the county of York, on the borders of Lancaſhire,

WHAN ſhaws beene ſheene, and ſhraddes full fayre,
And leaves both large and longe,
Itt's merrye walkyng in the fayre forrèſt
To heare the ſmall birdes ſonge.

The woodweele ſang, and wold not ceaſe,
Sitting upon the ſpraye,
Soe lowde, he wakened Robin Hood,
In the greenwood where he lay.

V. 1. "*It ſhould perhaps be* ſwards: i. e. *the ſurface of the ground:* viz. "*when the fields are in their beauty.*" PERCY. *Rather,* ſhrobbes *(ſhrubs). The plural of* ſward *was never uſed by any writer whatever.*

Now, by my faye, ſayd jollye Robìn,
A ſweaven I had this night;
I dreamt me of tow wighty yemèn,
That faſt with me can fight.

Methought they did me beate and binde,
And tooke my bowe me froe;
Iff I be Robin alive in this lande,
Ile be wroken on them towe.

Sweavens are ſwift, ſayd Lyttle John,
As the wind blowes over the hill;
For iff itt be never ſo loude this night,
To-morrow it may be ſtill.

"Buſke yee, bowne yee, my merry men all,
And John ſhall goe with mee,
For Ile goe ſeeke yond wighty yeomèn,
In greenwood where they bee."

Then they caſt on theyr gownes of grene,
And tooke theyr bowes each one;
And they away to the greene forrèſt
A ſhooting forth are gone;

Untill they came to the merry greenwood,
Where they had gladdeſt to bee,
There they were ware of a wight yeomàn,
That leaned agaynſt a tree.

A ſword and a dagger he wore by his ſide,
Of manye a man the bane;
And he was clad in his capull hyde
Topp and tayll and mayne.

Stand ſtill, maſter, quoth Little John,
Under this tree ſo grene,
And I will go to yond wight yeomàn,
To know what he doth meane.

"Ah! John, by me thou ſetteſt noe ſtore,
And that I farley finde:
How often ſend I my men before,
And tarry my ſelfe behinde?

It is no cunning a knave to ken,
And a man but heare him ſpeake;
And it were not for burſting of my bowe,
John, I thy head wold breake."

As often wordes they breeden bale,
So they parted Robin and John:
And John is gone to Barneſdale;
The gates he knoweth eche one.

But when he came to Barneſdale,
Great heavineſſe there he hadd,
For he found tow of his own fellòwes,
Were ſlaine both in a ſlade.

And Scarlette he was flying a-foote
  Faſt over ſtocke and ſtone,
For the proud ſheriffe with ſeven ſcore men
  Faſt after him is gone.

One ſhoote now I will ſhoote, quoth John,
  With Chriſt his might and mayne;
Ile make yond ſheriffe that wends ſoe faſt,
  To ſtopp he ſhall be fayne.

Then John bent up his long bende-bowe,
  And fetteled him to ſhoote:
The bow was made of tender boughe,
  And fell downe at his foote.

"Woe worth, woe worth thee, wicked wood,
  That ever thou grew on a tree!
For now this day thou art my bale,
  My boote when thou ſhold bee."

His ſhoote it was but looſely ſhott,
  Yet flewe not the arrowe in vaine,
For itt mett one of the ſheriffes men,
  And William a Trent was ſlaine.

It had bene better of William a Trent
  To have bene abed with ſorrowe,
Than to be that day in the greenwood ſlade
  To meet with Little Johns arrowe.

But as it is ſaid, when men be mett
  Fyve can doe more than three,
The ſheriffe hath taken Little John,
  And bound him faſt to a tree.

"Thou ſhalt be drawen by dale and downe,
  And hanged hye on a hill."
But thou mayſt fayle of thy purpoſe, quoth John,
  If it be Chriſt his will.

Lett us leave talking of Little John,
  And thinke of Robin Hood,
How he is gone to the wight yeomàn,
  Where under the leaves he ſtood.

Good morrowe, good fellowe, ſayd Robin ſo fayre,
  Good morrowe, good fellow, quo' he:
Methinkes by this bowe thou beares in thy hande,
  A good archere thou ſholdſt bee.

I am wilfulle of my waye, quo' the yemàn,
  And of my morning tyde.
Ile lead thee through the wood, ſayd Robìn;
  Good fellow, Ile be thy guide.

V. 94. *Dr. Percy, by the marks he has beſtowed on this line, ſeems to conſider it as the yeomans reply: but it ſeems rather a repetition of Robins complimentary addreſs.*

I ſeeke an outlawe, the ſtraunger ſayd,
Men call him Robin Hood;
Rather Ild meet with that proud outlàwe
Than fortye pound ſoe good.

"Now come with me, thou wighty yemàn,
And Robin thou ſoone ſhalt ſee:
But firſt let us ſome paſtime find
Under the greenwood tree.

Firſt let us ſome maſterye make
Among the woods ſo even,
We may chance to meet with Robin Hood
Here at ſome unſett ſteven."

They cutt them down two ſummer ſhroggs,
That grew both under a breere,
And ſett them threeſcore rood in twaine,
To ſhoote the prickes y-fere.

Leade on, good fellowe, quoth Robin Hood,
Leade on, I do bidd thee.
Nay, by my faith, good fellowe, hee ſayd,
My leader thou ſhalt bee.

The firſt time Robin ſhot at the pricke,
He miſt but an inch it fro:
The yeoman he was an archer good
But he cold never do ſoe.

The ſecond ſhoote had the wightye yemàn,
He ſhot within the garlànd:
But Robin he ſhott far better than hee,
For he clave the good pricke-wande.

A bleſſing upon thy heart, he ſayd;
Good fellowe, thy ſhooting is goode;
For an thy hart be as good as thy hand,
Thou wert better than Robin Hoode.

Now tell me thy name, good fellowe, ſayd he,
Under the leaves of lyne.
Nay, by my faith, quoth bold Robin,
Till thou have told me thine.

I dwell by dale and downe, quoth hee,
And Robin to take Ime ſworne;
And when I am called by my right name
I am Guy of good Giſbòrne.

My dwelling is in this wood, ſayes Robin,
By thee I ſet right nought:
I am Robin Hood of Barnéſdale,
Whom thou ſo long haſt ſought.

He that had neyther beene kythe nor kin,
Might have ſeen a full fayre fight,
To ſee how together theſe yeomen went
With blades both browne and bright.

To ſee how theſe yeomen together they fought
  Two howres of a ſummers day :
Yett neither Robin Hood nor ſir Guy
  Them fettled to flye away.

Robin was reachles on a roote,
  And ſtumbled at that tyde ;
And Guy was quicke and nimble withall,
  And hitt him upon the ſyde.

Ah, deere ladye, ſayd Robin Hood tho,
  That art but mother and may,
I think it was never mans deſtinye
  To dye before his day.

Robin thought on our ladye deere,
  And ſoone leapt up againe,
And ſtrait he came with a[n] awkwarde ſtroke
  And he ſir Guy hath ſlayne.

V. 163. awkwarde.] *So, according to Percy, reads his MS. He has altered it to* ' backward.'

V. 164. *The title of* Sir, *Dr. Percy ſays, was not formerly peculiar to knights; it was given to prieſts, and ſometimes to very inferior perſonages. If the text did not ſeem to be in favour of the latter part of this aſſertion, one might reaſonably queſtion its truth. Another inſtance, at leaſt, it is believed, admitting this to be one, which is by no means certain, could not be produced.*

He took ſir Guys head by the hayre,
And ſtuck it upon his bowes end:
"Thou haſt beene a traytor all thy life,
Which thing muſt have an end."

Robin pulled forth an Iriſh knife,
And nicked ſir Guy in the face,
That he was never on woman born
Cold know whoſe head it was.

Sayes, Lye there, lye there, now ſir Guye,
And with me be not wrothe;
Iff thou have had the worſt ſtrokes at my hand,
Thou ſhalt have the better clothe.

Robin did off his gown of greene,
And on ſir Guy did throwe,
And he put on that capull hyde,
That cladd him topp to toe.

"Thy bowe, thy arrowes, and little horne,
Now with me I will beare;
For I will away to Barnéſdale,
To ſee how my men doe fare."

Robin Hood ſett Guyes horne to his mouth,
And a loude blaſt in it did blow:
That beheard the ſheriffe of Nottingham,
As he leaned under a lowe.

Hearken, hearken, ſayd the ſheriffe,
I heare nowe tydings good,
For yonder I heare ſir Guyes horne blow,
And he hath ſlaine Robin Hoode.

Yonder I heare ſir Guyes horne blowe,
Itt blowes ſoe well in tyde,
And yonder comes that wightye yeomàn,
Cladd in his capull hyde.

Come hyther, come hyther, thou good ſir Guy,
Aſke what thou wilt of mee.
O I will none of thy gold, ſayd Robin,
Nor I will none of thy fee:

But now I have ſlaine the maſter, he ſayes,
Let me goe ſtrike the knave;
For this is all the meede I aſke;
None other rewarde I'le have.

Thou art a madman, ſayd the ſheriffe,
Thou ſholdſt have had a knightes fee:
But ſeeing thy aſking hath beene ſoe bad,
Well granted it ſhal bee.

When Little John heard his maſter ſpeake.
Well knewe he it was his ſteven:
Now ſhall I be looſet, quoth Little John,
With Chriſt his might in heaven.

Fast Robin hee hyed him to Little John,
He thought to loose him blive;
The sheriffe and all his companye
Fast after him can drive.

Stand abacke, stand abacke, sayd Robìn;
Why draw you mee so neere?
It was never the use in our countryè,
Ones shrift another shold heere.

But Robin pulled forth an Irish knife,
And losed John hand and foote,
And gave him sir Guyes bow into his hand,
And bade it be his boote.

Then John he took Guyes bow in his hand,
His boltes and arrowes eche one:
When the sheriffe saw Little John bend his bow,
He fettled him to be gone.

Towards his house in Nottingham towne,
He fled full fast away;
And soe did all the companye:
Not one behind wold stay.

But he cold neither runne soe fast,
Nor away soe fast cold ryde,
But Little John with an arrowe soe broad,
He shott him into the 'backe'-syde.

V. 236. Sic *PC*. quere *the MS*.

V.

A
TRUE TALE OF ROBIN HOOD:

OR,

A briefe touch of the life and death of that renowned outlaw Robert earl of Huntingdon, vulgarly called Robin Hood, who lived and dyed in A. D. 1198.* being the 9th year of king Richard the first, commonly called Richard Cœur de Lyon.

Carefully collected out of the truest writers of our English Chronicles: and published for the satisfaction of those who desire truth from falshood.

BY MARTIN PARKER.

* *An absurd mistake, scarcely worth notice in this place, and which the reader will have it in his own power to correct.*

This poem, given from an edition in black letter, printed for I. Clarke, W. Thackeray, and T. Passinger, 1686, remaining in the curious library left by Anthony à Wood, appears to have been first entered on the hall-book of the stationers company, the 29th of February, 1631.

Martin Parker was a great writer of ballads, several of which, with his initials subjoined, are still extant in the Pepysian and other collections. (See "Ancient songs," 1790, p. 239.) Dr. Percy mentions a little miscellany intitled, "The garland of withered roses, by Martin Parker, 1656." The editor has, likewise, seen "The nightingale warbling forth her own disaster, or the rape of Philomela: newly written in English verse by Martin Parker, 1632;" and, on the 24th. of November, 1640, Mr. Oulton enters, at Stationers hall, "a book called The true story of Guy earle of Warwicke, in prose, by Martyn Parker."

At the end of this poem the author adds "The epitaph which the prioress of the monastry of Kirkslay in Yorkshire set over Robin Hood, which," he says, "(as is before mentioned) was to be read within these hundred years, though in old broken English, much to the same sence and meaning." He gives it thus:

"Decembris quarto die, 1198. anno regni Richardi primi 9.

"*Robert earl of Huntington*
"*Lies under this little stone,*

" No archer was like him ſo good;
" His wildneſs named him Robin Hood;
" Full thirteen years, and ſomething more,
" Theſe northern parts he vexed ſore;
" Such outlaws as he and his men
" May England never know again."

" Some other ſuperſtitious words," he adds, " were in, which I," ſays he, " thought fit to leave out." Now, under this preciſe gentlemans favour, one would be glad to know what theſe ſame " ſuperſtitious words" were; there not being anything of the kind in Dr. Gales copy, which ſeems to be the original, and which is ſhorter by two lines than the above.

BOTH gentlemen, and yeomen bold,
Or whatſoever you are,
To have a ſtately ſtory told
Attention now prepare:

It is a tale of Robin Hood,
Which i to you will tell,
Which being rightly underſtood,
I know will pleaſe you well.

This Robin (ſo much talked on)
Was once a man of fame,
Inſtiled earl of Huntington,
Lord Robin Hood by name.

In courtſhip and magnificence
His carriage won him praiſe,
And greater favour with his prince
Than any in our days.

In bounteous liberality
He too much did excell,
And loved men of quality
More than exceeding well.

His great revenues all he ſold
For wine and coſtly chear;
He kept three hundred bow-men bold,
He ſhooting lov'd ſo dear.

No archer living in his time
With him might well compare;
He practis'd all his youthful prime
That exerciſe moſt rare.

At laſt, by his profuſe expence,
He had conſum'd his wealth;
And, being outlaw'd by his prince,
In woods he liv'd by ſtealth.

The abbot of Saint Maries rich,
To whom he mony ought,
His hatred to the earl was ſuch
That he his downfal wrought.

So being outlaw'd (as 'tis told)
He with a crew went forth
Of lufty cutters ftout and bold,
And robbed in the North.

Among the reft one Little John,
A yeoman bold and free,
Who could (if it ftood him upon)
With eafe encounter three.

One hundred men in all he got,
With whom (the ftory fays)
Three hundred common men durft not
Hold combat any waies.

They Yorkfhire woods frequented much,
And Lancafhire alfo,
Wherein their practifes were fuch
That they wrought muckle woe.

None rich durft travel to and fro,
Though ne'r fo ftrongly arm'd,
But by thefe thieves (fo ftrong in fhow)
They ftill were rob'd and harm'd.

His chiefeft fpight to th' clergy was,
That liv'd in monftrous pride:
No one of them he would let pafs
Along the highway fide,

But firſt they muſt to dinner go,
And afterwards to ſhrift:
Full many a one he ſerved ſo,
Thus while he liv'd by theſt.

No monks nor fryers he would let go,
Without paying their fees:
If they thought much to be uſed ſo,
Their ſtones he made them leſe.

For ſuch as they the country fill'd
With baſtards in thoſe days:
Which to prevent, theſe ſparks did geld
All that came in their ways.

But Robin Hood ſo gentle was,
And bore ſo brave a mind,
If any in diſtreſs did paſs,
To them he was ſo kind,

That he would give and lend to them,
To help them in their need;
This made all poor men pray for him,
And wiſh he well might ſpeed.

The widow and the fatherleſs
He would ſend means unto;
And thoſe whom famine did oppreſs
Found him a friendly foe.

Nor would he do a woman wrong,
  But see her safe convey'd:
He would protect with power strong
  All those who crav'd his aid.

The abbot of Saint Maries then,
  Who him undid before,
Was riding with two hundred men,
  And gold and silver store:

But Robin Hood upon him set,
  With his couragious sparks,
And all the coyn perforce did get,
  Which was twelve thousand marks.

He bound the abbot to a tree,
  And would not let him pass,
Before that to his men and he
  His lordship had said mass:

Which being done, upon his horse
  He set him fast astride,
And with his face towards his arse
  He forced him to ride.

His men were forced to be his guide,
  For he rode backward home:
The abbot, being thus villify'd,
  Did sorely chafe and fume.

Thus Robin Hood did vindicate
His former wrongs receiv'd:
For 'twas this covetous prelàte
That him of land bereav'd.

The abbot he rode to the king,
With all the haſte he could;
And to his grace he every thing
Exactly did unfold;

And ſaid that if no eourſe were ta'n,
By force or ſtratagem,
To take this rebel and his train,
No man ſhould paſs for them.

The king proteſted by and by
Unto the abbot then,
That Robin Hood with ſpeed ſhould dye,
With all his merry men.

But e're the king did any ſend,
He did another feat,
Which did his grace much more offend,
The fact indeed was great:

For in a ſhort time after that
The kings receivers went
Towards London with the coyn they got,
For's highneſs northern rent:

Bold Robin Hood and Little John,
With the reſt of their train,
Not dreading law, ſet them upon,
And did their gold obtain.

The king much moved at the ſame,
And the abbots talk alſo,
In this his anger did proclaim,
And ſent word to and fro,

That whoſoever alive or dead
Could bring bold Robin Hood,
Should have one thouſand marks well paid
In gold and ſilver good.

This promiſe of the king did make
Full many yeomen bold
Attempt ſtout Robin Hood to take
With all the force they could.

But ſtill when any came to him
Within the gay green wood,
He entertainment gave to them
With veniſon fat and good;

And ſhew'd to them ſuch martial ſport
With his long bow and arrow,
That they of him did give report,
How that it was great ſorow

That ſuch a worthy man as he
Should thus be put to ſhift,
Being a late lord of high degree,
Of living quite bereft.

The king to take him more and more
Sent men of mickle might;
But he and his ſtill beat them ſore,
And conquered them in fight:

Or elſe with love and courteſie,
To him he won their hearts.
Thus ſtill he liv'd by robbery
Throughout the northern parts;

And all the country ſtood in dread
Of Robin Hood and's men:
For ſtouter lads ne'r liv'd by bread
In thoſe days, nor ſince then.

The abbot, which before i nam'd,
Sought all the means he could
To have by force this rebel ta'n,
And his adherents bold.

Therefore he arm'd five hundred men,
With furniture compleat;
But the outlaws ſlew half of them,
And made the reſt retreat,

The long bow and the arrow keen
They were ſo us'd unto
That ſtill he kept the forreſt green
In ſpight o' th' proudeſt ſoe.

Twelve of the abbots men he took,
Who came to have him ta'n,
When all the reſt the field forſook,
Theſe he did entertain

With banqueting and merriment,
And, having us'd them well,
He to their lord them ſafely ſent,
And will'd them him to tell,

That if he would be pleas'd at laſt
To beg of our good king,
That he might pardon what was paſt,
And him to favour bring,

He would ſurrender back again
The mony which before
Was taken by him ' and his' men
From him and many more.

Poor men might ſafely paſs by him,
And ſome that way would chuſe,
For well they knew that to help them
He evermore did uſe.

But where he knew a miſer rich
That did the poor oppreſs,
To feel his coyn his hands did itch,
He'd have it more or leſs:

And ſometimes, when the high-way fail'd,
Then he his courage rouzes,
He and his men have oft aſſaild
Such rich men in their houſes:

So that, through dread of Robin then,
And his adventurous crew,
The miſers kept great ſtore of men,
Which elſe maintain'd but few.

King Richard, of that name the firſt,
Sirnamed Cœur de Lyon,
Went to defeat the Pagans curſt,
Who kept the coaſts of Sion.

The biſhop of Ely chancellor,
Was left a vice-roy here,
Who, like a potent emperor,
Did proud domineer.

Our chronicles of him report,
That commonly he rode
With a thouſand horſe from court to court,
Where he would make abode.

He, riding down towards the north,
With his aforeſaid train,
Robin and his men did iſſue forth,
Them all to entertain;

And with the gallant gray-gooſe wing
They ſhew'd to them ſuch play
That made their horſes kick and fling,
And down their riders lay.

Full glad and fain the biſhop was,
For all his thouſand men,
To ſeek what means he could to paſs
From out of Robins ken.

Two hundred of his men were kill'd,
And fourſcore horſes good,
Thirty, who did as captives yield,
Were carried to the green wood;

Which afterwards were ranſomed,
For twenty marks a man:
The reſt ſet ſpurs to horſe and fled
To th' town of Warrington.

The biſhop, ſore inraged, then
Did, in king Richards name,
Muſter up a power of northern men,
Theſe outlaws bold to tame.

But Robin with his courteſie
So won the meaner ſort,
That they were loath on him to try
What rigour did import.

So that bold Robin and his train
Did live unhurt of them,
Until king Richard came again
From fair Jeruſalem:

And then the talk of Robin Hood
His royal ears did fill;
His grace admir'd that i' th' green wood
He was continued ſtill.

So that the country far and near
Did give him great applauſe;
For none of them need ſtand in fear,
But ſuch as broke the laws.

He wiſhed well unto the king,
And prayed ſtill for his health,
And never practis'd any thing
Againſt the common-wealth.

Only, becauſe he was undone
By th' cruel clergy then,
All means that he could think upon
To vex ſuch kind of men,

He enterpriz'd with hateful ſpleen;
For which he was to blame,
For fault of ſome to wreak his teen
On all that by him came.

With wealth that he by roguery got
Eight alms-houſes he built,
Thinking thereby to purge the blot
Of blood which he had ſpilt.

Such was their blind devotion then,
Depending on their works;
Which if 'twere true, we Chriſtian men
Inferiour were to Turks.

But, to ſpeak true of Robin Hood,
And wrong him not a jot,
He never would ſhed any mans blood
That him invaded not.

Nor would he injure huſbandmen,
That toil at cart and plough;
For well he knew wer't not for them
To live no man knew how.

The king in perſon, with ſome lords,
To Nottingham did ride,
To try what ſtrength and ſkill affords
To cruſh this outlaws pride.

And, as he once before had done,
  He did again proclaim,
That whoſoever would take upon
  To bring to Nottingham,

Or any place within the land,
  Rebellious Robin Hood,
Should be preferr'd in place to ſtand
  With thoſe of noble blood.

When Robin Hood heard of the ſame,
  Within a little ſpace,
Into the town of Nottingham
  A letter to his grace

He ſhot upon an arrow head,
  One evening cunningly;
Which was brought to the king, and read
  Before his majeſty.

The tenour of this letter was
  That Robin would ſubmit,
And be true liegeman to his grace
  In any thing that's fit,

So that his highneſs would forgive
  Him and his merry men all;
If not, he muſt i' th' green wood live,
  And take what chance did fall.

The king would feign have pardoned him,
But that ſome lords did ſay,
This preſident will much condemn
Your grace another day.

While that the king and lords did ſtay
Debating on this thing,
Some of theſe outlaws fled away
Unto the Scottiſh king.

For they ſuppos'd, if he were ta'n
Or to the king did yield,
By th' commons all the reſt of 's train
Full quickly would be quell'd.

Of more than full an hundred men,
But forty tarried ſtill,
Who were reſolv'd to ſtick to him
Let Fortune work her will.

If none had fled, all for his ſake
Had got their pardon free;
The king to favour meant to take
His merry men and he.

But e're the pardon to him came
This famous archer dy'd:
His death and manner of the ſame
I'le preſently deſcribe.

For, being vext to think upon
His followers revolt,
In melancholy paſſiòn
He did recount his fault.

Perfidious traytors! ſaid he then,
In all your dangers paſt
Have i you guarded as my men,
To leave me thus at laſt!

This ſad perplexity did cauſe
A feaver, as ſome ſay,
Which him unto confuſion draws,
Though by a ſtranger way.

This deadly danger to prevent,
He hie'd him with all ſpeed
Unto a nunnery, with intent
For his healths-ſake to bleed.

A faithleſs fryer did pretend
In love to let him blood,
But he by falshood wrought the end
Of famous Robin Hood.

The fryer, as ſome ſay, did this
To vindicate the wrong
Which to the clergy he and his
Had done by power ſtrong.

Thus dyed he by treachery,
  That could not die by force:
Had he liv'd longer, certainly
  King Richard, in remorſe,

Had unto favour him receiv'd,
  'His' brave men elevated:
'Tis pitty he was of life bereav'd
  By one which he ſo hated.

A treacherous leach this fryer was,
  To let him bleed to death;
And Robin was, methinks, an aſs
  To truſt him with his breath.

His corps the prioreſs of the place,
  The next day that he dy'd,
Cauſed to be buried, in mean caſe,
  Cloſe by the high-way ſide.

And over him ſhe cauſed a ſtone
  To be fixt on the ground,
An epitaph was ſet thereon,
  Wherein his name was found;

The date o' th' year and day alſo,
  She made to be ſet there:
That all, who by the way did go,
  Might ſee it plain appear.

That ſuch a man as Robin Hood
Was buried in that place ;
And how he lived in the green wood
And robbed for a ſpace.

It ſeems that though the clergy he
Had put to mickle woe,
He ſhould not quite forgotten be,
Although he was their foe.

This woman, though ſhe did him hate,
Yet loved his memory ;
And thought it wondrous pitty that
His fame ſhould with him dye.

This epitaph, as records tell,
Within this hundred years,
By many was diſcerned well,
But time all things out-wears.

His followers, when he was dead,
Were ſome repriev'd to grace ;
The reſt to foreign countries fled,
And left their native place.

Although his funeral was but mean,
This woman had in mind,
Leaſt his fame ſhould be buried clean
From thoſe that came behind.

For certainly, before nor ſince,
No man e're underſtood,
Under the reign of any prince,
Of one like Robin Hood.

Full thirteen years, and ſomething more,
Theſe outlaws lived thus;
Feared of the rich, loved of the poor:
A thing moſt marvellous.

A thing impoſſible to us
This ſtory ſeems to be;
None dares be now ſo venturous,
But times are chang'd we ſee.

We that live in theſe later days
Of civil government,
If need be, have an hundred ways
Such outlaws to prevent.

In thoſe days men more barbarous were,
And lived leſs in awe;
Now (god be thanked) people fear
More to offend the law.

No waring guns were then in uſe,
They dreamt of no ſuch thing;
Our Engliſhmen in fight did uſe
The gallant gray-gooſe wing:

In which activity theſe men,
  Through practiſe, were ſo good,
That in thoſe days none equal'd them,
  Eſpecially Robin Hood.

So that, it ſeems, keeping in caves,
  In woods and foreſts thick,
They'd beat a multitude with ſtaves,
  Their arrows did ſo prick:

And none durſt neer unto them come,
  Unleſs in courteſie;
All ſuch he bravely would ſend home
  With mirth and jollity:

Which courteſie won him ſuch love,
  As i before have told,
'Twas the chief cauſe that he did prove
  More proſperous than he could.

Let us be thankful for theſe times
  Of plenty, truth and peace;
And leave out great and horrid crimes,
  Leaſt they cauſe this to ceaſe.

I know there's many feigned tales
  Of Robin Hood and 's crew;
But chronicles, which ſeldome fails,
  Reports this to be true.

V. 460. i. e. *than he could otherwiſe have been.*

Let none then think this is a lye,
For, if 'twere put to th' worſt,
They may the truth of all deſcry
I' th' reign of Richard the firſt.

If any reader pleaſe to try,
As i direction ſhow,
The truth of this brave hiſtory,
He'l find it true I know.

And i ſhall think my labour well
Beſtow'd to purpoſe good,
When't ſhall be ſaid that i did tell
True tales of Robin Hood.

GLOSSARY

TO

THE PRESENT VOLUME.

AIR. *p.* 107. *early.*

Alderbeſt. *p.* 51. *beſt of all. This phraſe, which occurs in Chaucer, is corrupted in de Wordes edition to* "al ther" *and* "al theyre," *which Coplande has changed to* "al of the;" *whence it may be infered that the expreſſion was become already obſolete, and conſequently that the poem is of much greater antiquity than* 1520: *and yet Shakſpeare above half a century after, puts the word* Alderliefeſt *into the mouth of queen Margaret.*

Anker. *p.* 36. *hermit, anchorite.*

Ar. *p.* 85. *ere.*

Aſay. *p.* 90. Aſayed. *p.* 31. *eſſayed, tryed, proved.*

A ſound. *p.* 112. *in a ſwoon.*

Aunſetters. *p.* 10. *anceſtors.*

Avow. *p.* 33. Avowe. *p.* 29. *vow.*

Avowe. *p.* 57. *maintain,* verbum juris.

Avowè. *p.* 42. *founder, patron, protector. See Spelmans gloſſary,* v. ADVOCATUS.

Awayte. awayte me ſcathe. *p.* 37. *lye in wait to do me harm.*

Awayted. *p.* 59. *lay in wait for.*

Awet. *p.* 93. *wit, know.*

Awkwarde. *p.* 123. *backward.* An awkwarde ſtroke *ſeems to mean an unuſual or out of the way ſtroke, one which the receiver could not foreſee, be aware of, or guard againſt; a ſort of left or back hand ſtroke.*

Ayenſt. *p.* 74. *againſt.*

Baiſt. *p.* 102. Baſte. *p.* 113. *baſted, belaboured.*

Baith. *p.* 106. *both.*

Bale. *p.* 117. *miſchief.—p.* 118. *woe, ſorrow, miſery.*

Banis *p.* 80. *bane, deſtruction.*

Bear. *p.* 103. *moan, lamentation, outcry.*

Bedene. *p.* 34. *behind, one after another?*

Bedyng. *p.* 88. *aſking.* Your bedyng ſhall be doyn, *Your invitation ſhall be complyed with.*

Beforen. *p.* 93. *before.*

Begeck. *p.* 108. give them a begeck, *play them a trick, make fools of them.*

Behote. *p.* 53. *promiſed.*

Bent. *p.* 84.

Beſcro. *p.* 86. *beſhrew.*

Beſtad. ferre and friend beſtad. *p.* 26. *far from home and without a friend. The paſſage, however, ſeems corrupt.*

Beſtead *p.* 104. *beſet, put to it.*

Beth. *p.* 11. *are, be.*

Blate. *pp.* 99, 112. *ſheepiſh or fooliſh, as we ſhould now ſay.*

Blive. *p.* 125. *belive, immediately.*

Bloſchems. *p.* 82. *bloſſoms.*

Bluter. *p.* 105.

Blyve. *p.* 53. *faſt, quickly, briſkly.*

Bocking. *p.* 103. *pouring flowing.*

Bode. *p.* 40. *bidden, invited.*

Bolt. *p.* 90. Bolte. *p.* 40. Boltes. *p.* 125. Boltys. *p.* 89. *A bolt was an arrow of a particular kind, uſed for ſhooting at a mark or at birds.*

Boote. *p.* 118. *help.*

Booting. *p.* 97.

Borde. *p.* 4. *table.*

Borowe. *p.* 13. *pledge, ſurety.*

Borowehode. *p.* 43. *ſuretyſhip.*

Boſkyd. *p.* 92. *buſked, prepared, got ready.*

Bottys. *p.* 89. *buts.*

Bou. *p.* 82. *bow.*

Bound. *p.* 101. *betook.*—*p.* 102. *went.* boldly bound away. *p.* 111. *briſkly ſcamper'd off.*

Bowe. *p.* 82. *bough.*

Bown. *p.* 110. *ready.*

Bowne ye. *p.* 116. *prepare ye, get ready.*

Boyt. *p.* 82. *both.*

Breyde. *p.* 83. *ſtarted, ſteped haſtyly.*

Breyde. *p.* 85. *ſtart, quick or haſty ſtep.*

Broke. *p.* 48. *brook, enjoy, uſe, keep.*

Bronde. *p.* 37. *brand, ſword.*

Buſhement. *p.* 54. *ambuſh.*

Buſke. *p.* 12. I wyll me buſke, i. e. *go, betake myſelf.*—*p.* 51. buſke you. *addreſs or prepare yourſelves, make ready.*

Bydene. *p.* 62. *one after another.*

Cankardly. *p.* 99. *peeviſhly, with ill temper.*

Capull hyde. *p.* 117. *horſe hide.*

Carel, *p.* 110. *carle, old fellow.*

Caward. *p.* 84. *awkward, or backward. See* Awkwarde.

Cerſtyn. *p.* 89. *chriſtian.*

Chaffar. *p.* 87. *chaffer, merchandiſe. p.* 93. *commodity.*

Chepe. better chepe. *p.* 46. *cheaper*; à meilleur marché, *F.* gret chepe. *p.* 87. *very cheap*; à tres bon marché.

Chepe. *p.* 86. *cheapen, buy.* Chepyd. *p.* 87. *cheapened, bought.*

Cheys. *p.* 90. *chooſe.*

Chorle. *p.* 40. *churl, peaſant, clown.*

Cla'd. *p.* 104. *ſcratched.*

Clock. *p.* 98. *cloak.*

Clouted. *p.* 98. *patched.*

Cole. *p.* 66.

Come. *p.* 16. (*pronounced* com) *came.*

Commytted. *p.* 77. *accounted.*

Coreſed. *p.* 20.

Corteſſey. *p.* 82.. *courteous.*

Cote a pye. *p.* 35. *upper garment, ſhort cloke*; courtepy, *Chaucer. See Tyrwhitts note*, iv. 201.

Coud. *p.* 33. *knew. underſtood.*

Covent. *p.* 17. *convent*; *whence our* Covent-garden.

Cowed. *p.* 88. *could, knew.* Cowed of curteyſey. *underſtood good manners.*

Crack. *p.* 102. *boaſt.*

Craftely *p.* 80. *ſkilfully,* ſecundum artem.

Crouſe. *p.* 102. *briſk.*

Cun. *p.* 44. *con, owe, give.*

Curn. *p.* 100.

Curteyſe. *p.* 3. *courteous.*

Cutters. *p.* 130. *ſharking fellows,*

Dear. *p.* 109. *harm.*

Demed. *p.* 19. *judged.*

Derne. *p.* 6. *privy, ſecret.*

Deyell. *p.* 94. *devil.*

Deythe. *p.* 92. *dight, dreſſed.*

Donne. *p.* 73. *dun.*

Doyt. *p.* 82. *doth, do.*

Dreyffe. *p.* 85. *drive.*

Dub. *p.* 106. *ſhallow mirey pool,*

Dung. *p.* 105. *beaten, overcome.*

Durk. *p.* 106. *dagger.*

Dyght. *p.* 6. *dreſſed.—p.* 57. *done.*

Dyghtande. *p.* 69.

Dyſgrate. *p.* 10. *diſgraced.* hath be dyſgrate. *hath fallen into poverty.*

Een. *p.* 102. *eyes.*

Eftſones, *p.* 43. *hereafter, afterward,*

Eild. *p.* 105. *age.*

Ender. *p.* 85. *under.*

Ere. *p.* 43. *before.*

Eylde. *p.* 92. *yield.*

Eyr. *p.* 93. *year.*

Fail. but fail. *p.* 102. *without fail, without doubt.*

Failyd. *p.* 63. *wanted, miſſed.*

Fair. *p.* 101. *fare, ado.*

Farley. *p.* 117. *fairly, plainly.*
Fay. *p.* 26. *faith.*
Fayne. *p.* 37. *glad.*
Fe. *p.* 76. *fee, wages.*
Feardeſt. *p.* 107. *fearfuleſt, moſt frightened or afraid.*
Feders. *p.* 51, *feathers.*
Fend. fend I godys forbode. *p.* 94.
Fende. *p.* 21, *defend.*
Fered. *p.* 86. *fared, lived.*
Ferre. *p.* 5. *far.* ferre dayes. *far in the day*; grand jour, *F.*
Fette. *p.* 32. *fetched.*
Fetteled him. *p.* 118. *made him ready, prepared himſelf, ſet about.* Fettled. them fettled. *p.* 122. *attempted, ſet about.*
Feyffe. *p.* 88. *five.*
Flee. *p.* 108. *fly.*
Flinders. *p.* 101. *ſplinters.*
Fone. *p.* 21. *foes.*
Forbode. *p.* 94. *commandment.*
Forgone. *p.* 44. *forego, loſe.*
Fors. *p.* 4. *care. See p.* 41.
Forſoyt, *p.* 91. *forſooth, truely.*
Foryete. *p.* 29. *forgoten.*
Foſtere. *p.* 65. *foreſter.*
Fothe. *p.* 90. *foot.*
Frae. *p.* 98. *from.*
Frebore. *p.* 2. *free born, gentle.*
Freſe. *p.* 39.

Fynly. *p.* 51. *goodly.*

Gae. *p.* 109. *go.*

Gan. *p.* 56. gan they gone. *are they gone, did they go.*

Gang. *p.* 98. Gange. *p.* 70. *go.*

Gate. *p.* 106. *way.* Gates *p.* 117. "*ways, paſſes, paths, ridings.* Gate *is a common word in the north for way.*" P.

Geffe. *p.* 89. *given.*

Ger. *p.* 90. *gear, ſtuff, goods, property, effects.*

Gereamarſey. *p.* 88. *See* Gramercy.

Glen. *p.* 106. *valley.*

God. *p.* 95. *good, goods, property.*

Godamarſey. *p.* 88. *See* Gramercy.

Godde. *p.* 94. *See* God.

Gorney. *p.* 85. *journey.*

Goy. *p.* 92. *joy.*

Gramarſey. *p.* 92. *See* Gramercy.

Gramercy. *p.* 8. *thanks, or many thanks*; grand merci, *F.*

Gree. *p.* 21. *ſatisfaction.*

Gret. *p.* 88. *greeted, ſaluted.*

Gripped. *p.* 106. *graſped, laid hold of.*

Grome. *p.* 3. *a common man?*

Hail. all hail. *p.* 110. *wholely, entirely.*

Halds. *p.* 105. *holds, holding places, ſupports.*

Halke. *p.* 65. *perhaps, haugh, low ground by the ſide of a river? See the gloſſary to Bp. Douglas's Virgil,* v. Hawchis. Halke, *with Chaucer, ſignifies a corner; but ſeems here uſed in oppoſition to* hill.

Halfendell. *p.* 68. *half.*

Hals. *p.* 110. *neck.*

Hambellet. *p.* 94. *ambleth.*

Hanſell. *p.* 87. *The vender of any wares is ſaid to receive* hanſel *of his firſt cuſtomer; but the meaning of the text,* Haffe hanſell for the mar, *is not underſtood; unleſs it can be thought to imply,* Give me hanſel, i. e. *buy of my pots.*

Hawt. *p.* 92. *aught, anything, ſomething.*

Hayt. *p.* 82. *hath.*

Held. *p.* 98. *kept, preſerved.*

Hende. *p.* 7. *gentle, courteous.*

Hent. *p.* 84. *took, caught.*

Hepe. *p.* 37. *hip, haw, the fruit of the white thorn. So in* Gil Morice, *a Scotiſh balad:*

> " *I was once* AS FOW *of Gill Morrice*
> " AS THE HIP IS O' THE STEAN."

Her. *p.* 92. *their.*

Het. *p.* 83. *it.*

Het. *p.* 92. *eat.*

Heynd. *p.* 86. *gentle, courteous.*

Heyt war howte. *p.* 86.

Holde. *p.* 18. *keep.*

Holde. *p.* 21. *v.* 101. *held, retained, of council.*

Holy. *p.* 19. *wholely.*

Hos. *p.* 94. Hus. *p.* 83. *us.*

Hotys. *p.* 87. *oats.*

Houſband. *p.* 10. *manager.*

Houſbonde. *p.* 4. *huſbandman, peaſant.*

How. *p.* 106. *hill.*

Howt. *p.* 84. *out.*

Hyght. *p.* 78. *vowed, promiſed.*

Hynde. *p.* 30. *knave.*

Ibent. *p.* 51. *bent.*

Ibonde. *p.* 59. *bound.*

Ichaunged. *p.* 31. *changed.*

Idyght. *p.* 69. *dight, dreſſed, made ready.*

Ifedered. *p.* 49. *feathered.*

Ilke. *p.* 111. *each.*

In fere. *p.* 17. *together.*

Inocked. *p.* 25. *nocked, notched.*

Ipyght. up ipyght. *p.* 26.

Iquyt. *p.* 61. *acquitted, ſet at liberty.*

Iſwore. *p.* 37. *ſworn.*

Itake. *p.* 50. *taken.*

Japes. *p.* 13. *tricks.*

Keſt. *p.* 74. *caſt.*

Knave. *p.* 16. *ſervant, man.*

Kod. *p.* 92. *quod, quoth, ſaid.*

Kyrtell. *pp.* 35, 53. *waiſtcoat?*

Kythe nor kin. *p.* 122. *acquaintance nor kindred.*

Lappe. *pp.* 14, 35. *wrap.*

Late. *p.* 106. *lake, play, game?*

Launſgay. *p.* 205. *a ſort of lance.*

Leaſynge. *p.* 57. *lying, falſehood.*

Lede. *p.* 65. *v.* 58. *train, ſuite.*

Ledesman. *p.* 65. *guide.*

Lefe. *p.* 41. *willing.* whether he were loth or lefe. *whether he would or not.*

Leffe. *p.* 84. *leave.* Leffe. *p.* 92. *left.*

Leffes. *p.* 92. *leaves.*

Lende. *p.* 70. *meet, encounter.*

Lene. *pp.* 15, 16, 22. *lend.*

Lere. *p.* 5. *learn.*

Lere. *p.* 7. *cheek.*

Lefe. *p.* 12. *lofe.*

Let. *p.* 9. *omit.—p.* 85. *v.* 88. *hinder.—v.* 92. *hindered.*

Leugh. *p.* 49. *laughed.*

Lever. *p.* 17. *rather.*

Lewtè. *pp.* 29, 53. *loyalty, faith, truth*; leauté, *F.*

Leythe. *p.* 92. *light.*

Lithe. *p.* 2. *attend, hear, hearken.*

Loffe. *p.* 82. *love.*

Lore. *p.* 11. *loft.*

Lough. *p.* 15. Loughe. *p.* 76. Low. *p.* 84. *laughed.*

Lowe. *p.* 124. "*a little hill.*" P.

Lown. *p.* 107. *villain, knave, bafe fellow.*

Luft. *p.* 3. *defire, inclination.*

Lyght. *p.* 15. *light*; *or, perhaps, for* lyte, *little.*

Lynde. *p.* 66. Lyne. *p.* 121. *the lime or linden tree*; *or collectively lime trees*; *or trees in general.*

Lyth. *p.* 97. *See* Lithe.

Lyveray. *p.* 14. *livery, habit.—p.* 30. *livery, delivery: the mefs, portion, or quantity of provifions delivered out at a time by the butler was called* a livery.

Mafars. *p.* 32. *cups, veffels.*

Mafterye. *p.* 120. "*a trial of fkill, high proof of fkill.*" P.

Mair. *p.* 101. *more.*

Maney. *p.* 82. *See* Meynè.

May. *p.* 122. *maid.*

Me. That ever yet fawe I me. *p.* 34. *a gallicifm*; que jamais j'ai vû moi.

Meal. *p.* 110. *oat-meal.*

Meal-poke. *p.* 98. *meal bag, bag in which oat-meal is put.*

Meat rife. *p.* 112.

Mede. to quyte hym well his mede. *p.* 29. *to reward him to ſome purpoſe.*

Medys. *p.* 87. *midſt, middle.*

Meede. *p.* 124. *reward.*

Met. *p.* 15. Mete. *p.* 14. *meaſured.*

Methe. *p.* 89. *meat.*

Meynè. *p.* 8. *attendants, retinue*; meſnie, *F.*

Meythe. *p.* 92. *might.*

Mickle. *p.* 135. *much.*

Might. *p.* 104. *power.*

Miſters. *p.* 113. *need: r.* miſter.

Molde. *p.* 27. *earth.*

Mot. *p.* 95. *might.*

Mote. *p.* 44. *might, may.*

Mote. *p.* 45. *meeting, aſſembly, court, audit.*

Mountenaunce. *p.* 31. *amount, duration, ſpace.*

Mowe. *p.* 5. *may.*

Muckle. *p.* 130. *See* Mickle.

Myrthes. *p.* 38. *mirth, merriment.* a man that myrthes can. *a minſtrel, fiddler, juggler, or the like.*

Myſter. *p.* 44. *need.*

Nane. *p.* 103. *none.*

Nar. *p.* 93. *nor, than.*

Ner. *p.* 90. *ear.*

Ner. *p.* 94. (ne wer it.) *were it not.*

Nip. *p.* 100.

Nips. *p.* 100.

Nobellys. *p.* 95. *nobles. The* noble *was a gold coin value* 6*s.* 8*d.*

Nombles. *p.* 8. Numbles. *p.* 32. *entrails; those parts which are usually baked in a pye: now, corruptly, called* humbles *or* umbles: nombles, *F.*

Okerer. *p.* 10. *usurer.*

Os. *p.* 89. *us.*

Owthe. *p.* 90. *out.*

Paid. *p.* 102, *beat.—p.* 105. *beaten.*

Passe. *p.* 63. *extent, bounds, limits, district; as the* pas de Calais. *Coplands edition reads* compas.

Pauage. *p.* 83. Pavag. Pavage. *p.* 84. Pawage. *p.* 82. *a toll or duty payable for the liberty of passing over the soil or territory of another:* paagium, *L.*

Pay. *p.* 13. *content, satisfaction.*

Pay. *p.* 20. *money.*

Peces. *p.* 32.

Pecocke. With pecocke well y dyght. *p.* 25. *handsomely dressed with peacock feathers. Thus Chaucer, describing his "squires yeman:"*

> " *A shefe of* peacocke arwes *bright and kene,*
> " *Under his belt he bare ful thriftely.*"

Plucke buffet. *p.* 75.

Polle. *p.* 90. *pull.*

Poke. *p.* 109. *bag.*

Preke. *p.* 91. *prick, a piece of wood in the center of the target.*

Prese. *p.* 40. *company.*

Preſt. *p.* 89. *ready, ready to go.—p.* 92.

Puding-pricks. *p.* 100. *ſkewers that faſten the pudding-bag.*

Pyne. goddes pyne. *p.* 69. *Chriſts paſſion or crucifixion.*

Quequer. *p.* 9. *a quick or quickſet hedge.*

Queyt. *p.* 92. *quit, recompenſe.*

Raked. *p.* 105. *walked apace.*

Ray. *p.* 92. *array, put in order.*

Raye. *p.* 42.

Reachles. *p.* 122. *careleſs, regardleſs, unobſervant.*

Red. *p.* 111. *clear.*

Reuth. *p.* 26. *pity, compaſſion.*

Reve. *p.* 4. *take by force.*

Reves. *p.* 46. *bailiffs, receivers.*

Ripe. *p.* 111. *cleanſe.* Riped. *p.* 112. *cleanſed.*

Rode. *p.* 90. *rood, croſs.*

Rung. *p.* 105. *ſtaff.*

Ruthe. *p.* 13. *pity, compaſſion.*

Ryall. *p.* 23. *royal.*

Ryalty. *p.* 39. *royalty.*

Ryghtwys. *p.* 43. *righteous, juſt.*

Sair. *p.* 101. *ſore.*

Salved. (ſalued ?) *p.* 20. *ſaluted.*

Scathe. *p.* 37. *harm.*

Schetyng. *p.* 92. *ſhooting.*

Schomer. *p.* 82. *ſummer.*

Sclo. *p.* 85. *ſlay.*

Scoper. *p.* 92. *ſupper.*

Scouth. *p.* 105.

Screfe. Screffe. *p.* 88. *ſherif.*

Se. *p.* 33. Vide See.

Seche. *p.* 13. *ſeek.*

See. *p.* 34. *regard.*

Seker. *p.* 39. *ſure.*

Selerer. *p.* 18. *The* cellarer (celerier, cellararius, *or* cellarius) *was that officer who furniſhed the convent with proviſions,* cui potus et eſcæ cura eſt, qui cellæ vinariæ et eſcariæ prœeſt, promus. (Du Cange.) *He appears to have been a perſon of conſiderable truſt, and to have had a principal concern in the management of the ſocietys revenues. See Spelmans gloſſary, Fullers church-hiſtory,* &c.

Semblaunte. *p.* 6. *ſemblance, appearance.*

Sene. *p.* 92. *ſee.*

Sete. *p.* 25.

Sette. *p.* 11. *mortgaged.*

Shawe. *p.* 5. Shaw *is uſually explained by* little wood, *but* green-wood little wood *would be mere tautology; it may therefore mean* ſhade, *which appears its primitive ſignification:* Scuwa, *Saxon.*—Shaws. *p.* 115. "*little woods.*" P.

Shende. *p.* 26. *hurt, annoy.* Shente. *p.* 70. *hurt, wounded.*

Shet. *p.* 30. *ſhut.*

Shete. *p.* 27. *ſhoot.*

Shope. *p.* 1 . *ſhaped, made.*

Shraddes. *p.* 115. *See the note.*

Shrewde. *p.* 30. Shrewed. *p.* 20. *unlucky.*

Shrift. *p.* 125. *confeſſion.*

Shroggs. *p.* 120. "*ſhrubs, thorns, briars. G. Doug.* ſcroggis." P.

Shyt. *p.* 56. *ſhut.*

Skaith. *p.* 106. *hurt, harm.* They feared for its ſkaith, i. e. *for the harm it might do them.*

Slade. *p.* 118. "*a ſlip of greenſwerd between plow-lands, or woods,* &c." P.

Slawe. *p.* 54. Slone. *p.* 75. *ſlain.*

Sle. *p.* 80. Sloo. *p.* 34. *ſlay.*

Somers. *p.* 39. *ſumpter-horſes.*

Sorowe. *p.* 19. *ſorry.*

Sothe. *p.* 13. *ſooth, truth.*

Sound. *See* A ſound.

Soyt. *p.* 85. *ſooth, truth.*

Spear. *p.* 103. *aſk.* Speer'd. *p.* 112. *aſked, enquired.*

Stalward. *p.* 90. Stalworthe. *p.* 72. *ſtout, well made.*

Stane. *p.* 102. *ſtone.*

Stark. *p.* 98. *ſtiff.*

Stede. *p.* 25. *time.*

Steven. *p.* 120. At ſome unſett ſteven. *at ſome unlooked for time, by ſome odd accident, by mere chance.*—*p.* 125. *voice.*

Stime. *p.* 111. *ſpark, particle or ray of light.*

Strang. *p.* 98. *ſtrong.*

Strete. *p.* 6. *lane, path, way.*

Sweaven. *p.* 116. *dream.*

Sweer. *p.* 100.

Syne. *p.* 102. *after, afterward, then.*

Syth. *p.* 46. *afterward.*

Takles. *p.* 51. *arrows.*

Takyll. *p.* 70. *arrow.*

Tarpe. *p.* 68.

Tene. *p.* 15. *grief, ſorrow, diſtreſs.—p.* 38. *vexation.*

Tene. *p.* 84. *grieve.*

The. *p.* 42. *thrive, proſper.*

Thes. *p.* 87. *thus.—p.* 89. *this.*

Thos. *p.* 88. *thus.*

Throwe. *p.* 79. *ſpace.*

Tortyll. *p.* 91. *wreathed, twined, twirled, twiſted*; tortillé, *F.*

Tray. *p.* 38. *anger.*

Tree. *p.* 101. *ſtaff.*

Treyffe. *p.* 95. *thrive.*

Trow. *p.* 89. *true.*

Trowet. *p.* 85. *troth.*

True. *p.* 105. *trow, believe.*

Tryſtell. *pp.* 49, 51, 53, 68. Tryſtyll. *p.* 73.

Tynde. *p.* 34. *tyndes, tines, antlers, the pointed branches that iſſue from the main beam of a ſtag.* "In Ynglond ther ys a ſhepcote, the wyche ſchepekote hayt ix dorys, & at yeuery dor ſtondet ix ramys, & every ram hat ix ewys, & yevery ewe hathe ix lambys, & yevery lambe hayt ix hornes, & every horne hayt ix TYNDES: what ys the ſomm of all thes belle?" (MSS. More, Ee. 4. 35.)

Win. *p.* 107. *get.*

Wiſt. *p.* 137. *knew.*

Unketh. *p.* 3. *uncouth, ſtrange.*

Unneth. *p.* 64. *ſcarcely.*

Up chaunce. *p.* 5. *by chance.*

Wan. wonnynge wan. *p.* 28. *dwelling-place.*

Wan. *p.* 106. *got.*

Warſe. *p.* 108. *worſe.*

Was. *p.* 89. *waſh.* "*And afterward the juſtices ariſe and* WASSE, *and geffe thanks onto the new ſerjaunts for ther gode dyner.*" (Origines juridiciales, *p.* 116.) *This ceremony, which, in former times, was conſtantly practiſed as well before as after meat, ſeems to have fallen into diſuſe on the introduction of forks, about the year* 1620; *as before that period our anceſtors ſupplyed the place of this neceſſary utenſil with their fingers.*

Wed. *p.* 83. Wedde. *p.* 53. *pawn, pledge, or depoſit.*—to wedde. *p.* 11. *in mortgage.*—lay my life to wedde. *p.* 39. *pawn my life.*

Welt. *p.* 65. welt them at his wyll; *did as he pleaſed with them, uſed them at his pleaſure.*

Wende. *p.* 5. *go.*

Weneſt. *p.* 13. *thinkeſt.*

Went. *p.* 16. *wended, gone.*

Werſchep. *p.* 82. *worſhiped, reverenced, reſpected.*

Weſt. *p.* 92. *wiſt, known.*

Wete. *p.* 26. *know.*

Whang. leathern whang. *p.* 98. *leather thong or ſtring.*

Wight. Wighty. *p.* 116. *ſtrong.* N. B. *The latter word ſeems every where a miſtake for the former.*

Wilfulle. *p.* 120. *doubtful.*

Wode. *p.* 93. *mad.*

Wodys. *p.* 82. *woods.*

Wolwarde. *p.* 78. *wearing a ſlanel ſhirt, by way of penance. See Steevens's Shakſpeare,* 1793, v. 360.

Woneſt. *p.* 56. *dwelleſt.*

Woodweele. *p.* 115. "*the golden ouzle, a bird of the thruſh kind.*" P.

Worthe. Wo worthe the. *p.* 35. *Woe be to thee.*

Wrack. *p.* 108. *ruin, deſtruction.*

Wroken. *p.* 116. *wreaked, revenged.*

Wyght. *p.* 28. *ſtrong, ſtout.*

Wynne. *p.* 56. *go.*

Wys. *p.* 36. *trow; there is no modern word preciſely ſynonimous.*

Wyte. *p.* 42. Wytte. *p.* 57. *know.*

Y. *p.* 83. *I.*

Yede. *p.* 30. Yeed. *p.* 109. *went.*

Yeff. *p.* 85. *if.*

Yeffell. *p.* 83. *evil.*

Yeft. *p.* 53. *gift.*

Yemenry. *p.* 85. *yeomanry.* Thow ſeys god yemenry, *Thou ſpeakeſt honeſtly, fairly, ſenſibly, like a good yeoman.*

Yend. *p.* 84. *yon.*

Yerdes. *p.* 70. *rods.*

Yever. *p.* 82. *ever.*

Yfere. *p.* 120. *together.*

Ylke. *p.* 32. *ſame.* Ylke ſame. *very ſame.*—*p.* 54. *ſame, very.*

Ynowe. *p.* 45. *enough.*

Yode. *p.* 57. *went.*

Yole. *p.* 74. *Christmass.*

Yonder. *p.* 92. *under.*

Yong men. *pp.* 36, 51, 69, 79. *yeomen (which is every where substituted in Coplands edition). See Spelmans glossary, in the words* Juniores, Yeoman; *Tyrwhitts edition of the* Canterbury tales, iv. 195; *Shakspeares* Plays, 1793, xiv. 347.

THE END OF VOLUME I.

CPSIA information can be obtained
at www.ICGtesting.com
Printed in the USA
LVOW10s0426230118
563548LV00001B/65/P

9 781108 078160